Python Graphics

A Reference for Creating 2D and 3D Images

B.J. Korites

Apress®

Python Graphics

B.J. Korites
Duxbury, Massachusetts, USA

ISBN-13 (pbk): 978-1-4842-3377-1   ISBN-13 (electronic): 978-1-4842-3378-8
https://doi.org/10.1007/978-1-4842-3378-8

Library of Congress Control Number: 2018946635

Managing Director, Apress Media LLC: Welmoed Spahr
Acquisitions Editor: Todd Green
Development Editor: James Markham
Coordinating Editor: Jill Balzano

Cover designed by eStudioCalamar

Cover image designed by Freepik (www.freepik.com)

Distributed to the book trade worldwide by Springer Science+Business Media New York, 233 Spring Street, 6th Floor, New York, NY 10013. Phone 1-800-SPRINGER, fax (201) 348-4505, e-mail orders-ny@springer-sbm.com, or visit www.springeronline.com. Apress Media, LLC is a California LLC and the sole member (owner) is Springer Science + Business Media Finance Inc (SSBM Finance Inc). SSBM Finance Inc is a **Delaware** corporation.

For information on translations, please e-mail rights@apress.com, or visit www.apress.com/rights-permissions.

Apress titles may be purchased in bulk for academic, corporate, or promotional use. eBook versions and licenses are also available for most titles. For more information, reference our Print and eBook Bulk Sales web page at www.apress.com/bulk-sales.

Any source code or other supplementary material referenced by the author in this book is available to readers on GitHub via the book's product page, located at www.apress.com/9781484233771. For more detailed information, please visit www.apress.com/source-code.

Printed on acid-free paper

For Pam

Table of Contents

About the Author ix

About the Technical Reviewer xi

Acknowledgments xiii

Chapter 1: Essential Python Commands and Functions 1

    1.1 Programming Style 2

    1.2 The Plotting Area 3

    1.3 Establishing the Size of the Plotting Area 4

    1.4 Importing Plotting Commands 6

    1.5 Displaying the Plotting Area 8

    1.6 The Plotting Grid 8

    1.7 Saving a Plot 8

    1.8 Grid Color 9

    1.9 Tick Marks 9

    1.10 Custom Grid Lines 11

    1.11 Labelling the Axes 13

    1.12 The Plot Title 14

    1.13 Colors 15

        1.13.1 Color Mixing 16

        1.13.2 Color Intensity 19

    1.14 Overplotting 20

    1.15 Background Color 23

    1.16 The Plotting Area Shape 23

    1.17 How to Correct Shape Distortions 26

        1.17.1 Applying a Scale Factor When Plotting 27

        1.17.2 The Best Way: Scaling the Axes in plt.axis( ) 27

1.18 Coordinate Axes 29

1.19 Commonly Used Plotting Commands and Functions 30

　1.19.1 Points and Dots Using scatter() 31

　1.19.2 Lines Using plot() 32

　1.19.3 Arrows 33

　1.19.4 Text 34

　1.19.5 Lists, Tuples, and Arrays 36

　1.19.6 Arrays 41

　1.19.7 arange( ) 42

　1.19.8 range( ) 43

1.20 Summary 43

Chapter 2: Graphics in Two Dimensions **45**

2.1 Lines from Dots 45

2.2 Dot Art 50

2.3 Circular Arcs from Dots 52

2.4 Circular Arcs from Line Segments 59

2.5 Circles 60

2.6 Dot Discs 64

2.7 Ellipses 68

2.8 2D Translation 75

2.9 2D Rotation 78

2.10 Summary 100

Chapter 3: Graphics in Three Dimensions **101**

3.1 The Three-Dimensional Coordinate System 101

3.2 Projections onto the Coordinate Planes 104

3.3 Rotation Around the y Direction 106

3.4 Rotation Around the x Direction 109

3.5 Rotation Around the z Direction 111

3.6 Separate Rotations Around the Coordinate Directions 113

3.7 Sequential Rotations Around the Coordinate Directions 121

3.8 Matrix Concatenation 129

3.9 Keyboard Data Entry with Functional Program Structure 133

3.10 Summary 141

Chapter 4: Perspective **143**

4.1 Summary 152

Chapter 5: Intersections **153**

5.1 Line Intersecting a Rectangular Plane 153

5.2 Line Intersecting a Triangular Plane 166

5.3 Line Intersecting a Circle 181

5.4 Line Intersecting a Circular Sector 181

5.5 Line Intersecting a Sphere 187

5.6 Plane Intersecting a Sphere 196

5.7 Summary 201

Chapter 6: Hidden Line Removal **203**

6.1 Box 203

6.2 Pyramid 212

6.3 Planes 218

6.4 Sphere 225

6.5 Summary 233

Chapter 7: Shading **235**

7.1 Shading a Box 236

7.2 Shading a Sphere 246

7.3 Summary 253

Chapter 8: 2D Data Plotting **255**

8.1 Linear Regression 265

8.2 Function Fitting 269

8.3 Splines 275

8.4 Summary 283

Chapter 9: 3D Data Plotting 285

9.1 3D Surfaces.. 297

9.2 3D Surface Shading 305

9.3 Summary.. 319

Chapter 10: Demonstrations 321

10.1 Saturn 321

10.2 Solar Radiation.. 331

10.2.1 Photons and the Sun 331

10.2.2 Max Planck's Black Body Radiation................................ 333

10.2.3 The Sun's Total Power Output... 334

10.3 Earth's Irradiance.. 344

10.3.1 The Earth Sun Model 346

10.4 Summary.. 351

Appendix A: Where to Get Python 353

Appendix B: Planck's Radiation Law and the Stefan-Boltzmann Equation........... 355

Index... 359

About the Author

B.J. Korites has been involved in engineering and scientific applications of computers for his entire career. He has been an educator, consultant, and author of more than ten books on geometric modelling, computer graphics, artificial intelligence, simulation of physical processes, structural analysis, and the application of computers in science and engineering. He has been employed by Northrop Corporation, the Woods Hole Oceanographic Institute, Arthur D. Little, Itek, and Worcester Polytech. He has consulted for Stone and Webster Engineering, Gould Inc, Wyman Gordon, CTI Cryogenics, the US Navy, Aberdeen Proving Grounds, and others. Early in his career he developed mathematics and software that would find physical interferences between three-dimensional solid objects. This found wide application in the design of nuclear power plants, submarines, and other systems with densely packed spaces. He enjoys sailing and painting maritime landscapes in oils. He holds degrees from Tufts and Yale.

About the Technical Reviewer

 **Andrea Gavana** has been programming in Python for almost 15 years and dabbling with other languages since the late nineties. He graduated from university with a Master's degree in Chemical Engineering, and he is now a Senior Reservoir Engineer working for Maersk Oil in Copenhagen, Denmark.

Andrea enjoys programming at work and for fun, and he has been involved in multiple open source projects, all Python-based. One of his favorite hobbies is Python coding, but he is also fond of cycling, swimming, and cozy dinners with family and friends.

Acknowledgments

I would like to thank my wife, Pam, for her patience during the many long days and nights that I spent writing this book and for her understanding of the distant stare I sometimes had while off in another world thinking of math and Python, two of life's great joys. I would also like to thank everyone at Apress, especially editors Todd Green and Jill Balzano, who made the production of this book a fast and seamless process.

Acknowledgments

CHAPTER 1

Essential Python Commands and Functions

In this chapter, you will learn the essential Python commands and functions you will need to produce the illustrations shown in this book. You will learn how to use Python's basic plotting functions, set up a plotting area, create a set of two-dimensional coordinate axes, and use basic plotting primitives (the dot, the line, and the arrow), which are the building blocks you will use to construct images throughout this book. In Chapter 2, you will learn how to use these primitives to build two-dimensional images and then translate and rotate them. In Chapter 3, you will extend these concepts to three dimensions. Also in this chapter you will learn about colors, how to apply text to your plots, including the use of Latex commands, and the use of lists and arrays. By the last chapter, you will be able to create images such as Figure 1-1.

Figure 1-1. *Saturn*

© B.J. Korites 2018
B.J. Korites, *Python Graphics*, https://doi.org/10.1007/978-1-4842-3378-8_1

1.1 Programming Style

First a note on the programming style used in this book. We all have preferences when it comes to style. I favor a clear, top-down, open style. Many programmers try to reduce their code to as few lines as possible. That may be fine in practice but in an instructional text, such as we have here, I believe it is better to proceed slowly in small, simple steps. The intention is to keep everything clear and understandable. Since I do not know the skill level of the readers, and since I want to make this book accessible to as wide an audience as possible, I generally start each topic from an elementary level, although I do assume some familiarity with the Python language. If you are just learning Python, you will benefit from the material in this first chapter. If you are an accomplished Pythoner, you could probably skip it and move on to Chapter 2.

Some Python developers advocate using long descriptive names for variables such as "temperature" rather than "T." I find excessively long variable names make the code difficult to read. It's a matter of preference. With relatively short programs such as we have in this book, there's no need for complex programming. Try to adopt a style that is robust rather than elegant but fragile.

My programs usually have the same structure. The first few statements are generally **import numpy as np**, **import matplotlib.pyplot as plt**, and so on. Sometime I will import from the **math** library with **from math import sin, cos, radians, sqrt**. These are commonly used functions in graphics programming. Importing them separately in this way eliminates the need to use prefixes as in **np.sin()**; you can just use **sin()**. Then I most often define the plotting area with **plt.axis([0,150,100,0])**. As explained in Section 1.2, these values, where the x axis is 50% wider than the y axis, produce a round circle and a square square without reducing the size of the plotting area. At this point, axes can be labelled and the plot titled if desired. Next, I usually define parameters (such as diameters, time constants, and so on) and lists. Then I define functions. Finally, in lengthy programs, at the bottom I put a control section that invokes the functions in the proper order.

Including **plt.axis('on')** plots the axes; **plt.grid(True)** plots a grid. They are very convenient options when developing graphics. However, if I do not want the axes or grid to show in the final output, I replace these commands with **plt.axis('off')** and **plt.grid(False)**. The syntax must be as shown here. See Section 1.10 to learn how to create your own grid lines if you are not satisfied with Python's defaults.

I often begin development of graphics by using the **scatter()** function which produces what I call *scatter dots*. They are fast and easy to use and are very useful in the development stage. If kept small enough and spaced closely together, dots can produce acceptable lines and curves. However, they can sometimes appear a bit fuzzy so, after I have everything working right, I will often go back and replace the dots with short line segments using either arrows via **plt.arrow()** or lines via **plt.plot()**. There is another aspect to the choice of dots or lines: which overplots which. You don't want to create something with dots and then find lines covering it up. This is discussed in Section 1.14.

Some variants of Python require the **plt.show()** statement at the end to plot graphics. My setup, Anaconda with Spyder and Python 3.5 (see Appendix A for installation instructions), does not require this but I include it anyway since it serves as a marker for the end of the program. Finally, press the F5 key or click on the Run button at the top to see what you have created. After you are satisfied, you can save the plot by right-clicking it and specifying a location.

Regarding the use of lists, tuples and arrays, they can be a great help, particularly when doing graphics programming that involves a lot of data points. They are explained in Section 1.19.5. An understanding of them, together with a few basic graphics commands and techniques covered in this chapter, are all you need to create the illustrations and images you see in this book.

1.2 The Plotting Area

A computer display with a two-dimensional coordinate system is shown in Figure 1-2. In this example, the origin of the x,y coordinate axes, (x=0, y=0), is located in the center of the screen. The positive x axis runs from the origin to the right; the y axis runs from the origin vertically downward. As you will see shortly, the location of the origin can be changed as can the directions of the x and y axes. Also shown is a point p at coordinates (x,y), which are in relation to the x and y axes.

The direction of the y axis pointing down in Figure 1-2 may seem a bit unusual. When plotting data or functions such as y=cos(x) or y=exp(x), we usually think of y as pointing up. But when doing technical graphics, especially in three dimensions, as you will see later, it is more intuitive to have the y axis point down. This is also consistent with older variants of BASIC where the x axis ran along the top of the screen from left to right and the y axis ran down the left side. As you will see, you can define y to point up or down, whichever best suits what you are plotting.

1.3 Establishing the Size of the Plotting Area

The plotting area contains the graphic image. It always appears the same *physical* size when displayed in the Spyder output pane. Spyder is the programming environment (see Appendix A). However, the *numerical* size of the plotting area, and of the values of the point, line, and arrow definitions within the plotting area, can be specified to be anything. Before doing any plotting, you must first establish the area's *numerical* size. You must also specify the location of the coordinate system's origin and the directions of the coordinate axes. As an illustration, Listing 1-1 uses the **plt.axis([x1,x2,y1,y2])** function in line 8 to set up an area running from x=-10 to +10; y=−10 to +10. The rest of the script will be explained shortly.

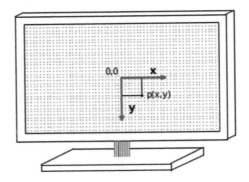

Figure 1-2. *A two-dimensional x,y coordinate system with its origin (0,0) centered in the screen. A point p is shown at coordinates (x,y) relative to x,y.*

Listing 1-1. Program PLOTTING_AREA

```
1  import numpy as np
2  import matplotlib.pyplot as plt
3
4  x1=-10
5  x2=10
6  y1=-10
7  y2=10
8  plt.axis([x1,x2,y1,y2])
9
10 plt.axis('on')
```

```
11 plt.grid(True)
12
13 plt.show()
```

Listing 1-1 produces the plotting area shown in Figure 1-3. It has a horizontal width of 20 and a vertical height of 20. I could have made these numbers 200 and 200, and the area would appear in an output pane as the same physical size but with different numerical values on the axes. Line 13 contains the command **plt.show()**. The purpose of this is to display the program's results in the output pane. With modern versions of Python it isn't required since the plots are automatically displayed when the program is run. With older versions it may or may not be displayed. **plt.show()** can also be placed within a program in order to show plots created during execution. Even though it may not be necessary, it's a good idea to include this command at the end of your script since it can serve as a convenient marker for the end of your program. Lines 1, 2, 10, and 11 in Listing 1-1 will be explained in the following sections. These commands, or variations of them, will appear in all of our programs.

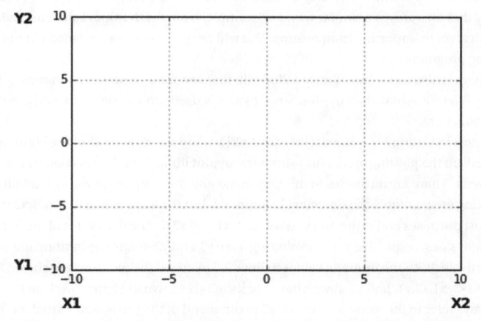

***Figure 1-3.** Plotting area produced by Listing 1-1 with (0,0) located in the center of the area*

1.4 Importing Plotting Commands

While Python has many built-in commands and functions available, some math and graphics commands must be imported. Lines 1 and 2 in Listing 1-1 do this. The **import numpy as np** statement in line 1 imports math functions such as **sin(ϕ)**, **e^α**, and so on. The **np** in this statement is an abbreviation that may be used when referring to a **numpy** function. When used in a program, these functions must be identified as coming from **numpy**. For example, if you were to code **v=e^α**, the program statement would be **v=np.exp(α)** where α would have been previously defined. You don't have to write out the full length **numpy.exp(α)** since you defined the shorthand **np** for **numpy** in line 1. Graphics commands are handled similarly. The statement **import matplotlib.pyplot as plt** imports the library **pyplot,** which contains graphics commands. **plt** is an abbreviation for **pyplot**. For example, if you want to plot a dot at x,y you would write **plt.scatter(x,y)**. I will talk more about **plt.scatter()** shortly.

Functions may also be imported directly from **numpy**. The statement **from numpy import sin, cos, radians** imports the **sin()**, **cos()**, and **radians()** functions. When imported in this manner they may be used without the **np** prefix. There is also a **math** library that operates in a similar way. For example, **from math import sin, cos, radians** is equivalent to importing from **numpy**. You will be using all these variations in the coming programs.

There is also a graphics library called **glib** that contains graphics commands. **glib** uses a different syntax than **pyplot**. Since **pyplot** is used more widely, you will use it in your work here.

Line 8 in Listing 1-1, **plt.axis([x1,x2,y1,y2])**, is the standard form of the command that sets up the plotting area. This is from the **pyplot** library and is preceded by the **plt.** prefix. There are attributes to this command and there are other ways of defining a plotting area, notably the **linspace()** command, but the form in line 8 is sufficient for most purposes and is the one you will use. x1 and x2 define the values of the left and right sides, respectively, of the plotting area; y1 and y2 define the bottom and top, respectively. With the numeric values in lines 8-11 you get the plotting area shown in Figure 1-3. x1,x2,y1, and y2 always have the locations shown in Figure 1-3. That is, x1 and y1 always refer to the lower left corner, y2 to other end of the y axis, and x2 to the other end of the x axis. Their values can change, but they always refer to these locations. They may be negative, as shown in Figure 1-4.

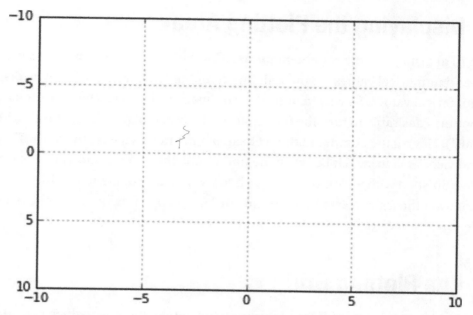

Figure 1-4. *Plotting area with (0,0) located in the center, positive y direction pointing down*

Because the x and y values specified in lines 4-7 are symmetric in both the x and y directions (i.e. −10, +10), this plotting area has the (x=0, y=0) point halfway between. In this case, the center of the area will be the origin used as reference for plotting coordinates. Since x1 < x2, the positive direction of the x axis will run horizontally from left to right. Similarly, since y1 < y2, the positive direction of the y axis will go vertically up. But earlier I said we want the positive y direction to go vertically down. You can do that by reversing the y values to y1=10, y2=−10. In this case, you get the area shown in Figure 1-4 where the positive x axis still goes from left to right but the positive y axis now points down. The center is still in the middle of the plotting area.

You could move the origin of the coordinate system off center by manipulating x1, x2,y1, and y2. For example, to move the x=0 point all the way to the left side, you could specify x1=0, x2=20. To move the (x=0, y=0) point to the lower left corner, you could specify x1=0, x2=20, y1=0, y2=20. But that would make the positive y direction point up; you want it to point down, which you can do by making y2=0, y1=20. This will make the origin appear in the *upper* left corner. You are free to position the (0,0) point anywhere, change the direction of positive x and y, and scale the numerical values of the coordinate axes to suit the image you will be trying to create. The numerical values you are using here could be anything. The physical size of the plot produced by Python will be the same; only the values of the image coordinates will change.

1.5 Displaying the Plotting Area

In line 10 of Listing 1-1 the statement **plt.axis('on')** displays the plotting area with its frame and numerical values. If you omit this command, the frame will still be displayed with numerical values. So why include this command? Because, when creating a plot it is sometimes desirable to turn the frame off. To do that, replace **plt.axis('on')** with **plt. axis('off')**. Having the command there ahead of time makes it easy to type **'off'** over **'on'** and vice versa to switch between the frame showing and not showing. Also, after you have finished with a plot, you may wish to use it in a document, in which case you may not want the frame. Note that **'on'** and **'off'** must appear in quotes, either single or double.

1.6 The Plotting Grid

Line 11 of Listing 1-1, **plt.grid(True),** turns on the dotted grid lines, which can be an aid when constructing a plot, especially when it comes time to position textual information. If you do not include this command, the grid lines will not be shown. To turn off the grid lines, change the **True** to **False**. Note the first letter in **True** and **False** is capitalized. **True** and **False** do *not* appear in quotations marks. As with **plt.axis()**, having the **plt. grid(True)** and **plt.grid(False)** commands there makes it easy to switch back and forth. Again, note that both **True** and **False** must have the first letter capitalized and do *not* appear in quotes.

1.7 Saving a Plot

The easiest way to save a plot that appears in the output pane is to put your cursor over it and right-click. A window will appear allowing you to give it a name and specify where it is to be saved. It will be saved the .png format. If you are planning to use it in a program such as Photoshop, the .png format works. Some word processing and document programs may require the .eps (encapsulated Postscript) format. If so, save it in the .png format, open it in Photoshop, and resave it in the .eps format. It's a bit cumbersome but it works.

1.8 Grid Color

There are some options to the **plt.grid()** command. You can change the color of the grid lines with the **color='color'** attribute. For example, **plt.grid(True, color='b')** plots a blue grid. More color options will be defined shortly.

1.9 Tick Marks

The **plt.grid(True)** command will create a grid with Python's own choice of spacing, which may not be convenient. You can alter the spacings with the **plt.xticks(xmin, xmax, dx)** and **plt.yticks(ymin, ymax, dy)** commands. **min** and **max** are the range of the ticks; **dx** and **dy** are the spacing. While normally you want the tick marks to appear over the full range of x and y, you can have them appear over a smaller range if you wish. These commands appear in lines 23 and 24 of Listing 1-2.

Listing 1-2. Program TICK_MARKS

```
1   import numpy as np
2   import matplotlib.pyplot as plt
3
4   #——————————plotting area
5   x1=-10
6   x2=140
7   y1=90
8   y2=-10
9   plt.axis([x1,x2,y1,y2])
10  plt.axis('on')
11
12  #——————————grid
13  plt.grid(True,color='b')
14  plt.title('Tick Mark Sample')
15
16  #——————————tick marks
```

```
17 xmin=x1
18 xmax=x2
19 dx=10
20 ymin=y1
21 ymax=y2
22 dy=-5
23 plt.xticks(np.arange(xmin, xmax, dx))
24 plt.yticks(np.arange(ymin, ymax, dy))
25
26 plt.show()
```

The output is shown in Figure 1-5. In line 23, **xmin** and **xmax** are the beginning and end of the range of ticks along the x axis, similarly for line 24, which controls the y axis ticks. **dx** in line 19 spaces the marks 10 units apart from x1=-10 (line 5) to x2=140 (line 6). **dy** in line 22 is -5. It is negative because y2=-10 (line 8) while y1=+90 (line 7). Thus, as the program proceeds from y1 to y2, y decreases in value; hence **dy** must be negative.

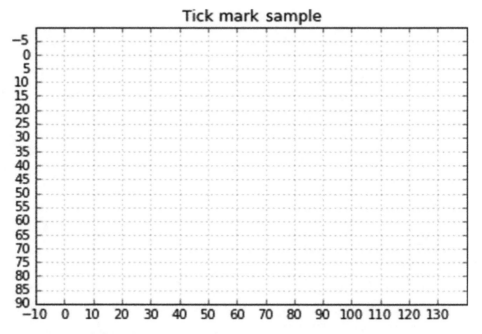

Figure 1-5. *User-defined tick mark*

1.10 Custom Grid Lines

The automatically generated grid that is produced by the **plt.grid(True)** command is not always satisfactory especially if you want to include text in your plot. It is often not fine enough to accurately place text elements. But if the **xtick()** and **ytick()** commands are used to reduce the spacing, the numbers along the axes can become cluttered. The numbers can be eliminated but then you do not have the benefit of using them to position textual information such as when labelling items on a plot. The grid shown in Figure 1-3 would be more helpful if the increments were smaller. You can produce your own grid lines and control them any way you want. The code in Listing 1-3 produces Figure 1-6, a plotting area with finer spacing between grid lines.

Listing 1-3. Program CUSTOM_GRID

```
 1   import numpy as np
 2   import matplotlib.pyplot as plt
 3
 4   x1=-5
 5   x2=15
 6   y1=-15
 7   y2=5
 8   plt.axis([x1,x2,y1,y2])
 9
10   plt.axis('on')
11
12   dx=.5                              #x spacing
13   dy=.5                              #y spacing
14   for x in np.arange(x1,x2,dx):      #x locations
15       for y in np.arange(y1,y2,dy):  #y locations
16       plt.scatter(x,y,s=1,color='grey')   #plot a grey point at x,y
17
18   plt.show()
```

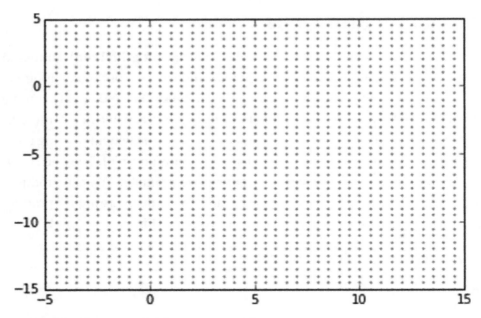

Figure 1-6. *Plotting area with custom grid*

The **scatter()** function in line 16 of Listing 1-3 plots a grey dot at every x,y location. I will discuss **scatter()** in more depth later. Note that **plt.grid(True)** is not used in this program. Lines 1-10 produce the plotting area with axes as before. This time, instead of using the **plt.grid(True)** command, you produce your own custom grid in lines 12-16. Lines 12 and 13 specify the spacing. The loop beginning at line 14 advances horizontally from left to right in steps **dx**. The loop beginning at line 15 does the same in the vertical direction. The size of the dot is specified as 1 by the **s=1** attribute in line 16. This could be changed: **s=.5** will give a smaller dot; **s=5** will give a larger one. The **color='grey'** attribute sets the dot color to grey. You can experiment with different size dots, colors, and spacings. Sometimes it can be beneficial to use the grid produced by **Grid(True)** along with a custom grid.

1.11 Labelling the Axes

Axes can be labelled with the **plt.xlabel('label')** and **plt.ylabel('label')** functions. As an example, the lines

```
plt.xlabel('this is the x axis')
plt.ylabel('this is the y axis')
```

when added to Listing 1-3 after line 10 produce Figure 1-7 where the custom grid dots have been changed to a lighter grey by using the attribute **color='lightgrey'** in the **plt. scatter()** function.

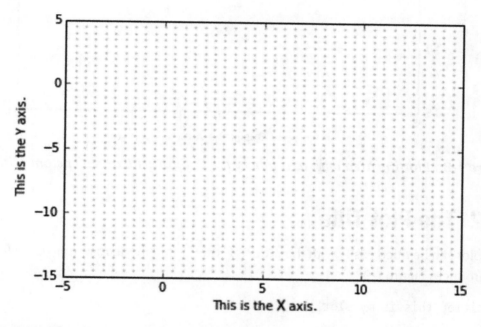

Figure 1-7. *Plotting area with axis labels and custom grid*

In Figure 1-8 you can see the matplotlib grid. This combination of Python's grid plus a custom grid makes a convenient working surface for locating elements.

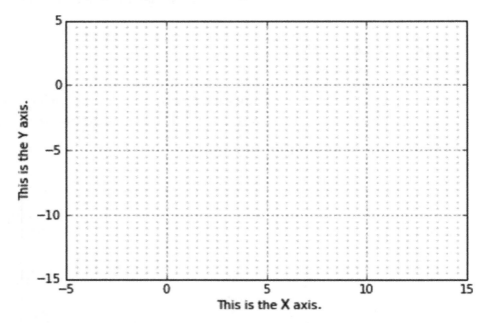

Figure 1-8. *Plotting area with axis labels, the Python grid, and a custom grid*

1.12 The Plot Title

Your plot can be titled easily with the **plt.title('title')** statement. Inserting the following line produces Figure 1-9:

```
plt.title('this is my plot')
```

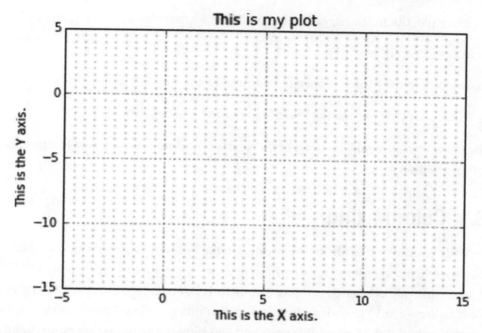

Figure 1-9. *Plotting area with axis labels, Python grid, custom grid, and title*

1.13 Colors

As you move along in this book, you will make good use of Python's ability to plot in color. Some of the colors available are

> 'k' for black
>
> 'b' for blue
>
> 'c' for cyan
>
> 'g' for green
>
> 'm' for magenta
>
> 'r' for red
>
> 'y' for yellow
>
> 'gray' or 'grey'
>
> 'lightgray' or 'lightgrey'

For example, the following statement will plot a green dot at coordinates x,y:

```
plt.scatter(x,y,color='g')
```

A swatch of many more colors can be found at

```
https://matplotlib.org/examples/color/named_colors.html.
```

The color attribute may be used in the **scatter()**, **plot()**, and **arrow()** functions along with other attributes.

1.13.1 Color Mixing

You can mix your own hues from the primary colors of red (r), green (g), and blue (b) with the specification **color=(r,g,b)** where r,g,b are the values of red, green, and blue in the mix, with values of each ranging from 0 to 1. For example **color=(1,0,0)** gives pure red; **color=(1,0,1)** gives magenta, a purplish mix of red and blue; **color=(0,1,0)** gives green; **color(.5,0.1)** gives more red and less blue in the magenta; **color(0,0,0)** gives black; and **color(1,1,1)** gives white. Keeping the r,g,b values the same gives a grey progressing from black to white as the values increase. That is, **color=(.1,.1,.1)** produces a dark grey, **color(.7,.7,.7)** gives a lighter grey, and **color(.5,.9,.5)** gives a greenish grey. Note that when specifying **'grey'** it can also be spelled **'gray'**.

Listing 1-4 shows how to mix colors in a program. Lines 7-9 establish the fraction of each color ranging from 0-1. The red component in line 7 depends on x, which ranges from 1-100. The green and blue components each have a value of 0 in this mix. Line 10 draws a vertical line at x from top to bottom having the color mix specified by the attribute **color=(r,g,b)**. The results are shown in Figure 1-10. The hue on the left side is almost black. This is because the amount of each color in the mix is 0 or close to it **(r=.01,g=0,b=0)**. The hue on the right is pure red since on that side **r=1,g=0,b=0**; that is, the red is full strength and is not contaminated by green or blue.

Listing 1-4. Program COLORS

```
1   import numpy as np
2   import matplotlib.pyplot as plt
3
```

```
4  plt.axis([0,100,0,10])
5
6  for x in np.arange(1,100,1):
7      r=x/100
8      g=0
9      b=0
10     plt.plot([x,x],[0,10],linewidth=5,color=(r,g,b))
11
12 plt.show()
```

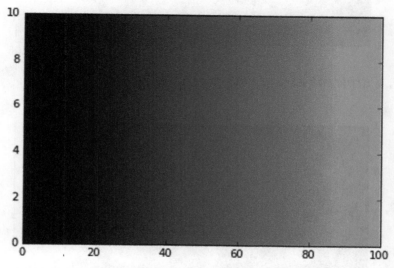

Figure 1-10. *Red color band produced by Listing 1-4 with r=x/100, g=0, b=0*

Figure 1-11 shows the result of adding blue to the mix. Figure 1-12 shows the result of adding green to the red. Mixing all three primary colors equally gives shades of grey ranging from black to white, as shown in Figure 1-13.

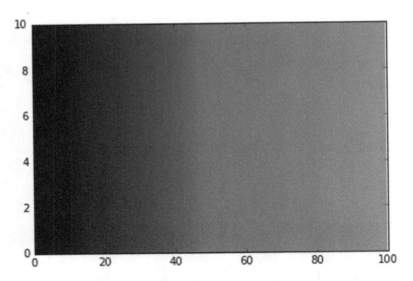

Figure 1-11. *Purple color band with r=x/100, g=0, b=x/100*

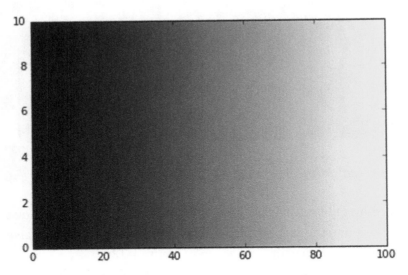

Figure 1-12. *Yellow color band with r=x/100, g=x/100, b=0*

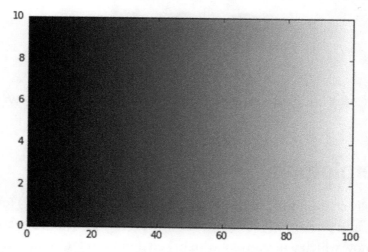

Figure 1-13. *Grey color band with r=x/100, g=x/100, b=x/100*

There are 256 values of each primary color available. Mixing them, as I did here, gives 256^3, which is almost 17 million different hues.

1.13.2 Color Intensity

The intensity of a color can be controlled with the **alpha** attribute, as shown in lines 6-8 in Listing 1-5, which produced Figure 1-14. **alpha** can vary from 0 to 1, with 1 producing the strongest hue and 0 the weakest.

Listing 1-5. Program COLOR_INTENSITY

```
1   import numpy as np
2   import matplotlib.pyplot as plt
3
4   plt.axis([0,100,0,10])
5
6   plt.scatter(60,50,s=1000,color='b',alpha=1)
7   plt.scatter(80,50,s=1000,color='b',alpha=.5)
8   plt.scatter(100,50,s=1000,color='b',alpha=.1)
9
10  plt.show()
```

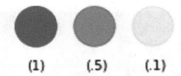

Figure 1-14. *Color intensity controlled by the attribute alpha shown in Listing 1-5*

1.14 Overplotting

You will normally create your graphics using the functions **plt.scatter()** for dots, **plt. plot()** for lines, and **plt.arrow()** for arrows and lines (arrows without heads). It is important to know which will overplot which. You don't want to create an elaborate image just to find it gets overplotted by something else. Figure 1-15 shows some examples. In (A), a red line (1) goes first, then a green one (2). Notice that the second line overplots the first. In (B), a blue dot (1) is plotted first and then a red line (2). The line overplots the dot. Then another blue dot (3) is plotted. It does not overplot the line. In (C), a red dot (1) is first plotted, then a blue one (2), then a yellow one (3). They overplot one another. In summary,

- New lines overplot old ones.

- Lines overplot dots.

- New dots overplot old ones.

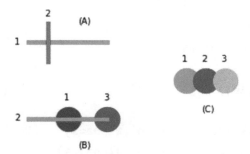

Figure 1-15. *Overplotting with lines and dots*

These examples were created by the following code:

```
#————————————————(A)
plt.text(45,10,'(A)')
plt.plot([20,60],[20,20],linewidth=5,color='r')
plt.text(13,21,'1')
plt.plot([30,30],[10,30],linewidth=5,color='g')
plt.text(28,6,'2')

#————————————————(B)
plt.text(45,75,'(B)')
plt.scatter(40,60,s=800,color='midnightblue')
plt.text(38,50,'1')
plt.plot([20,60],[60,60],linewidth=5,color='r')
plt.text(13,61,'2')
plt.scatter(60,60,s=800,color='b')
plt.text(58,50,'3')

#————————————————(C)
plt.text(108,56,'(C)')
plt.scatter(100,40,s=800,color='r')
plt.text(98,30,'1')
plt.scatter(110,40,s=800,color='b')
plt.text(108,30,'2')
plt.scatter(120,40,s=800,color='y')
plt.text(118,30,'3')
```

Figure 1-16 shows arrows. In (A) a red line is put down first and then a green arrow. The arrow does not overplot the line. Then a blue arrow is drawn. The red line still takes precedence and covers the blue arrow. In (B) a dark blue dot is plotted first and then a red arrow. The arrow covers the dark blue dot. Then a blue dot is drawn. The arrow still takes precedence and covers the blue dot. In (C) a red arrow is drawn first and then a blue one. The new blue arrow covers the old red one. As a result, we can conclude that

- Lines cover arrows.

- Arrows cover dots.

- New arrows cover old ones.

In general, we can say that lines overplot everything, even older lines; dots don't overplot anything except older dots; and arrows overplot dots and older arrows but not lines.

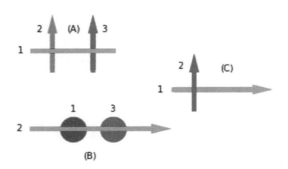

Figure 1-16.   *Overplotting with lines, arrows, and dots*

The code that produced Figure 1-16 is

```
#———————————————(A)
plt.plot([20,60],[20,20],linewidth=5,color='r')
plt.text(13,21,'1')
plt.arrow(30,30,0,-20,linewidth=5,head_length=4,head_width=2,color='g')
plt.text(22,10,'2')
plt.arrow(50,30,0,-20,linewidth=5,head_length=4,head_width=2,color='b')
plt.text(54,10,'3')
#———————————————(B)
plt.scatter(40,60,s=800,color='midnightblue')
plt.text(39,51,'1')
plt.arrow(20,60,60,0,linewidth=5,head_length=4,head_width=2,color='r')
plt.text(12,61,'2')
plt.scatter(60,60,s=800,color='b') plt.text(58,51,'3')
#———————————————(C)
plt.arrow(90,40,40,0,linewidth=5,head_length=4,head_width=2,color='r')
plt.text(82,41,'1')
plt.arrow(100,50,0,-20,linewidth=5,head_length=4,head_width=2,color='b')
plt.text(92,29,'2')
```

1.15 Background Color

The preceding section offers implications for painting a background. Normally, images are drawn on the computer screen in a color against a white background. It can sometimes be useful to plot against a dark background, such as black or midnight blue. Figure 1-17 shows an example taken from Chapter 6. The black background is obtained by first covering the plotting area with black lines. The sphere is then drawn with green lines, which overplot the black ones. You could also have painted the background with **scatter()** dots but lines take less computer processing time. If you had chosen to draw the sphere with dots, the background lines would have covered them up. If you did draw the sphere with dots, you could have painted the background with dots first and the newer sphere dots would have overplotted them.

Figure 1-17. *Sphere plotted against a black background*

1.16 The Plotting Area Shape

When using the **plt.axis()** command to set up a plotting area, it will normally appear in the output pane as rectangular rather than square, even though the x and y axes dimensions indicate it should be square. This is shown in Figure 1-18, which was created by Listing 1-6 where the values in Line 7 indicate the area should be square. This distortion may be problematic at times since it can distort objects. For example, a mathematically correct circle may appear as an oval or a mathematically correct square may appear as a rectangle, as shown in Figure 1-18.

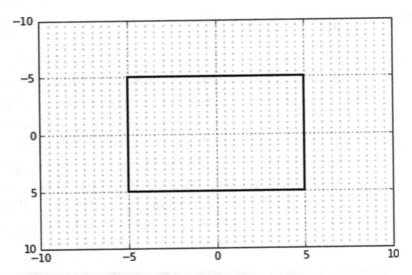

Figure 1-18. *Distortion of a mathematically correct square*

Listing 1-6. Program SQUARE

```
1   import numpy as np
2   import matplotlib.pyplot as plt
3
4   plt.grid(True)
5   plt.axis('on')
6
7   plt.axis([-10,10,10,-10])
8
9   #───────────────custom grid
10  x1=-10
11  x2=10
12  y1=10
13  y2=-10
14
15  dx=.5
16  dy=-.5
17  for x in np.arange(x1,x2,dx):
18      for y in np.arange(y1,y2,dy):
19          plt.scatter(x,y,s=1,color='lightgray')
20
```

24

```
21 #————————————square box
22 plt.plot([-5,5],[-5,-5],linewidth=2,color='k')
23 plt.plot([5,5],[-5,5],linewidth=2,color='k')
24 plt.plot([5,-5],[5,5],linewidth=2,color='k')
25 plt.plot([-5,-5],[5,-5],linewidth=2,color='k')
26
27 plt.show()
```

As shown in Figure 1-19, you can correct this distortion by including the command

```
plt.axes().set_aspect('equal')
```

in Listing 1-6 after line 7. This squares the box by squaring the plotting area. Unfortunately, it also shrinks the plotting area's width. This may not be convenient for certain images where you may want the full width of the plotting area without the accompanying distortions.

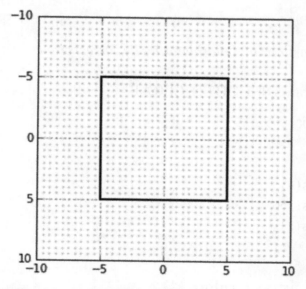

Figure 1-19. *Distortion corrected by equalizing axes*

1.17 How to Correct Shape Distortions

Figure 1-20 again illustrates the problem, this time when you try to plot a circle. You have a plotting area with numerically equal x and y dimensions, each of which is 100 units in extent. When you plot a mathematically correct circle, you get Figure 1-20, an ellipse. Listing 1-7 produced Figure 1-20.

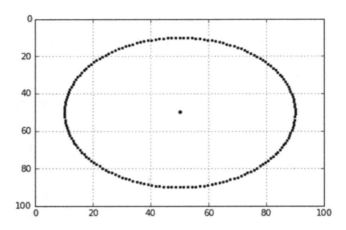

Figure 1-20. *Distortions of a mathematically correct circle*

Listing 1-7. Program DISTORTED_CIRCLE

```
1  plt.axis([0,100,100,0])
2
3  r=40
4  alpha1=radians(0)
5  alpha2=radians(360)
6  dalpha=radians(2)
7  xc=50
8  yc=50
9  plt.scatter(xc,yc,s=10,color='k')
10 for alpha in np.arange(alpha1,alpha2,dalpha):
11      x=xc+r*cos(alpha)
12      y=yc+r*sin(alpha)
13      plt.scatter(x,y,s=5,color='k')
```

Obviously, this is not going to work. You must find a way to get a true circle, not an ellipse.

1.17.1 Applying a Scale Factor When Plotting

The circle in Figure 1-20 is constructed with **scatter()** dots. You could try to apply a correction factor, a scale factor of sfx, to the x coordinate of each dot as it is plotted. How do you get sfx? Using a ruler, measure on the screen of your monitor Δx and Δy, which are the x and y displayed spans of the elliptical circle. You use a ruler for this since monitors differ in horizontal and vertical pixel spacing. Suppose these come out to be $\Delta x = 7.5$cm, $\Delta y = 5$cm. The scale factor to be applied to the x coordinate of each point would be sfx=$\Delta y/\Delta x = 5/7.5 \cong .67$. Replacing line 11 in Listing 1-6 with

$$x=xc+\textbf{sfx}*r*cos(alpha)$$

where sfx=.67, you get Figure 1-21. The problem with this method is every x coordinate that is to be plotted must be multiplied by sfx.

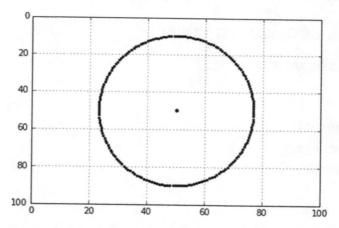

Figure 1-21. *Distortion corrected by applying a scale factor to each point as it is plotted*

1.17.2 The Best Way: Scaling the Axes in plt.axis()

The best way to correct the distortion is to apply a scale factor to the x axis through the **plt.axis()** function. Using the circle above as an example, the scale factor to be applied to the x-axis is $\Delta x/\Delta y = 7.5/5 = 1.5$. Using this in the **plt.axis()** function it becomes

```
plt.axis([0,150,100,0])
```

The circle code, which produced Figure 1-22, now becomes Listing 1-8.

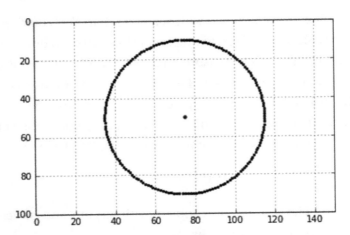

Figure 1-22. *Distortion corrected by applying a scale factor to the x axis*

Listing 1-8. THE_BEST_WAY_TO_CORRECT_DISTORTIONS

```
1  plt.axis([0,150,100,0])
2
3  r=40
4  alpha1=radians(0)
5  alpha2=radians(360)
6  dalpha=radians(2)
7  xc=75
8  yc=50
9  plt.scatter(xc,yc,s=10,color='k')
10 for alpha in np.arange(alpha1,alpha2,dalpha):
11     x=xc+r*cos(alpha)
12     y=yc+r*sin(alpha)
13     plt.scatter(x,y,s=5,color='k')
14
15 plt.show()
```

This gives you Figure 1-22, a true circle. Line 1 in Listing 1-8 makes sure the x axis is 1.5 times the y axis in numerical length. The y axis could have any numerical length. You will still get a true circle or a square square as long as the x axis is 1.5 times the y axis as defined by the **plt.axis()** function. For example, **plt.axis([0,1800,1200,0])** will work.

In most of the sample programs in the book, you will use a standard plotting area defined by **plt.axis([0,150,100,0])**. The 1.5 scaling factor may have to be fine tuned for your display.

1.18 Coordinate Axes

As you have seen, to construct graphic images, points, lines and arrows are placed on the plotting area at coordinates that have numerical values relative to an origin at x=0,y=0. While it is not necessary to show either the coordinate axes or their origin, they are often an aid when creating images since they indicate the location of the (0,0) point and the directions of positive x and y values. Figure 1-23 shows axes which are drawn using the **plt.arrow()** function in Listing 1-9 lines 23 and 24.

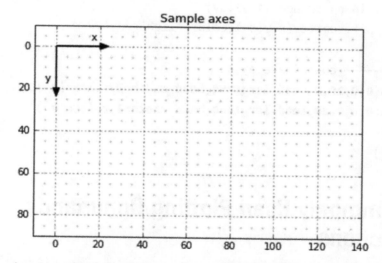

Figure 1-23. *A convenient working surface: 100x150 plotting area, Python grid, custom grid, frame out of the way*

Listing 1-9. Program COORDINATE_AXES

```
1  import numpy as np
2  import matplotlib.pyplot as plt
3
4  x1=-10 #—Δx=150
5  x2=140
```

```
6   y1=90  #--Δy=100
7   y2=-10
8   plt.axis([x1,x2,y1,y2])
9
10  plt.axis('on')
11  plt.grid(True)
12
13  plt.title('Sample Axes')
14
15  #——————————grid
16  dx=5
17  dy=-5
18  for x in np.arange(x1,x2,dx):
19      for y in np.arange(y1,y2,dy):
20          plt.scatter(x,y,s=1,color='lightgray')
21
22  #——————-coordinate axes
23  plt.arrow(0,0,20,0,head_length=4,head_width=3,color='k')
24  plt.arrow(0,0,0,20,head_length=4,head_width=3,color='k')
25
26  plt.show()
```

1.19 Commonly Used Plotting Commands and Functions

You saw the use of several plotting commands and functions in the previous sections. In the following sections, you will look at those commands, and others, in more depth. You will also learn some optional attributes for those functions. Note that I won't list all attributes available since most of them are often not used; I only include here the most important attributes that are required to create the illustrations in this book.

1.19.1 Points and Dots Using scatter()

`plt.scatter(x,y,s=`*size*`,color=`'*color* ')

scatter() plots a solid dot at coordinates x,y. **size** is the size of the dot: **s=.5** makes a small dot; **s=10** makes a bigger one. We use the term *point* to describe a small dot. The dot's physical size in relation to your plot will depend on the plotting area's scale. The best way to determine the most appropriate size of a dot is to experiment by making it larger or smaller until you get what you want. **color** is the dot's color. There are other attributes available for **scatter()** but we won't use them in this book.

I discussed colors earlier in the section on colors; for most normal applications, those colors should be satisfactory. For example, **color='r'** gives a red dot, **color='k'** gives a black one. You can also mix rgb colors, as explained earlier, with the statement **color=(r,g,b)** where r=red, g=green, and b=blue.

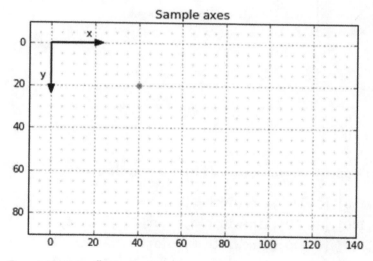

Figure 1-24. *Green scatter() dot at x=40,y=20*

The values of each of these three parameters can range from 0 to 1. While colors can sometimes be useful, much can be done with **'k'** (black), **'grey'**, and **'lightgrey'**. As a general rule, the addition of color to a plot can be a great aid in conveying information. However, too much color can create confusion. For an example of **scatter()**,

`plt.scatter(40,20,s=2,color='g')`

plots a green dot of size 2 at x=40,y=20, as shown in Figure 1-24. Note that these x,y coordinates are relative to the origin of the coordinate axes.

1.19.2 Lines Using plot()

plt.plot([x1,x2],[y1,y2],linewidth=*linewidth*,
                    color='*color* ',linestyle='*linestyle*')

This command draws a line from x1,y1 to x2,y2. It has a width specified by **linewidth**, a color by **color,** and a style by **linestyle**. Regarding **linewidth**, the appearance of a line's width will depend on the plot's scale so it can best be determined by experiment. Regarding **linestyle**, the ones shown in Figure 1-25 are usually sufficient.

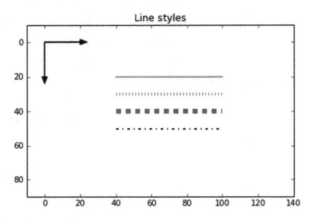

Figure 1-25. *Line styles*

The lines in Figure 1-25 were created by the following code:

```
plt.plot([40,100],[20,20],linewidth=2,color='r')
plt.plot([40,100],[30,30],linewidth=4,color='g',linestyle=':')
plt.plot([40,100],[40,40],linewidth=6,color='b',linestyle='-')
plt.plot([40,100],[50,50],linewidth=2,color='k',linestyle='-.')
```

There are other line styles available, which can be found with an Internet search.

1.19.3 Arrows

```
plt.arrow(x,y,Δx,Δy,line_width='linewidth',
                head_length='headlength',
                head_width='headwidth',
                color='color ')
```

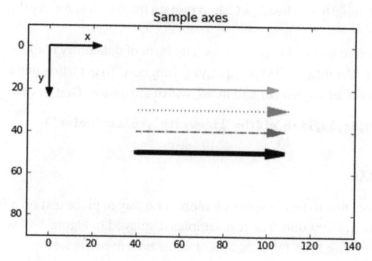

Figure 1-26. *Arrows*

The arrows shown in Figure 1-26 were drawn with the following commands:

```
plt.arrow(40,20,60,0,linewidth=1,color='r',head_length=5,
    head_width=3)
```

```
plt.arrow(40,30,60,0,linewidth=1,color='g',linestyle=':',
    head_length=10,head_width=5)
```

```
plt.arrow(40,40,60,0,linewidth=1,color='b',linestyle='-',
    head_length=8,head_width=4)
```

```
plt.arrow(40,50,60,0,linewidth=4,color='k',linestyle='-',
    head_length=8,head_width=3)
```

Δx and Δy are the changes in x and y from beginning to end of the arrow's shaft; the **linewidth** establishes the thickness of the arrow's shaft. The **head_width** specifies the width of the head; the **head_length** specifies its length. The arrow's head length adds to the overall length of the arrow. Adding the shaft length to the head length to get the total arrow length is not much of a problem with vertical and horizontal arrows. For example, to draw a horizontal arrow with an overall length of 13, you specify a Δx of 7, **head_length=3**. But it can be tricky when constructing oblique arrows that must fit within a specific length. The best thing to do in that case is to use a trial and error approach adjusting Δx, Δy, and **head_length** until it comes out right. Usually you will want **head_length** and **head_width** to remain fixed so it is Δx, Δy that usually get changed.

Arrows can also be used to draw lines. The form of data entry is sometimes more convenient than the **plt.plot([x1,x2],[y1,y2])** function. To get a line without the arrow head, just omit the **head_length** and **head_width** attributes. That is, write the following:

```
plt.arrow(x,y,Δx,Δy,line_width='linewidth',color='color')
```

1.19.4 Text

Python considers text to be a graphic element. The way to place text on a Python plot is to use the **plt.text()** function. The text samples displayed in Figure 1-27 were produced by the code in Listing 1-10. Lines 30 and 31 show how to rotate text:

```
plt.text(x,y,'text',color='color ',size='size',fontweight='fontweight ',
    fontstyle='fontstyle',rotation=degrees)
```

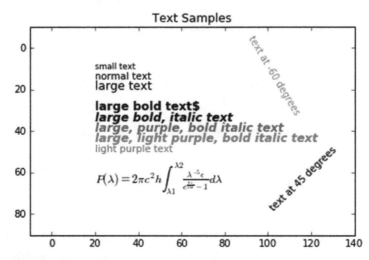

Figure 1-27. *Text samples*

Listing 1-10. Program TEXT_SAMPLES

```
1  import numpy as np
2  import matplotlib.pyplot as plt
3
4  x1=-10
5  x2=140
6  y1=90
7  y2=-10
8  plt.axis([x1,x2,y1,y2])
9
10 plt.axis('on')
11 plt.grid(False)
12
13 plt.title('Text Samples')
14
15
16 #───────────────text samples
17 plt.text(20,10,'small text',size='small')
18 plt.text(20,15,'normal text')
19 plt.text(20,20,'large text',size='large')
20
21 plt.text(20,30,'large bold text',size='large',fontweight='bold')
22 plt.text(20,35,'large bold,italic
23 text',size='large',fontweight='bold',fontstyle='italic')
24 plt.text(20,40,'large, pure, bold italic
25 text',size='large',fontweight='bold',fontstyle='italic',color=(.5,0,.5))
26 plt.text(20,45,'large, light purple, bold italic
27 text',size='large',fontweight='bold',fontstyle='italic',color=(.8,0,.8))
28 plt.text(20,50,'light purple text',color=(.8,0,.8))
29
30 plt.text(100,50,'text at 45 degrees',rotation=45,color='k')
31 plt.text(90,-3,'text at -60 degrees',rotation=-60,color='g')
32
```

```
33 plt.text(20,65,r'$P(\lambda)=2 \pi c^{2} h
      \int_{\lambda1}^{\lambda2}\frac{\lambda^{-5}\epsilon}
      {e^{\frac{hc}{\lambda k t}}-1}d\lambda$',size='large')
34
35 plt.show()
```

The equation at the bottom of Figure 1-27 is Max Planck's black body radiation equation which gives the power radiated by a black body for wavelengths from $\lambda1 \to \lambda2$. The text for this equation is plotted by line 33 in Listing 1-9. The ability of Python to display this equation illustrates some of Python's graphical power. Python can plot as text much of what can be accomplished with Latex. Notice in line 33 that the Latex text between the single quotes is preceded by the lower case **r**. The **r** in front tells Python to treat the string as a raw string, thus keeping the backward slashes needed by Latex. It is **matplotlib** that knows it is Latex because of the dollar sign. The Latex code is put between dollar signs. Obviously there is more Latex text that could be displayed. In fact, this entire book was written and formatted in Latex. All the illustrations in it have been created with Python.

1.19.5 Lists, Tuples, and Arrays

To draw an object such as a box with individual lines can often require a lot of typing. For example, to draw a square box you could define each edge with

```
plt.plot([-20,20],[-20,-20],linewidth=2,linestyle='-',color='r')
plt.plot([20,20],[-20,20],linewidth=2,linestyle='-',color='r')
plt.plot([20,-20],[20,20],linewidth=2,linestyle='-',color='r')
plt.plot([-20,-20],[20,-20],linewidth=2,linestyle='-',color='r')
```

A more efficient way is to use lists:

```
x=[-20,20,20,-20,-20]
y=[-20,-20,20,20,-20]
plt.plot(x,y,linewidth=2,linestyle='-',color='g')
```

Each x[i],y[i] pair in these lists represents the coordinates of a point. The **plt.plot(x,y...)** function automatically connects point x[i],y[i] with x[i+1], y[i+1]. The 5th element in these lists has the same coordinates as element 0. This closes the box.

Finite sequences of numbers enclosed in square brackets such as **x=[x1,x2,x3,x4,x5]** and **y=[y1,y2,y3,y4,y5]** are called **lists**. Lists are very useful, especially in computer graphics. The x,y pairs (x1,y1),(x2,y2),(x3,y3).... in these lists substitute for the syntax **([x1,x2],[y1,y2])** in individual **plt.plot** functions. You can draw virtually any shape with them; the lines will be connected in sequence.

List elements can be defined individually as above, or they can be specified as in the following structure:

```
1  x=[ ]
2  for i in range(10):
3       x.append(i*i)
4
5  print(x)
6
7  [0,1,4,9,16,25,36,49,64,81]
```

Line 1 defines an empty list x which contains no elements. The length of the list is not specified. The loop starting at line 2 increments i from 0 to 9 (10 elements). Line 3 adds i*i to the list as an additional element every cycle through the loop starting with element 0. Line 7 shows the results.

Another way to do this is to predefine the list elements, as in line 1 below. The numbers in the list could be anything; they just serve to define the length of the list. Line 4 changes the value of each element to i*i in the loop starting at line 3.

```
1  x=[0,1,2,3,4,5,6,7,8,9]
2
3  for i in range(10):
4       x[i]=(i*i)
5
6  print(x)
7
8  [0,1,4,9,16,25,36,49,64,81]
```

A list's length can also be defined by

g=[0]*10

where the list g is defined as having 10 elements each having a value 0. To get the length of a list, use the function

len(x)

which returns the length of list x, the length being the number of elements in the list. For example, in the following script, the loop will process all elements of list x from element 0 to the last element of x, adding 3 to each element:

```
x=[4,0,7,1]

for i in range(len(x)):
    x[i]=x[i]+3

print(x)

[7,3,10,4]
```

You will use all these methods in the programs that follow.

A **tuple**, which is a sequence of numbers such as **x=(x0,x1,x2,x3,x4)**, is similar to a list. The difference is, aside from the style of brackets, the elements inside a tuple are immutable, meaning they cannot be changed (mutated). The elements in a list, on the other hand, can be changed. Tuples can be used without the parentheses. For example, **v=7,12** is equivalent to **v=(7,12)**, which defines a tuple having two elements; the first having a value of 7, the second 12.

The use of lists and tuples is certainly a more efficient method of coding, as opposed to doing it the long way; that is, by using separate **np.plot()** lines for each leg of a figure. On the other hand, they can sometimes be problematic. For example, if you have long x and y lists or tuples, and your plot is not coming out right, it can be a tedious process to find the offending element. The long way can be speeded up by using copy and paste. Copy the first line and paste it into the code as the second, and then change the x and y coordinate values to produce the second line segment and so on for the remaining lines. Obviously, if you have a lot of points to deal with, you won't want to copy and paste the **plt.plot()** function over and over again, in which case a list or tuples may become a more viable option. Whether to use lists and tuples, or do it the long way, is a personal preference.

If you want to draw just one line segment you can use the syntax

```
x=[x1,x2]
y=[y1,y2]
plt.plot(x,y)
```

or

```
plt.plot([x1,x2],[y1,y2])
```

To draw two line segments, you can use

```
x=[x1,x2,x3]
y=[y1,y2,y3]
plt.plot(x,y)
```

or

```
plt.plot([x1,x2],[y1,y2])
plt.plot([x2,x3],[y2,y3])
```

and so on. Each method has its advantages. You will use both in this text.

In fact, Listing 1-11 uses both methods. It first plots a red square using individual **np.plot** commands for each side and then a green one using lists. The output is shown in Figure 1-28.

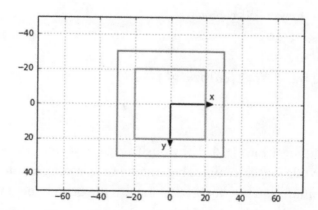

Figure 1-28. *Green box plotted using lists; red box plotted without lists*

Listing 1-11. Program LISTS

```
1   import numpy as np
2   import matplotlib.pyplot as plt
3
4   plt.axis([-75,75,50,-50])
5
6   plt.axis('on')
7   plt.grid(True)
8
9   plt.arrow(0,0,20,0,head_length=4,head_width=3,color='k')
10  plt.arrow(0,0,0,20,head_length=4,head_width=3,color='k')
11
12  plt.text(22,-3,'x')
13  plt.text(-5,25,'y')
14
15  #————————————red box
16  plt.plot([-20,20],[-20,-20],linewidth=2,color='r')
17  plt.plot([20,20],[-20,20],linewidth=2,color='r')
18  plt.plot([20,-20],[20,20],linewidth=2,color='r')
19  plt.plot([-20,-20],[-20,20],linewidth=2,color='r')
20
21  #————————————green list box
22  x=[-30,30,30,-30,-30]
23  y=[-30,-30,30,30,-30]
24  plt.plot(x,y,linewidth=2,color='g')
25
26  plt.show()
```

Doing it the long way (lines 16-19) obviously requires a lot more typing than using lists (lines 22-24). While lists and tuples have some time-saving features, they can be tricky to use. A common trap is to forget that in both the first element is not element 1, it is element 0. For example, with a list of

$$x = [1, 2, 3, 4, 5] \qquad (1.1)$$

if you were to include it in a program with the statement **print('x[4])=',x[4])**, you would get 5 for an answer. If you asked for **x[1]**, you would get 2. Tuples have the same idiosyncrasy. This peculiar feature is highly error-prone and must always be kept in mind when using lists and tuples. Incidentally, when asking for the value of an element in either a list *or* tuple you must use square brackets, not round ones. For example, to get the third element in x above you would ask for **x[2]**.

1.19.6 Arrays

The following is a typical array:

```
A=np.array([ [x0,y0,z0],[x1,y1,z1],[x2,y2,z2],............[xn,yn,zn] ])
```

array is a **numpy** function and must be preceded by the **np** prefix. As you see, the array A above has n+1 elements, each of which is a list containing three items. Each elements could represent the x,y,z coordinates of a point in three-dimensional space. Suppose you have an array holding three points as in

```
A=np.array([ [7,3,9],[34,21,65],[19,21,3] ])
```

where each element of A represents a point. To print the x,y,z coordinates of the second point (point 1) for example,

```
print(A[1])
```

```
34,21,65
```

The result isn't 7,3,9, of course, since that is point 0. To print the z coordinate of point 1,

```
print(A[1,2])
```

```
65
```

The 1 is point 1 (0,**1**,2); the 2 is the z coordinate (x,y,**z**). Other operations on arrays are similar to those used with lists. Arrays are very convenient to use when doing three-dimensional graphics. You will be using them in later chapters.

1.19.7 arange( )

arange() is a **numpy** function. It is useful for incrementing a floating point variable between limits. It must be used with the **np.** prefix unless it is imported explicitly with **from Numpy import arange**. The syntax is

```
for x in np.arange(start,stop,step):
```

This will produce values of x from **start** to **stop** in increments of **step**. All values are floats. The colon must be included at the end. As an example,

```
for x in np.arange(1,5,2):
    print(x)
1
3
```

What happened to the 5? Shouldn't you be getting 1, 1+2=3, 3+2=5? The 5 is lost to small roundoff errors within the computer. That is, when your computer adds 3+2, it may get something very slightly larger or smaller than 5, which means you may or may not get the 5. This illustrates one of the faults with **arange()**. The cure is to make the **stop** value slightly larger than what you want (or slightly smaller if going in the negative direction).

```
for x in np.arange(1,5.1,2):
    print(x)
1
3
5
```

If you are plotting a circle by incrementing an angle from 0 to 360 degrees and you find the circle isn't closing but is leaving a small gap, the round-off error in the **np.arange** function could be the problem.

start, **stop,** and **step** may have negative as well as positive values. If **stop** is less than **start**, **step** should be negative.

1.19.8 range( )

range() is useful, especially in loops, for incrementing an integer variable through a range. It is a standard Python function and does not need a prefix. The syntax is

```
for x in range(start,stop,step):
```

where all values are integers. As an example,

```
for x in range(1,5,1):
    print(x)
```

```
1
2
3
4
```

Again, what happened to the 5? Perversely, Python chooses to have **range()** return values only up to **one step less than stop**. To get the 5, you have to extend **stop** by one **step**.

```
for x in range(1,6,1):
    print(x)
```

```
1
2
3
4
5
```

As with **arange()**, **start**, **stop,** and **step** may have negative values. If **stop** is less than **start**, **step** should be negative.

1.20 Summary

In this chapter, you reviewed basic Python commands, those fundamental to Python as well as those specialized to graphics programming. You now have all the programming tools you will need to understand the following chapters and produce the illustrations shown in this book. All the graphics were create by the proper use of three fundamental building blocks: the dot, the line, and the arrow. Once you understand how to use them in a Python program, the main difficulties become the use of two and three-dimensional vector math and geometry, which will be ubiquitous in the work that follows.

CHAPTER 2

Graphics in Two Dimensions

In this chapter, you will learn how to construct two-dimensional images using points and lines. You learned the basic tools for creating images with Python in Chapter 1. In this chapter, you will expand on that and learn methods to create, translate and rotate shapes in two dimensions. You will also learn about the concept of relative coordinates, which will be used extensively throughout the remainder of this book. As usual, you will explore these concepts through sample programs.

2.1 Lines from Dots

You saw how to create a line with the command

```
plt.plot([x1,x2],[y1,y2],attributes)
```

This draws a line from (x1,y1) to (x2,y2) with *attributes* specifying the line's width, color, and style. At times it may be desirable to construct a line using dots. Figures 2-1 and 2-2 show the geometry: an inclined line beginning at point 1 and ending at point 2. Its length is Q. Shown on the line in Figure 2-2 is point p at coordinates x,y. To draw the line, you start at 1 and advance toward 2 in steps, calculating coordinates of p at each step and plotting a dot at each step as you go. This analysis utilizes vectors, which will be used extensively later.

Note that you do not have coordinate axes in these models. This analysis is generic; it is applicable to any two-dimensional orthogonal coordinate directions.

© B.J. Korites 2018
B.J. Korites, *Python Graphics*, https://doi.org/10.1007/978-1-4842-3378-8_2

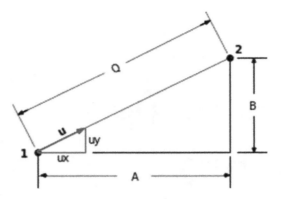

Figure 2-1. *Geometry for creating a line from dots (a)*

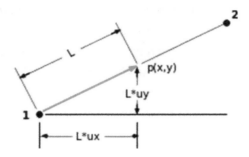

Figure 2-2. *Geometry for creating a line from dots (b)*

To advance from point 1 toward point 2, you must first determine the direction from 1 to 2. This will be expressed as a unit vector **û** (unit vectors will be shown in bold with a hat; full vectors in bold):

$$\hat{\mathbf{u}} = ux\hat{\mathbf{i}} + uy\hat{\mathbf{j}} \tag{2-1}$$

where $\hat{\mathbf{i}}$ and $\hat{\mathbf{j}}$ are unit vectors in the x and y directions; ux and uy are the *scalar* components of **û** in the x and y directions.

ux is the cosine of the angle between **û** and the x axis; uy is the cosine of the angle between **û** and the y axis. ux and uy are often referred to as direction cosines. It is easy to show they are cosines: the cosine of the angle between **û** and the x axis is ux/|**û**| , where |**û**| is the scalar magnitude of **û**. Since **û** is a unit vector, |**û**|=1;. The cosine of the angle is then ux/(1)=ux. Similarly for uy.

It is important to remember that

$$|\hat{\mathbf{u}}| = 1 \qquad (2\text{-}2)$$

since this feature enables you to multiply **û** by a magnitude to get a position vector. For example, you can get a vector from point 1 to p, **v1p**, by multiplying **û** by L where L is the distance from 1 to p. L gives the vector its magnitude, **û** gives its direction. A vector from point 1 to p is then

$$\mathbf{v1p} = L\left(ux\hat{\mathbf{i}} + uy\hat{\mathbf{j}}\right) \qquad (2\text{-}3)$$

You can calculate ux and uy from coordinate values as

$$ux = A/Q = (x2 - x1)/Q \qquad (2\text{-}4)$$
$$uy = B/Q = (y2 - y1)/Q \qquad (2\text{-}5)$$

where (x1,y1) and (x2,y2) are the coordinates of points 1 and 2, and

$$Q = \sqrt{(x2 - x1)^2 + (y2 - y1)^2} \qquad (2\text{-}6)$$

Listing 2-1 gives two examples of lines drawn with dots. The results are shown in Figure 2-3. Smaller dots and closer spacing will produce a finer line (green), which is almost as good the line obtained by using the **plt.plot([x1,x2],[y1,y2])** function.

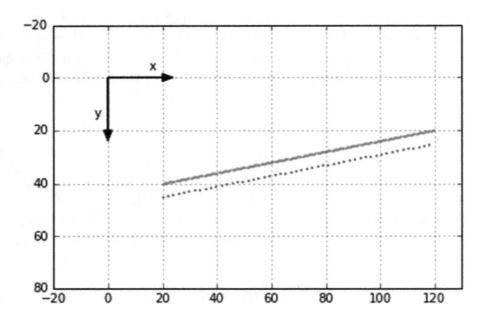

Figure 2-3. *Dot lines created by Listing 2-1*

Listing 2-1. Program DOTLINE

```
1    """
2    DOTLINE
3    """
4
5    import matplotlib.pyplot as plt
6    import numpy as np
7
8    plt.axis([-20,130,80,-20])
9
10   plt.axis('on')
11   plt.grid(True)
12
13   plt.arrow(0,0,20,0,head_length=4,head_width=3,color='k')
14   plt.arrow(0,0,0,20,head_length=4,head_width=3,color='k')
15   plt.text(15,-3,'x')
16   plt.text(-5,15,'y')
17
```

```
18   #——————————————green line
19   x1=20
20   x2=120
21   y1=40
22   y2=20
23
24   q=np.sqrt((x2-x1)**2+(y2-y1)**2)
25   ux=(x2-x1)/q
26   uy=(y2-y1)/q
27
28   for l in np.arange(0,q,.5):
29          px=x1+l*ux
30          py=y1+l*uy
31          plt.scatter(px,py,s=1,color='g')
32
33   #——————————————————————————————blue line
34   x1=20
35   x2=120
36   y1=45
37   y2=25
38
39   q=np.sqrt((x2-x1)**2+(y2-y1)**2)
40   ux=(x2-x1)/q
41   uy=(y2-y1)/q
42
43   for l in np.arange(0,q,2):
44          px=x1+l*ux
45          py=y1+l*uy
46          plt.scatter(px,py,s=1,color='b')
47
48   plt.show()
```

This program should be self-explanatory since the definitions are consistent with the prior analysis.

2.2 Dot Art

Interesting patterns can be created by arranging dots in a geometric pattern. Figure 2-4 shows some examples. In all three cases, the dots are arranged in a two-dimensional x,y matrix. You can vary the size of the dots, colors, and the x and y limits of the matrix. Each matrix is created with nested **for** loops, as shown in Listing 2-2, lines 20-22, 25-35, and 40-45. These nested loops sweep in the x direction then, at each x, in the y direction, thus filling out a rectangular area. Mondrian is composed of three separate dot rectangles plus a large red dot.

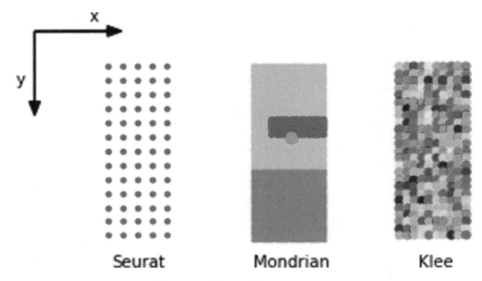

Figure 2-4. *Dot art created created by Listing 2-2*

In line 7, you import **random**. This is a library of random functions that you use in lines 42, 43, and 44 to produce random primary r,g,b color components. They are mixed in line 45. You will use **random**'s **random.randrange(a,b,c)** function to obtain the random values. You could also use the random functions that are included in **numpy**, although the syntax is a bit different. The **random** library is being used here to illustrate that there are other math libraries besides **numpy**.

random.randrange(a,b,c) returns a random number between a and b in increments c. a, b, and c must be integers. To obtain a wide selection of random numbers, let a=1, b=100, and c=1 in lines 42-44. But rr in line 42 must be between 0 and 1.0 so you divide by 100 in line 42. This provides a random value for rr, the red component of the color mix, between 0 and 1.0. Similarly for rg and rb, the green and blue components, in lines 43 and 44. As you can see, the results in Klee are quite interesting.

Listing 2-2. Program DOTART

```
1    """
2    DOTART
3    """
4
5    import matplotlib.pyplot as plt
6    import numpy as np
7    import random
8
9    plt.axis([10,140,90,-10])
10
11   plt.axis('off')
12   plt.grid(False)
13
14   plt.arrow(0,0,20,0,head_length=4,head_width=3,color='k')
15   plt.arrow(0,0,0,20,head_length=4,head_width=3,color='k')
16   plt.text(15,-3,'x')
17   plt.text(-5,15,'y')
18
19   #————————————————————————————————-plot Seurat
20   for x in np.arange(20,40,4):
21       for y in np.arange(10,60,4):
22           plt.scatter(x,y,s=8,color='b')
23
24   #————————————————————————————————-plot Mondrian
25   for x in np.arange(60,80,1):
26       for y in np.arange(10,40,1):
27           plt.scatter(x,y,s=8,color='y')
28
29   for x in np.arange(60,80,1):
30       for y in np.arange(40,60):
31           plt.scatter(x,y,s=8,color='g')
32
33   for x in np.arange(65,80,1):
34       for y in np.arange(25,30,1):
35           plt.scatter(x,y,s=8,color='b')
```

```
36
37  plt.scatter(70,30,s=50,color='r')
38
39  #—————————————————————————————plot Klee
40  for x in np.arange(100,120,2):
41          for y in np.arange(10,60,2):
42                  rr=random.randrange(0,100,1)/100 #-random red 0<=rr<=1
43                  rg=random.randrange(0,100,1)/100 #-random green 0<=rg<=1
44                  rb=random.randrange(0,100,1)/100 #-random blue 0<=rb<=1
45          plt.scatter(x,y,s=25,color=(rr,rg,rb))
46
47  #———————————————————————————————labels
48  plt.text(105,67,'Klee')
49  plt.text(60,67,'Mondrian')
50  plt.text(21,67,'Seurat')
51
52  plt.show()
```

2.3 Circular Arcs from Dots

Listing 2-3 draws a circular arc using points. This is your first program dealing with circular coordinates, angles, and trig functions. The geometry used by Listing 2-3 is shown in Figure 2-5. The output is shown in Figure 2-6.

Lines 25-31 in Listing 2-3 plot the arc. The center of curvature is at (xc,yc) as defined in lines 20 and 21. The radius of curvature is r in line 22. The arc starts at point 1, which is at an angle p1 relative to the x axis. It ends at point 2, which is at an angle p2. These angles, 20 and 70 degrees respectively, are set in lines 25 and 26 where they are converted to radians, the units required by **np.sin()** and **np.cos()**. In later programs, you will use the **radians()** function, which converts an argument from degrees to radians. The points on the arc are spaced an angular increment dp apart, as shown in line 27. dp is set to the total angle spanned by the arc, p2-p1, divided by 100. A wider spacing, say (p2-p1)/20, especially when combined with a smaller dot size, will give a more coarse arc. The loop running from line 28 to 31 advances the angle of each point by the increment dp using the **arange()** function. Lines 29 and 30 calculate the coordinates of each point relative to the *global* x,y system, which has its origin at (0,0). The global coordinates are those used for plotting. **xp=r*np.cos(p)** and **yp=r*np.(sin(p)** are the coordinates of p along the arc relative to the arc's center of curvature at (xc,yc). These are *local* coordinates. The coordinates of the center of curvature (xc,yc) must be added to the local coordinates to obtain the global coordinates relative to x=0,y=0. This is done in lines 29 and 30. Line 31 plots a green dot of size 1 at each location using the global coordinates. The results are shown in Figure 2-5 and the code is shown in Listing 2-4.

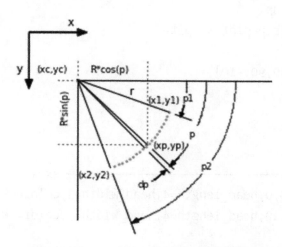

Figure 2-5. *Geometric model used for creating a circular arc with scatter() dots, created by Listing 2-4*

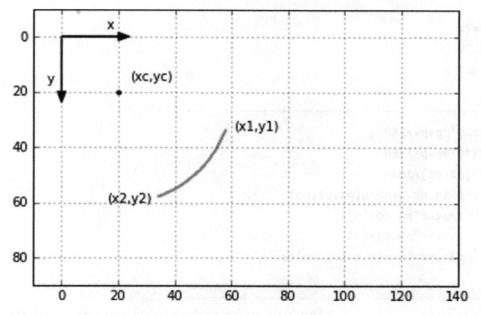

Figure 2-6. *Circular arc created with np.scatter() dots*

Listing 2-3. Program PARC

```
1    """
2    PARC
3    """
4
5    import numpy as np
6    import matplotlib.pyplot as plt
7
8    plt.axis([-10,140,90,-10])
9
10   plt.axis('on')
11   plt.grid(True)
12
13   #———————————————————————————————axes
14   plt.arrow(0,0,20,0,head_length=4,head_width=3,color='k')
15   plt.arrow(0,0,0,20,head_length=4,head_width=3,color='k')
16
17   plt.text(16,-3,'x')
18   plt.text(-5,17,'y')
19
20   xc=20
21   yc=20
22   r=40
23
24   #———————————————————————————————plot arc
25   p1=20*np.pi/180
26   p2=70*np.pi/180
27   dp=(p2-p1)/100
28   for p in np.arange(p1,p2,dp):
29       x=xc+r*np.cos(p)
30       y=yc+r*np.sin(p)
31       plt.scatter(x,y,s=1,color='g')
32
33   #———————————————————————————————labels
34   plt.text(61,34,'(x1,y1)')
```

```
35   plt.text(16,60,'(x2,y2)')
36   plt.scatter(xc,yc,s=10,color='k')
37   plt.text(xc+4,yc-4,'(xc,yc)',color='k')
38
39   plt.show()
```

(The following is the program that created Figure 2-5)

Listing 2-4. Program PARCGEOMETRY

```
1    """
2    PARCGEOMETRY
3    """
4
5    import numpy as np
6    import matplotlib.pyplot as plt
7
8    plt.axis([-10,140,90,-10])
9
10   plt.axis('off')
11   plt.grid(False)
12
13   #————————————————————————————coordinate axes
14   plt.arrow(0,0,20,0,head_length=4,head_width=3,color='k')
15   plt.arrow(0,0,0,20,head_length=4,head_width=3,color='k')
16
17   #————————————————————————————labels
18   plt.text(16,-3,'x')
19   plt.text(-5,17,'y')
20
21   #————————————————————————————main arc
22   xc=20
23   yc=20
24   r=40
25   plt.scatter(xc,yc,color='b',s=5)
26
27   phi1=20*np.pi/180.
```

```
28   phi2=70*np.pi/180.
29   dphi=(phi2-phi1)/20.
30   for phi in np.arange(phi1,phi2,dphi):
31       x=xc+r*np.cos(phi)
32       y=yc+r*np.sin(phi)
33       plt.scatter(x,y,s=2,color='g')
34
35   plt.plot([xc,xc+r*np.cos(phi1)],[yc,yc+r*np.sin(phi1)],color='k')
36
37   x1=xc+(r+3)*np.cos(phi1)
38   x2=xc+(r+10)*np.cos(phi1)
39   y1=yc+(r+3)*np.sin(phi1)
40   y2=yc+(r+10)*np.sin(phi1)
41   plt.plot([x1,x2],[y1,y2],color='k')
42
43   x1=xc+(r+3)*np.cos(phi2)
44   x2=xc+(r+30)*np.cos(phi2)
45   y1=yc+(r+3)*np.sin(phi2)
46   y2=yc+(r+30)*np.sin(phi2)
47   plt.plot([x1,x2],[y1,y2],color='k')
48
49   plt.plot([xc,xc+r*np.cos(phi2)],[yc,yc+r*np.sin(phi2)],color='k')
50
51   phihalf=(phi1+phi2)*.5
52   phi3=phihalf-dphi/2
53   phi4=phihalf+dphi/2
54
55   plt.plot([xc,xc+r*np.cos(phi3)],[yc,yc+r*np.sin(phi3)],color='k')
56   plt.plot([xc,xc+r*np.cos(phi4)],[yc,yc+r*np.sin(phi4)],color='k')
57
58   x1=xc+(r+3)*np.cos(phi3)
59   x2=xc+(r+15)*np.cos(phi3)
60   y1=yc+(r+3)*np.sin(phi3)
61   y2=yc+(r+15)*np.sin(phi3)
62   plt.plot([x1,x2],[y1,y2],color='k')
63
```

```
64   x1=xc+(r+3)*np.cos(phi4)
65   x2=xc+(r+15)*np.cos(phi4)
66   y1=yc+(r+3)*np.sin(phi4)
67   y2=yc+(r+15)*np.sin(phi4)
68   plt.plot([x1,x2],[y1,y2],color='k')
69
70   #————————————————————————————————————P1 arc
71   dphi=(phi3)/100.
72   for phi in np.arange(0,phi1/2-3.2*np.pi/180,dphi):
73       x=xc+(r+5)*np.cos(phi)
74       y=yc+(r+5)*np.sin(phi)
75       plt.scatter(x,y,s=.1,color='k')
76
77   for phi in np.arange(phi1/2+3.3*np.pi/180,phi1,dphi):
78       x=xc+(r+5)*np.cos(phi)
79       y=yc+(r+5)*np.sin(phi)
80       plt.scatter(x,y,s=.1,color='k')
81
82   #————————————————————————————————————P2 arc
83   dphi=(phi3)/100.
84   for phi in np.arange(0,phi2/2-3.2*np.pi/180,dphi):
85       x=xc+(r+25)*np.cos(phi)
86       y=yc+(r+25)*np.sin(phi)
87       plt.scatter(x,y,s=.1,color='k')
88
89   dphi=(phi3)/100.
90   for phi in np.arange(phi2/2+3.2*np.pi/180,phi2,dphi):
91       x=xc+(r+25)*np.cos(phi)
92       y=yc+(r+25)*np.sin(phi)
93       plt.scatter(x,y,s=.1,color='k')
94
95   #————————————————————————————————————P arc
96   dphi=(phi3)/100.
97   for phi in np.arange(0,phi3/2-.5*np.pi/180,dphi):
98       x=xc+(r+13)*np.cos(phi)
99       y=yc+(r+13)*np.sin(phi)
```

```
100        plt.scatter(x,y,s=.1,color='k')
101
102 dphi=(phi3)/100.
103 for phi in np.arange(phi3/2+9.*np.pi/180,phi3,dphi):
104        x=xc+(r+13)*np.cos(phi)
105        y=yc+(r+13)*np.sin(phi)
106        plt.scatter(x,y,s=.1,color='k')
107
108 #─────────────────────────────────────dp arc
109 dphi=(phi3)/100.
110 for phi in np.arange(phi3+5*dphi,phi3+25*dphi,dphi):
111        x=xc+(r+13)*np.cos(phi)
112        y=yc+(r+13)*np.sin(phi)
113        plt.scatter(x,y,s=.1,color='k')
114
115 plt.plot([xc,100],[yc,yc],'k')
116 plt.plot([xc,xc],[yc,80],'k')
117
118 #─────────────────────────────────────labels
119 plt.text(71,58,'p2',size='small')
120 plt.text(66,44,'p',size='small')
121 plt.text(63,29,'p1',size='small')
122 plt.text(45,66,'dp',size='small')
123 plt.text(41,26,'r')
124 plt.text(3,17,'(xc,yc)',size='small')
125 plt.plot([xc+r*np.cos(phi3),xc+r*np.cos(phi3)],[yc-8,yc+r*np.
    sin(phi3)],'k:')
126 plt.plot([xc,xc],[yc-2,yc-8],'k:')
127 plt.text(25,17,'R*cos(p)',size='small')
128
129 plt.plot([xc-8,xc+r*np.cos(phi3)],[yc+r*np.sin(phi3),yc+r*np.
    sin(phi3)],'k:')
130 plt.plot([xc-2,xc-8],[yc,yc],'k:')
131 plt.text(13,27,'R*sin(p)',size='small',rotation=90)
132
133 plt.text(49,30,'(x1,y1)',size='small')
```

```
134 plt.text(20,62,'(x2,y2)',size='small')
135 plt.text(51,49,'(xp,yp)',size='small')
136
137 #————————————————————————arrow heads
138 plt.arrow(47,79,-2,1,head_length=3,head_width=2,color='k')
139 plt.arrow(62,53,-2,2,head_length=2.9,head_width=2,color='k')
140 plt.arrow(64,31,-.9,3,head_length=2,head_width=2,color='k')
141 plt.arrow(52,63,3,-3,head_length=2,head_width=2,color='k')
142
143 plt.show()
```

2.4 Circular Arcs from Line Segments

Instead of plotting dots with **np.scatter()** at points along the arc, you can create a finer arc using straight-line segments between points. If you replace the "plot arc" routine in Listing 2-3, beginning at line 24, with

```
24  #————————————————————plot arc
25  p1=20*np.pi/180
26  p2=70*np.pi/180
27  dp=(p2-p1)/100
28  xlast=xc+r*np.cos(p1)
29  ylast=yc+r*np.sin(p1)
30  for p in np.arange(p1+dp,p2,dp):
31      x=xc+r*np.cos(p)
32      y=yc+r*np.sin(p)
33      plt.plot([xlast,x],[ylast,y],color='g')
34      xlast=x
35      ylast=y
```

you get the arc shown in Figure 2-7. In lines 28 and 29 of the code above you define **xlast** and **ylast**. These are the last x and y coordinate values plotted at the end of the previous line segment. Since you are just starting to plot the arc before the loop begins, these are initially set equal to the arc's starting point where p=p1. You will need them to plot the first arc segment in line 33. Parameters p, p1, p2, and dp are the same as before. Imagine the loop 30-35 is just starting to run. Lines 31 and 32 calculate the global coordinates of the *end* of the first line segment, which is dp into the arc. Using the previously set values **xlast** and **ylast**, which are the coordinates of the beginning of that line segment in 28 and 29, line 33 plots the first line segment. Lines 34 and 35 update the end coordinates of the first segment as **xlast, ylast**. These will be used as the beginning coordinates of the second line segment. The loop continues to the end of the arc using the end of the preceding segment as the beginning of the next one. Notice in line 30 the loop begins at p1+dp, the end angle of the first line segment. This isn't actually necessary and the beginning of the loop could be set to p1 as before, in which case the first line segment would have zero length. The loop would continue to the end of the arc as before.

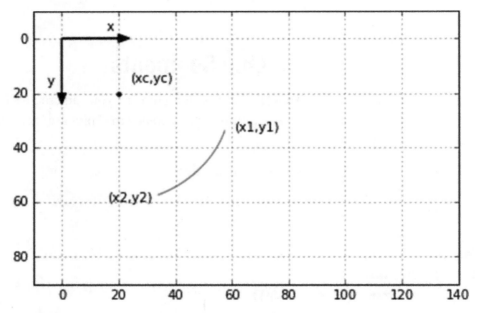

Figure 2-7. *Circular arc created with plt.plot() line segments*

In future work, you will sometimes use curves constructed of dots instead of line segments. Even though dots do not produce as fine results, they avoid complicating the plotting algorithm, which can sometimes obscure the logic of the script. However, line segments do produce superior results so you will use them as well.

2.5 Circles

A full circle is just a 360° arc. You can make a full circle by changing the beginning and end angles of the arc in the previous section to p1=0 and p2=360 degrees. This is done in lines 24 and 25 of Listing 2-5. The output is shown in Figure 2-8. Three circles and a solid disc are plotted at different locations. They have different colors and widths. Half the green circle is plotted with solid-line segments, the other half with dashed lines 29-37. The decision to plot a solid or dashed line is made by the **if** logic between lines 32 and 35. This changes the **linestyle** attribute in line 33. The blue solid disc is made by plotting concentric circles with radii from r1=0 to the disc's outer radius r2. You could, of course, also make a solid disk with the **np.scatter()** function. You should be able to follow the logic used here to create the various circles by examining the script in Listing 2-5.

This program could have been shortened by the use of functions. It has been left open for the sake of clarity by using cut and paste to reproduce sections of redundant code.

Listing 2-5. Program CIRCLES

```
1    """
2    CIRCLES
3    """
4
5    import numpy as np
6    import matplotlib.pyplot as plt
7
8    plt.axis([-75,75,50,-50])
9
10   plt.axis('on')
11   plt.grid(True)
12
13   plt.arrow(0,0,20,0,head_length=4,head_width=3,color='k')
14   plt.arrow(0,0,0,20,head_length=4,head_width=3,color='k')
15
16   plt.text(16,-3,'x')
17   plt.text(-5,17,'y')
18
19   #————————————————————————green circle
20   xc=0
21   yc=0
22   r=40
23
24   p1=0*np.pi/180
```

```
25  p2=360*np.pi/180
26  dp=(p2-p1)/100
27  xlast=xc+r*np.cos(p1)
28  ylast=yc+r*np.sin(p1)
29  for p in np.arange(p1,p2+dp,dp):
30      x=xc+r*np.cos(p)
31      y=yc+r*np.sin(p)
32      if p > 90*np.pi/180 and p < 270*np.pi/180:
33          plt.plot([xlast,x],[ylast,y],color='g',linestyle=':')
34      else:
35          plt.plot([xlast,x],[ylast,y],color='g')
36      xlast=x
37      ylast=y
38
39  plt.scatter(xc,yc,s=15,color='g')
40
41  #————————————————————————————red circle
42  xc=-20
43  yc=-20
44  r=10
45
46  p1=0*np.pi/180
47  p2=360*np.pi/180
48  dp=(p2-p1)/100
49  xlast=xc+r*np.cos(p1)
50  ylast=yc+r*np.sin(p1)
51  for p in np.arange(p1,p2+dp,dp):
52      x=xc+r*np.cos(p)
53      y=yc+r*np.sin(p)
54      plt.plot([xlast,x],[ylast,y],linewidth=4,color='r')
55      xlast=x
56      ylast=y
57
58  plt.scatter(xc,yc,s=15,color='r')
59
```

```
60   #─────────────────────────────────────purple circle
61   xc=20
62   yc=20
63   r=50
64
65   p1=0*np.pi/180
66   p2=360*np.pi/180
67   dp=(p2-p1)/100
68   xlast=xc+r*np.cos(p1)
69   ylast=yc+r*np.sin(p1)
70   for p in np.arange(p1,p2+dp,dp):
71       x=xc+r*np.cos(p)
72       y=yc+r*np.sin(p)
73       plt.plot([xlast,x],[ylast,y],linewidth=2,color=(.8,0,.8))
74       xlast=x
75       ylast=y
76
77   plt.scatter(xc,yc,color=(.5,0,.5))
78
79   #─────────────────────────────────────blue disc
80   xc=-53
81   yc=-30
82   r1=0
83   r2=10
84   dr=1
85
86   p1=0*np.pi/180
87   p2=360*np.pi/180
88   dp=(p2-p1)/100
89   xlast=xc+r1*np.cos(p1)
90   ylast=yc+r1*np.sin(p1)
91   for r in np.arange(r1,r2,dr):
92       for p in np.arange(p1,p2+dp,dp):
93           x=xc+r*np.cos(p)
94           y=yc+r*np.sin(p)
95           plt.plot([xlast,x],[ylast,y],linewidth=2,color=(0,0,.8))
```

```
96              xlast=x
97              ylast=y
98
99  plt.show()
```

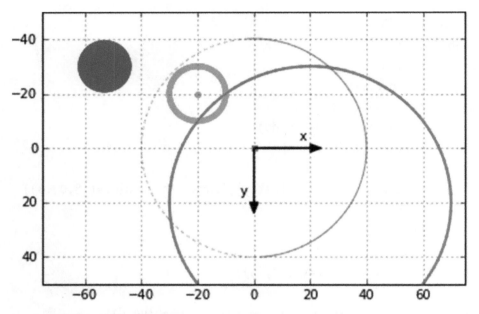

Figure 2-8. *Circles created by Listing 2-5*

2.6 Dot Discs

Two discs created with different dot patterns are shown in Figure 2-9. The disc labelled "r,p" is drawn by placing dots in a traditional polar r,p array where r is the radius from the center and p is the angle. The algorithm starts at line 21 in Listing 2-6. The script in Listing 2-6 should be self-explanatory. The only issue with this plot is that the dots are not uniformly spaced but are further apart as the radius increases. This may be undesirable in some situations.

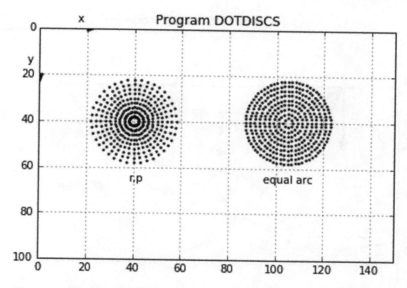

Figure 2-9. *Discs created by different dot patterns in Listing 2-6 where "r,p" contains simple polar coordinates and "equal arc" has modified polar coordinates*

The "equal arc" disc, beginning in line 38, appears better visually. As with the "r,p" disc, the dots are equally spaced in the radial direction. However, in the "equal arc" disc, the number of dots in the circumferential direction at each radial location becomes larger as the radius increases, thus keeping the circumferential arc spacing between dots constant. The model used is shown in Figure 2-10. dc is the circumferential spacing between dots a and b at rmax, the outer edge of the disk. dp is the angular spacing between radii to a and b. To achieve more uniform spacing across the disc, you hold dc constant at all radii. A typical radial location is shown at r=rmax/2. dc at this radius is the same as at rmax and is equal to dc. To accommodate this spacing, the angle between adjacent dots must increase to drp.

In line 44 of Listing 2-6, the disc's outer radius is set to 20. The radial spacing is set to 2 in line 45. Keeping in mind that the circumferential spacing between two points on a circular arc is r×dp where r is the radius and dp is the angle between the points, line 46 calculates dc where you have arbitrarily set the number of dots at rmax to 40 per π radians (80 around the complete circumference). The loop beginning at line 48 starts at r=dr and advances in the radial direction to rmax in steps dr. At each value or r, the angle between dots dpr required to keep the circumferential spacing equal to dc is calculated in line 49. The loop beginning at line 50 then places the dots circumferentially.

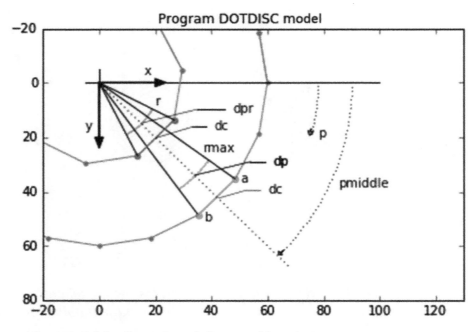

Figure 2-10. *Model for "equal arc" disc used by Listing 2-6*

Listing 2-6. Program DOTDISCS

```
1    """
2    DOTDISCS
3    """
4
5    import matplotlib.pyplot as plt
6    import numpy as np
7    import random as rnd
8
9    plt.axis([0,150,100,0])
10
11   plt.axis('off')
12   plt.grid(False)
13
14   plt.arrow(0,0,20,0,head_length=4,head_width=3,color='k')
15   plt.arrow(0,0,0,20,head_length=4,head_width=3,color='k')
16
17   plt.text(16,-3,'x')
```

```
18   plt.text(-5,17,'y')
19
20   #──────────────────────────────────simple r,p dot pattern
21   xc=40
22   yc=25
23
24   p1=0
25   p2=2*np.pi
26   dp=np.pi/20
27
28   rmax=20
29   dr=2
30
31   for r in np.arange(dr,rmax,dr):
32        for p in np.arange(p1,p2,dp):
33             x=xc+r*np.cos(p)
34             y=yc+r*np.sin(p)
35             plt.scatter(x,y,s=2,color='k')
36
37   #──────────────────────────────equal arc length dot pattern
38   xc=40
39   yc=70
40
41   p1=0
42   p2=2*np.pi
43
44   rmax=20
45   dr=2
46   dc=np.pi*rmax/40
47
48   for r in np.arange(dr,rmax,dr):
49       dpr=dc/r
50       for p in np.arange(p1,p2,dpr):
51            x=xc+r*np.cos(p)
52            y=yc+r*np.sin(p)
53            plt.scatter(x,y,s=2,color='k')
```

```
54
55  #————————————————————————————————labels
56  plt.text(38,66,'r,p')
57  plt.text(95,66,'equal arc')
58
59  plt.show()
```

2.7 Ellipses

Ellipses are shown in Figure 2-12. They were drawn by Listing 2-7. The model used by Listing 2-7 is shown in Figure 2-11. This was drawn by Listing 2-8. The dimension a is called the semi-major since it refers to half the greater width; b is the semi-minor. 2a and 2b are the major and minor dimensions.

The equation of an ellipse, which we are all familiar with, is,

$$\frac{x^2}{a^2} + \frac{y^2}{b^2} = 1 \qquad (2\text{-}7)$$

In the special case where a=b=r, this degenerates to a circle, as in

$$x^2 + y^2 = r^2 \qquad (2\text{-}8)$$

where r is the radius.

A possible strategy to use when plotting an ellipse is to start at x=-a and advance in the +x direction using Equation 2-7 to calculate y at each x, and then plot either a dot or a line segment from the last step, as you have done in the past. The y coordinate is easily derived from Equation 2-7 as

$$y = b\sqrt{1 - \frac{x^2}{a^2}} \qquad (2\text{-}9)$$

This seems easy enough. The green ellipse in Figure 2-12 was drawn this way. However, there is a problem. Look at Listing 2-7, lines 48, 49, and 50; the square root in Equation 2-9 and in line 48 gives uncertain results as x approaches +a and line 48 tries to take the square root of a number very close to zero. This is caused by roundoff errors in Python's calculations. The manifestation of this shows up as a gap at the +a side of the ellipse. In the algorithm for the green ellipse, this gap is closed by lines 54 and 55. You can get a decent ellipse this way but you have to be careful.

Another way is to use polar coordinates, as shown in Figure 2-11. You want to determine the coordinates (xp,yp) for a point on the ellipse as a function of the angle p. By varying p, you will have the information you need to plot the ellipse. To determine (xp,yp) vs. p, you note that it lies on the intersection of the ellipse and the radial line. This point is indicated by the red dot. Incidentally, the dot does not appear to lie exactly at the intersection, as can be seen. This is because the scale factor used to adjust the x axis values in line 8 of Listing 2-8 is a bit off. You used a rough measurement with a ruler and then you rounded off the results of the calculation to determine the scale factor. The resulting slight errors are showing up here. The equation of the line can be determined from the following:

$$xp = r cos(p) \tag{2-10}$$

$$yp = r sin(p) \tag{2-11}$$

Combining the above,

$$\frac{yp}{xp} = \frac{r sin(p)}{r cos(p)} = tan(p) \tag{2-12}$$

$$yp = xp tan(p) \tag{2-13}$$

You know that (xp,yp) lies at the intersection of the line and the ellipse. This is where the equations for both the line and the ellipse are satisfied by xp and yp. You can determine the coordinates of this point by substituting Equation 2-13 into Equation 2-7,

$$\frac{xp^2}{a^2} + \frac{xp^2 tan^2 p}{b^2} = 1 \tag{2-14}$$

which works out to

$$xp = ab \left[b^2 + a^2 tan^2(p) \right]^{-\frac{1}{2}} \tag{2-15}$$

$$yp = ab \left[a^2 + b^2 \frac{1}{tan^2(p)} \right]^{-\frac{1}{2}} \tag{2-16}$$

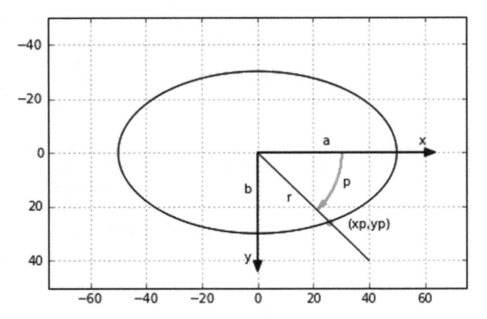

Figure 2-11. *Model created by Listing 2-8 and used by Listing 2-7*

Equations 2-15 and 2-16 are implemented in Listing 2-7 to draw the red ellipse between lines 20 and 36, the green ellipse between lines 39 and 55, and the blue ellipse in lines 58 and 69. The output is shown in Figure 2-12. When drawing the green ellipse, the program loops from -a to +a and uses Equation 2-9 to calculate y values. As mentioned, this can lead to roundoff errors near the extremity of the ellipse at x=+a, which leaves a gap in the ellipse. This is corrected in lines 54 and 55, which draw short lines to close the gap. Note that the blue ellipse is filled in. This is accomplished by line 69, which plots vertical lines from the top to the bottom of the ellipse.

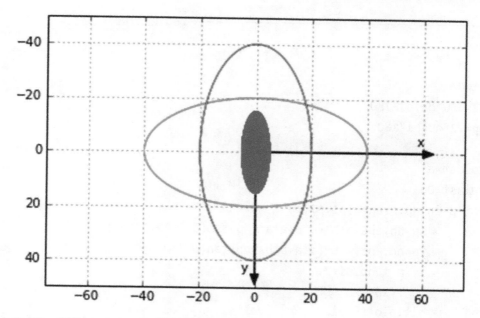

Figure 2-12. *Ellipses created by Listing 2-7*

Listing 2-7. Program ELLIPSES

```
1    """
2    ELLIPSES
3    """
4
5    import numpy as np
6    import matplotlib.pyplot as plt
7
8    plt.axis([-75,75,50,-50])
9
10   plt.axis('on')
11   plt.grid(True)
12
13   plt.arrow(0,0,60,0,head_length=4,head_width=3,color='k')
14   plt.arrow(0,0,0,45,head_length=4,head_width=3,color='k')
15
16   plt.text(58,-3,'x')
17   plt.text(-5,44,'y')
18
```

```
19   #————————————————————red ellipse
20   a=40
21   b=20.
22   p1=0
23   p2=180*np.pi/180
24   dp=.2*np.pi/180
25
26   xplast=a
27   yplast=0
28   for p in np.arange(p1,p2,dp):
29           xp=np.abs(a*b*(b*b+a*a*(np.tan(p))**2.)**-.5)
30           yp=np.abs(a*b*(a*a+b*b/(np.tan(p)**2.))**-.5)
31           if p > np.pi/2:
32               xp=-xp
33           plt.plot([xplast,xp],[yplast,yp],color='r')
34           plt.plot([xplast,xp],[-yplast,-yp],color='r')
35           xplast=xp
36           yplast=yp
37
38   #————————————————————green ellipse
39   a=20.
40   b=40.
41   xp1=-a
42   xp2=a
43   dx=.1
44
45   xplast=-a
46   yplast=0
47   for xp in np.arange(xp1,xp2,dx):
48       yp=b*(1-xp**2./a**2.)**.5
49       plt.plot([xplast,xp],[yplast,yp],linewidth=1,color='g')
50       plt.plot([xplast,xp],[-yplast,-yp],linewidth=1,color='g')
51       xplast=xp
52       yplast=yp
53
```

```
54   plt.plot([xplast,a],[yplast,0],linewidth=1,color='g'
55   plt.plot([xplast,a],[-yplast,0],linewidth=1,color='g'
56
57   #──────────────────────────────blue ellipse
58   a=5.
59   b=15.
60   p1=0
61   p2=180*np.pi/180
62   dp=.2*np.pi/180
63
64   for p in np.arange(p1,p2,dp):
65       xp=np.abs(a*b*(b*b+a*a*(np.tan(p))**2.)**-.5)
66       yp=np.abs(a*b*(a*a+b*b/(np.tan(p)**2.))**-.5)
67       if p > np.pi/2:
68           xp=-xp
69       plt.plot([xp,xp],[yp,-yp],linewidth=1,color='b')
70
71   plt.show()
```

(The following program was used to create Figure 2-11.)

Listing 2-8. Program ELLIPSEMODEL

```
1    """
2    ELLIPSEMODEL
3    """
4
5    import numpy as np
6    import matplotlib.pyplot as plt
7
8    plt.axis([-75,75,50,-50])
9
10   plt.axis('on')
11   plt.grid(True)
12
13   plt.arrow(0,0,60,0,head_length=4,head_width=3,color='k')
14   plt.arrow(0,0,0,40,head_length=4,head_width=3,color='k')
```

```
15
16  plt.text(58,-3,'x')
17  plt.text(-5,40,'y')
18
19  #————————————————————————ellipse
20  a=50.
21  b=30.
22  p1=0.
23  p2=180.*np.pi/180.
24  dp=(p2-p1)/180.
25
26  xplast=a
27  yplast=0
28  for p in np.arange(p1,p2+dp,dp):
29      xp=np.abs(a*b*(b*b+a*a*(np.tan(p))**2.)**-.5)
30      yp=np.abs(a*b*(a*a+b*b/(np.tan(p)**2.))**-.5)
31      if p > np.pi/2:
32          xp=-xp
33      plt.plot([xplast,xp],[yplast,yp],color='k')
34      plt.plot([xplast,xp],[-yplast,-yp],color='k')
35      xplast=xp
36      yplast=yp
37
38  #————————————————————————line
39  plt.plot([0,40],[0,40],color='k')
40
41  #————————————————————————point
42  p=45.*np.pi/180.
43  xp=np.abs(a*b*(b*b+a*a*(np.tan(p))**2.)**-.5)
44  yp=np.abs(a*b*(a*a+b*b/(np.tan(p)**2.))**-.5)
45  plt.scatter(xp,yp,s=20,color='r')
46
47  #————————————————————————labels
48  plt.text(23,-3,'a',color='k')
49  plt.text(-5,15,'b',color='k')
50  plt.text(32,28,'(xp,yp)')
```

74

```
51  plt.text(30,12,'p')
52  plt.text(10,18,'r')
53
54  #──────────────────────────────────p arc
55  p1=0
56  p2=45*np.pi/180
57  dp=(p2-p1)/180
58  r=30
59  for p in np.arange(p1,p2,dp):
60      x=r*np.cos(p)
61      y=r*np.sin(p)
62      plt.scatter(x,y,s=.1,color='r')
63
64  plt.arrow(25,17.5,-1,1,head_length=3,head_width=2,color='r')
65
66  plt.show()
```

2.8 2D Translation

In two dimensions, an object has three independent degrees of freedom: it can rotate around one axis direction which is perpendicular to the plane and it can translate in two directions (x and y) within the plane. Pure translation implies the object is moved without rotation; pure rotation implies the object is rotated without translation. The objects in Figure 2-13 are examples of pure translation. The triangle (black) has been translated (moved) to the right (green) without rotation and then down (red). This is a simple thing to accomplish with Python, especially when using lists as in Listing 2-9. For example, to move an object to the right in an amount of dx, just add dx to the x coordinates and replot it. Similarly for the y direction, just add dy to the y coordinates and replot. The small blue boxes were translated across the plotting area by incrementing the x coordinates by 10 units in the loop beginning in line 45.

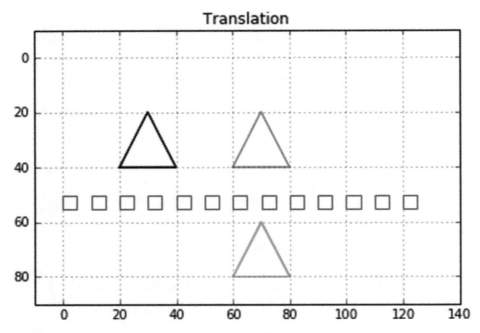

Figure 2-13. *Examples of translation created by Listing 2-9*

Listing 2-9. Program 2DTRANSLATION

```
1    """
2    2DTRANSLATION
3    """
4
5    import numpy as np
6    import matplotlib.pyplot as plt
7
8    x1=-10
9    x2=140
10   y1=90
11   y2=-10
12   plt.axis([x1,x2,y1,y2])
13
14   plt.axis('on')
15   plt.grid(True)
```

```
16
17  plt.title('Translation')
18
19  #————————————————————————————————triangle
20  x=[20,30,40,20]
21  y=[40,20,40,40]
22  plt.plot(x,y,color='k')
23  plt.plot(x,y,color='k')
24  plt.plot(x,y,color='k')
25
26  #————————————————————————translate triangle dx=60
27  x=[60,70,80,60]
28  plt.plot(x,y,color='g')
29  plt.plot(x,y,color='g')
30  plt.plot(x,y,color='g')
31
32  #————————————————————————translate triangle dy=40
33  y=[80,60,80,80]
34  plt.plot(x,y,color='r')
35  plt.plot(x,y,color='r')
36  plt.plot(x,y,color='r')
37
38  #————————————————————————————————————box
39  x=[0,0,5,5,0]
40  y=[55,50,50,55,55]
41  plt.plot(x,y,'b')
42
43  #————————————————————————————translate box
44  y=[55,50,50,55,55]
45  for x in np.arange(0,130,10):
46      x=[x,x,x+5,x+5,x]
47      plt.plot(x,y,'b')
48
49  plt.show()
```

2.9 2D Rotation

So far in this chapter, you have seen how to construct images on a two-dimensional plane using points and lines. In this section, you'll learn how to rotate a two-dimensional planar object within its own plane. A 2D object that you might want to rotate, a rectangle for example, or something more complicated which will normally consist of any number of points and lines. Lines, of course, are defined by their end points or a series of points if constructed from dots. As you have seen, curves can also be constructed from line segments or dots. If you can determine how to rotate a point, you will then be able to rotate any planar object defined by points. In Chapter 3, you will extend these concepts to the rotation of three-dimensional objects around three coordinate directions.

Figure 2-14 shows three coordinate systems: the blue xg,yg system is the *global* coordinate system. Its numerical size and the location of the global origin (xg=0, yg=0) are defined by the values in the **plt.axis([x1,x2,y1,y2])** statement. This is the system you use when plotting. All plotting coordinates should relate to this system. For example, if writing **plt.scatter(xg,yg)**, xg and yg should be relative to the blue xg,yg system as shown.

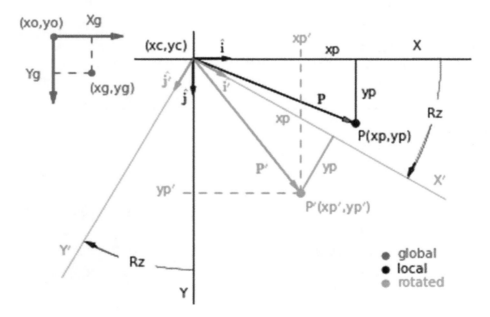

Figure 2-14. *2D rotation model*

The black x,y system is the *local* system. A position (xp,yp) in the local system is equivalent to (xc+xp, yc+yp) in the global system. You use the local system to construct shapes by specifying the coordinates of the points that comprise them. For example, if you want to plot a circle somewhere in the plotting area, you could place (xc,yc) at the circle's center, calculate the points defining the circle around it in reference to the local (black) system, and then relate them back to the xg,yg (blue) system for plotting by translating each point by xc and yc.

Figure 2-14 shows a point P that is rotated through a clockwise angle Rz to a new position at P'. The red coordinate system rotates through the angle Rz. P rotates along with it. The coordinates of P' in the rotated system, (xp,yp), are the same as they were in the local system. However, in the global system, they are obviously different. Your goal now is to determine the coordinates of P' in the local system and then in the global system, so you can plot it.

I am using the terminology Rz for the angle because a clockwise rotation in the x,y plane is actually a rotation about the z direction, which points into the plane of the paper. This was illustrated in Chapter 1. It will be explained in more detail in Chapter 3.

Figure 2-14 shows point P in its unrotated position. Its coordinates in relation to the local x,y system (black) are (xp,yp). Its location is defined by the vector **P**,

$$\mathbf{P} = xp\hat{\mathbf{i}} + yp\hat{\mathbf{j}} \tag{2-17}$$

where $\hat{\mathbf{i}}$ and $\hat{\mathbf{j}}$ are unit vectors in the x and y directions.

After **P** is rotated through the angle Rz, it reaches a new position P' (red) at coordinates (x',y') in relation to the x,y (black) system. P' is defined by the vector **P'** (red) as,

$$\mathbf{P'} = xp'\hat{\mathbf{i}} + yp'\hat{\mathbf{j}} \tag{2-18}$$

The coordinates of P' in relation to the rotated x',y' system are (xp,yp). The position of P' is thus also defined by the vector

$$\mathbf{P'} = xp\hat{\mathbf{i}}' + yp\hat{\mathbf{j}}' \tag{2-19}$$

where $\hat{\mathbf{i}}'$ and $\hat{\mathbf{j}}'$ are unit vectors in the x' and y' directions.

Your task now is to determine relations for $\hat{\mathbf{i}}'$ and $\hat{\mathbf{j}}'$ in relation to $\hat{\mathbf{i}}$ and $\hat{\mathbf{j}}$ and then substitute them into Equation 2-19. This will give you the coordinates of P' in relation to the local x,y system. By simply adding xc and yc you will then get the coordinates of P' in the global system, which you need for plotting.

Four unit vectors are shown at (xc,yc). $\hat{\mathbf{i}}$ and $\hat{\mathbf{j}}$ point in the x and y directions; $\hat{\mathbf{i}}'$ and $\hat{\mathbf{j}}'$ point in the x' and y' directions. By examining Figure 2-14, you can see that

$$\hat{\mathbf{i}}' = \underbrace{cos(Rz)\hat{\mathbf{i}}}_{X\ component} + \underbrace{sin(Rz)\hat{\mathbf{j}}}_{Y\ component} \tag{2-20}$$

$$\hat{\mathbf{j}}' = \underbrace{-sin(Rz)\,\hat{\mathbf{i}}}_{X\ component} + \underbrace{cos(Rz)\,\hat{\mathbf{j}}}_{Y\ component} \tag{2-21}$$

Plugging these into Equation 2-19, you get

$$\mathbf{P}' = xp\left[\,cos(Rz)\hat{\mathbf{i}} + sin(Rz)\hat{\mathbf{j}}\,\right] + yp\left[\,-sin(Rz)\hat{\mathbf{i}} + cos(Rz)\hat{\mathbf{j}}\,\right] \tag{2-22}$$

This can be separated into x and y components,

$$\mathbf{P}' = xp'\hat{\mathbf{i}} + yp'\hat{\mathbf{j}} \tag{2-23}$$

where

$$xp' = xp\left[\,cos(Rz)\,\right] + yp\left[\,-sin(Rz)\,\right] \tag{2-24}$$

$$yp' = xp\left[\,sin(Rz)\,\right] + yp\left[\,cos(Rz)\,\right] \tag{2-25}$$

These last two equations are all you need to rotate a point from (xp,yp) through the angle Rz to new coordinates (xp',yp'). Note that both sets of coordinates, (xp,yp) and (xp',yp'), are in reference to the local x,y axes. They can then be easily translated by xc and yc to get them in the global system for plotting.

In the special case where yp=0, that is when P, before rotation, lies on the x axis at x=xp, Equations 2-24 and 2-25 degenerate to

$$xp' = xpcos(Rz) \tag{2-26}$$

$$yp' = xpsin(Rz) \tag{2-27}$$

which can be easily verified from Figure 2-14. You are, of course, concerned with rotating a generic point that initially is anywhere in the x,y plane so you need the full formulation contained in Equations 2-24 and 2-25. These can be expressed in matrix form as

$$\begin{bmatrix} xp' \\ yp' \end{bmatrix} = \begin{bmatrix} cos(Rz) & -sin(Rz) \\ sin(Rz) & cos(Rz) \end{bmatrix} \begin{bmatrix} xp \\ yp \end{bmatrix} \tag{2-28}$$

which can be abbreviated as

$$[P'] = [Rz][P] \tag{2-29}$$

The [P'] and [P] matrices are often termed *column vectors* since they contain the components of vectors **P** and **P'**. [Rz] is a transformation matrix; it transforms the **P** vector into the **P'** vector, in this case by rotation through the angle Rz. These vectors are shown in Figure 2-15 where **P** defines the location of the unrotated point P1 (black) and the rotated point **P'** (red) at P3. You can rewrite [Rz] as

$$[Rz] = \begin{bmatrix} C(1,1) & C(1,2) \\ C(2,1) & C(2,2) \end{bmatrix} \tag{2-30}$$

$$C(1,1) = cos(Rz) \tag{2-31}$$

$$C(1,2) = -sin(Rz) \tag{2-32}$$

$$C(2,1) = sin(Rz) \tag{2-33}$$

$$C(2,2) = cos(Rz) \tag{2-34}$$

The definitions in Equations 2-31 through 2-34 will be used in the Python programs that follow. They represent a rotation in the x,y plane in the clockwise direction; use a negative value of Rz to rotate in the counterclockwise direction. Note that [Rz] is purely a function of the angle of rotation, Rz.

To convert xp' and yp' to xg and yg, you simply add xc to xp' and yc to yp', as in

$$xg = xc + xp' \tag{2-35}$$
$$yg = yc + yp' \tag{2-36}$$

In matrix form,

$$\begin{bmatrix} xg \\ yg \end{bmatrix} = \begin{bmatrix} xc \\ yc \end{bmatrix} + \begin{bmatrix} \cos(Rz) & -\sin(Rz) \\ \sin(Rz) & \cos(Rz) \end{bmatrix} \begin{bmatrix} xp \\ yp \end{bmatrix}$$

(2-37)

which can be abbreviated as

$$\underbrace{[Pg]}_{global} = \underbrace{[C]}_{center} + \underbrace{[Rz][P]}_{local}$$

(2-38)

or in vector form, as shown in Figure 2-15,

$$\mathbf{Pg} = \mathbf{C} + \mathbf{P}'$$

(2-39)

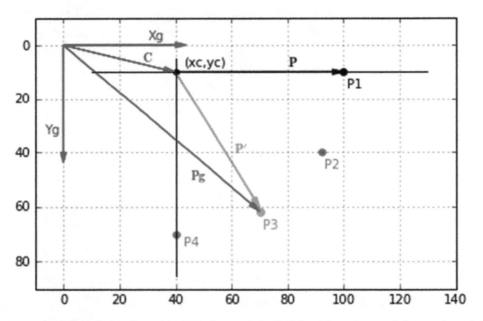

Figure 2-15. *Rotation of a point P1 from Rz=0° (black) to Rz=30° (green), 60° (red), and 90° (grey). Vectors drawn from xg=0, yg=0 to Point 3 at Rz=60° illustrating Equation 2-38. Plotted by Listing 2-10.*

As an illustration of the above concepts, Listing 2-10 rotates a point P1 about (xc,yc) from its original unrotated location at (xp,yp)=(60,0) in 30 degree increments. Results are shown in Figure 2-15. The coordinates of the center of rotation, (xc,yc), are set in lines 16 and 17.

Lines 28-37 of Listing 2-10 define a function **rotz(xp1,yp1,Rz)**, which uses the elements of the transformation matrix [Rz] in Equations 2-31 through 2-34 and the angle of rotation Rz to calculate and return the transformed (rotated and translated) coordinates (xg,yg). Lines 35 and 36 in function **rotz** relate the local coordinates to the xg,yg system for plotting. Note that **rotz** rotates each point and simultaneously translates it by xc and yc in lines 35 and 36. This puts the coordinates in the *global* system ready for plotting. You are rotating the point four times: Rz=0,30,60,90. The use of the function **rotz(xp,yp,Rz)** enables you to avoid coding the transformation for every point.

Lines 39 and 40 set the original coordinates of P to (60,0). It is important to note that these coordinates are relative to the center of rotation (xc,yc). Line 43 starts the calculation of the first point. This is at Rz=0. Line 44 converts Rz from degrees to radians. Later, I will show how to use the **radians()** function to do this. Line 45 invokes the function **rotz(xp,yp,Rz)**. xp and yp were set in lines 39 and 40; Rz was set in line 43. The function returns the coordinates of the rotated point (xg,yg) in line 37. Since Rz was zero in this first transformation, they are the same as the coordinates of the unrotated point P1.

The plotting of point P2 begins in line 50. You set the angle of rotation to 30 degrees in line 50. The routine is the same as before and P2 is plotted as a grey point. Sections P3 and P4 increase Rz to 60 and 90 degrees, plotting the red and final grey point.

Lines 74, 77, 80, and 83 illustrate the use of Latex in printing text on a plot. Looking at line 74, for example,

```
plt.text(28,6,r'$\mathbf{C}$',color='k')
```

the text starts at coordinates xg=28, yg=6. As discussed in Chapter 1, the **r** tells Python to treat the string as raw. This keeps the backward slashes needed by the Latex code between the dollar signs; in this case, $\mathbf{C}$. \mathbf{} makes whatever is between the braces {} bold. In line 80, ^{\prime} places a superscript prime next to P. This won't work if the prefix **r** is not included.

Listing 2-10.   Program 2DROT1

```
1
2     """
3     2DROT1
4     """
5     import matplotlib.pyplot as plt
6     import numpy as np
```

```
7
8   plt.axis([-10,140,90,-10])
9   plt.axis('on')
10  plt.grid(True)
11
12  #——————————————————-axes
13  plt.arrow(0,0,40,0,head_length=4,head_width=2,color='b')
14  plt.arrow(0,0,0,40,head_length=4,head_width=2,color='b')
15
16  xc=40
17  yc=10
18
19  plt.plot([xc-30,xc+90],[yc,yc],linewidth=1,color='k') #--X
20  plt.plot([xc,xc],[yc-5,yc+75],linewidth=1,color='k') #--Y
21
22  plt.text(30,-2,'Xg',color='b')
23  plt.text(-7,33,'Yg',color='b')
24  plt.scatter(xc,yc,s=20,color='k')
25  plt.text(xc+3,yc-2,'(xc,yc)')
26
27  #————————————————define rotation matrix rz
28  def rotz(xp,yp,rz): #---xp,yp=un-rotated coordinates relative to xc,yc
29      c11=np.cos(rz)
30      c12=-np.sin(rz)
31      c21=np.sin(rz)
32      c22=np.cos(rz)
33      xpp=xp*c11+yp*c12 #--xpp,ypp=rotated coordinates relative to xc,yc
34      ypp=xp*c21+yp*c22
35      xg=xc+xpp #--xg,yg=rotated coordinates relative to xg,yg
36      yg=yc+ypp
37      return [xg,yg]
38
39  xp=60 #————————————-coordinates of first point P1 relative to xc,yc
40  yp=0
41
42  #————————————————————P1
```

84

```
43  rz=0
44  rz=rz*np.pi/180
45  [xg,yg]=rotz(xp,yp,rz)
46  plt.scatter(xg,yg,s=30,color='k' )
47  plt.text(xg+1,yg+6,'P1',color='k')
48
49  #————————————————————————P2
50  rz=30
51  rz=rz*np.pi/180
52  [xg,yg]=rotz(xp,yp,rz)
53  plt.scatter(xg,yg,s=30,color='grey')
54  plt.text(xg+1,yg+6,'P2',color='grey')
55
56  #————————————————————————P3
57  rz=60
58  rz=rz*np.pi/180
59  [xg,yg]=rotz(xp,yp,rz)
60  plt.scatter(xg,yg,s=30,color='r')
61  plt.text(xg+1,yg+6,'P3',color='r')
62  xpp3=xg #——save for later in line 76
63  ypp3=yg
64
65  #————————————————————————P4
66  rz=90
67  rz=rz*np.pi/180
68  [xg,yg]=rotz(xp1,yp1,rz)
69  plt.scatter(xg,yg,s=30,color='grey')
70  plt.text(xp2+1,yp2+6,'P4',color='grey')
71
72  #————————————————————————————plot vectors
73  plt.arrow(0,0,xc-4,yc-1,head_length=4,head_width=2,color='k')
74  plt.text(28,6,r'$\mathbf{C}$',color='k')
75
76  plt.arrow(0,0,xpp3-3,ypp3-3,head_length=4,head_width=2,color='b')
77  plt.text(45,50,r'$\mathbf{Pg}$',color='b')
78
```

```
79   plt.arrow(xc,yc,xpp3-2-xc,ypp3-5-yc,head_length=4,head_
     width=2,color='r')
80   plt.text(61,40,r'$\mathbf{P^{\prime}}$',color='r')
81
82   plt.arrow(xc,yc,xp-4,yp,head_length=4,head_width=2,color='k')
83   plt.text(80,yc-2,r'$\mathbf{P}$',color='k')
84
85   plt.show()
```

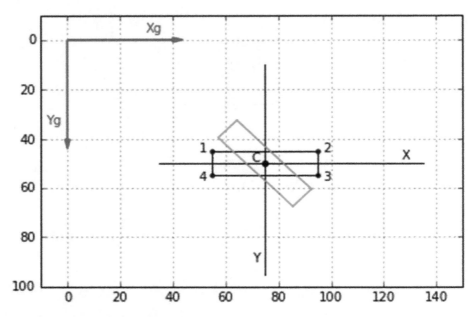

Figure 2-16. *Rotation of a rectangle around its center from Listing 2-11*

Next, you rotate a rectangle around its center, as shown in Figure 2-16. The center of rotation is point c at (xc,yc). The black rectangle shows the rectangle in its unrotated orientation. Its corners are numbered 1-4, as shown. The program plots the unrotated rectangle and then rotates it around point c to the rotated position and displays it in red.

Since the rectangle is defined by its corner points, you can rotate it by rotating the corners around c. The methodology is detailed in Listing 2-11. First, you plot the unrotated rectangle (black). The local coordinates of its four corner points are specified relative to the center of rotation c in lines 42-49. The points are labelled and plotted as dots in lines 51-58 where the local coordinates are converted to global by adding xc and yc in lines 55-58.

Next, you connect the corners by lines. Lines 61-68 translate the local corner coordinates by xc and yc. These points are labelled xg and yg to indicate that they are relative to the global plotting axes. They are set up as lists in lines 70 and 71, and then plotted in line 73, which draws lines between sequential xg,yg pairs.

Note the sequence of coordinate pairs in lines 70 and 71. When line 73 is invoked, it connects (xg1,yg1) to (xg2,yg2), then (xg2,yg2) to (xg3,yg3), and so on. But when it gets to corner 4, it has to connect corner 4 back to corner 1 in order to close the rectangle; hence you have (xg4,yg4) connected to (xg1,yg1) at the end of 70 and 71.

The plotting of the rotated rectangle begins at line 76. Rz is the angle of rotation. It is set to 45 degrees here and then converted from degrees to radians in line 77 (you could have used the **radians()** function to do this).

The function **rotz(xp,yp,Rz)** is defined in lines 29-38. The elements of the rotation transformation matrix shown in Equations 2-31 through 2-34 are evaluated in lines 30-33. xp and yp are the coordinates of an unrotated point. xpp and ypp (xp′ and yp′), coordinates in the rotated system, are evaluated in lines 34 and 35 using Equations 2-24 and 2-25. xg and yg, the coordinates in the global system after rotation and translation, are evaluated in lines 36-37 in accordance with Equations 2-35 and 2-36. Note that these lines rotate the points and simultaneously translate them relative to point c. The transformed coordinates are returned as a list in line 38.

Lines 80-101 transform each of the corner coordinates one by one by invoking function **rotz(xp,yp,Rz)**. For example, lines 80-83 transform corner 1 from local, unrotated coordinates xp1,yp1 to global coordinates xg and yg. The remaining three points are transformed in the same way. The lines connecting the corners are plotted in red in lines 104-107 using lists.

Listing 2-11. Program 2DROTRECTANGLE

```
1    """
2    2DROTRECTANGLE
3    """
4
5    import matplotlib.pyplot as plt
6    import numpy as np
7
8    plt.axis([-10,150,100,-10])
9    plt.axis('on')
```

```
10   plt.grid(True)
11
12   #——————————————————————————————-axes
13   plt.arrow(0,0,40,0,head_length=4,head_width=2,color='b')
14   plt.arrow(0,0,0,40,head_length=4,head_width=2,color='b')
15   plt.text(30,-3,'Xg',color='b')
16   plt.text(-8,34,'Yg',color='b')
17
18   xc=75 #————————————-center of rotation
19   yc=50
20   plt.plot([xc-40,xc+60],[yc,yc],linewidth=1,color='grey') #–-X
21   plt.plot([xc,xc],[yc-40,yc+45],linewidth=1,color='grey') #–-Y
22   plt.text(127,48,'X')
23   plt.text(70,90,'Y')
24
25   plt.scatter(xc,yc,s=20,color='k') #–plot center of rotation
26   plt.text(70,49,'c')
27
28   #————————————————————-define function rotz
29   def rotz(xp,yp,rz):
30       c11=np.cos(rz)
31       c12=-np.sin(rz)
32       c21=np.sin(rz)
33       c22=np.cos(rz)
34       xpp=xp*c11+yp*c12 #———-relative to xc,yc
35       ypp=xp*c21+yp*c22
36       xg=xc+xpp #–-relative to xg,yg
37       yg=yc+ypp
38       return [xg,yg]
39
40   #——————————————————————-plot unrotated rectangle
41   #——————————-rectangle corner coordinates in X,Y system
42   xp1=-20
43   xp2=+20
44   xp3=+20
45   xp4=-20
```

```
46   yp1=-5
47   yp2=-5
48   yp3=+5
49   yp4=+5
50
51   plt.text(50,45,'1') #————-label
52   plt.text(97,45,'2')
53   plt.text(97,57,'3')
54   plt.text(50,57,'4')
55   plt.scatter(xp1+xc,yp1+yc,s=10,color='k')
56   plt.scatter(xp2+xc,yp2+yc,s=10,color='k')
57   plt.scatter(xp3+xc,yp3+yc,s=10,color='k')
58   plt.scatter(xp4+xc,yp4+yc,s=10,color='k')
59
60   #————————————————-plot unrotated rectangle
61   xg1=xc+xp1 #————-corner coordinates in Xg,Yg system
62   yg1=yc+yp1
63   xg2=xc+xp2
64   yg2=yc+yp2
65   xg3=xc+xp3
66   yg3=yc+yp3
67   xg4=xc+xp4
68   yg4=yc+yp4
69
70   xg=[xg1,xg2,xg3,xg4,xg1]
71   yg=[yg1,yg2,yg3,yg4,yg1]
72
73   plt.plot((xg),(yg),color='k')
74
75   #————————————————-rotate rectangle corner coordinates
76   rz=45
77   rz=rz*np.pi/180
78
79   #————————————————————-point 1
80   xp=xp1
81   yp=yp1
```

```
82  [xg,yg]=rotz(xp,yp,rz)
83  [xg1,yg1]=[xg,yg]
84
85  #——————————————————————————————point 2
86  xp=xp2
87  yp=yp2
88  [xg,yg]=rotz(xp,yp,rz)
89  [xg2,yg2]=[xg,yg]
90
91  #——————————————————————————————point 3
92  xp=xp3
93  yp=yp3
94  [xg,yg]=rotz(xp,yp,rz)
95  [xg3,yg3]=[xg,yg]
96
97  #——————————————————————————————point 4
98  xp=xp4
99  yp=yp4
100 [xg,yg]=rotz(xp,yp,rz)
101 [xg4,yg4]=[xg,yg]
102
103 #——————————————————————————————plot rotated rectangle
104 xg=[xg1,xg2,xg3,xg4,xg1]
105 yg=[yg1,yg2,yg3,yg4,yg1]
106
107 plt.plot(xg,yg,color='r')
108
109 plt.show()
```

To summarize the procedure, you first construct the object, in this case a simple rectangle, using points located at coordinates xp,yp in the local x,y system. This is done by specifying the coordinates relative to the center of rotation at c. Next, you specify Rz, evaluate the elements of the transformation matrix, transform each coordinate by Rz, translate the rotated points by xc,yc to get everything into the global xg,yg system, and then plot. The transformations are carried out by the function **rotz(xp,yp,rz),** which simultaneously rotates and translates the coordinates into the xg,yg system for plotting. In this case, you transformed all the coordinates first and then plotted at the end using lists. In some programs, you will plot points or lines immediately after transforming.

Next, you rotate a rectangle about its lower left corner. This is shown in Figure 2-17. The program that does this (not listed) is similar to Listing 2-11 except the center of rotation is changed to

$$xc = 55 \qquad\qquad (2\text{-}40)$$
$$yc = 55 \qquad\qquad (2\text{-}41)$$

and the corner coordinates are changed to

$$xp1 = 0 \qquad\qquad (2\text{-}42)$$

$$xp2 = +50 \qquad\qquad (2\text{-}43)$$

$$xp3 = +50 \qquad\qquad (2\text{-}44)$$

$$xp4 = 0 \qquad\qquad (2\text{-}45)$$

$$yp1 = -10 \qquad\qquad (2\text{-}46)$$

$$yp2 = -10 \qquad\qquad (2\text{-}47)$$

$$yp3 = +0 \qquad\qquad (2\text{-}48)$$

$$yp4 = +0 \qquad\qquad (2\text{-}49)$$

These dimensions are relative to the center of rotation, (xc,yc).

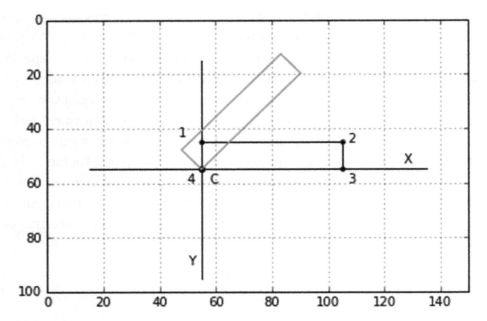

Figure 2-17. *Rotation of a rectangle about a corner*

The center of rotation c does not have to be contiguous with the object; you could put it anywhere as long as the corner coordinates relative to the center of rotation are updated.

Figure 2-18 shows an example of constructing and rotating a circular object. Obviously, without some distinctive feature, you wouldn't be able to see if a circle had been rotated so you make the top half of the starting circle green and the bottom half red. You also add a bar across the diameter with dots at each end. Figure 2-19 shows the model used by Listing 2-12 to generate Figure 2-18.

As shown in Figures 2-19 and 2-18, and referring to Listing 2-12, you construct the starting circle with a center at xcc,ycc in program lines 41 and 42. It has a radius r=10, which is set in line 43. The angle p starts at p1=0 and goes to $p2=2\pi$ in steps dp in lines 45-47. Note that you are not using the angle definition Rz since p is a local angle about point xcc,ycc (the center of the circle), not xc,yc, the center of rotation. Points along the circle's perimeter are calculated in lines 55 and 56 in local coordinates. When **alpha**=0, this produces the starting circle.

The use of **alpha** in the function call in line 57 illustrates that you can use any name for the angle, even though Rz was used in the function definition in line 29. You are passing a number from a function call to a function. It doesn't matter what name it has on either end; the value received by the function will be the same as in the call to that function.

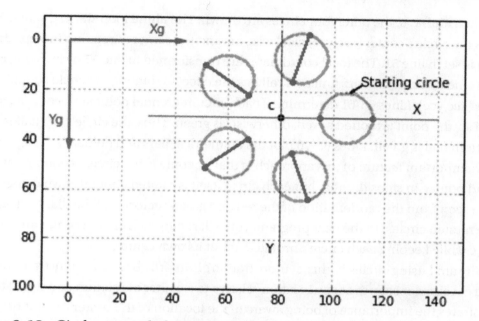

Figure 2-18. *Circles rotated about point c from Listing 2-12*

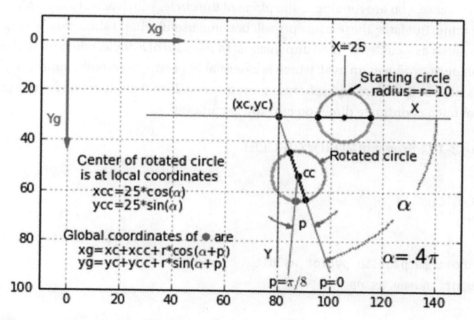

Figure 2-19. *Model used by Listing 2-12*

When **alpha**>0, the other four circles are drawn. The **alpha** loop starting at line 53 moves the circle's center (xcc,ycc) clockwise around the center of rotation in steps **dalpha**, which is set in line 51. The local coordinates are transformed in line 57 by invoking **rotz**. Alpha's inclusion in the **rotz** function call has the effect of rotating the circle about its own center (xcc,ycc). Lines 58-61 determine if each circumferential point lies between p=0 and p=π. If so, the point is plotted as red, otherwise as green. Thus, the circle's top half is red, its bottom half is green. Lines 62-70 plot the diametrical bars and points.

An important feature of this approach is that not only is the circle's center rotated around point c in steps **dalpha**, but each circle itself is rotated about its own center, as can be seen from the reorientation of the red and green sectors and the diametrical bars in the rotated circles. In the next program, you will rotate each circle's center around point c while keeping each circle unrotated about its own center.

Why am I using circles in this demonstration? Primarily because it illustrates how to construct circular shapes at any location relative to a center of rotation and rotate them. It illustrates the importance of being aware of the location of the center of rotation; it isn't necessarily the same as the center of the circle.

In this case, you are rotating in the plane of the circle, which admittedly isn't very illuminating. But later, these concepts will become useful when I show how to rotate objects, such as a circle, in three dimensions. In the case of a circle, when rotated out of its plane, it produces an oval, which is essential in portraying circular and spherical objects such as cylinders and spheres in three dimensions. Simply rotate a circle out of plane about a coordinate direction and you get an oval.

Listing 2-12. Program 2DROTCIRCLE1

```
1    """
2    2DROTCIRCLE1
3    """
4
5    import matplotlib.pyplot as plt
6    import numpy as np
7
8    plt.axis([-10,150,100,-10])
9    plt.axis('on')
10   plt.grid(True)
11
```

```
12   #————————————————————————————————————axes
13   plt.arrow(0,0,40,0,head_length=4,head_width=2,color='b')
14   plt.arrow(0,0,0,40,head_length=4,head_width=2,color='b')
15   plt.text(30,-3,'Xg',color='b')
16   plt.text(-8,34,'Yg',color='b')
17
18   xc=80 #————————————center of rotation
19   yc=30
20   plt.plot([xc-50,xc+60],[yc,yc],linewidth=1,color='grey') #--X
21   plt.plot([xc,xc],[yc-35,yc+60],linewidth=1,color='grey') #--Y
22   plt.text(xc+50,yc-2,'X')
23   plt.text(xc-5,yc+55,'Y')
24
25   plt.scatter(xc,yc,s=20,color='k') #-plot center of rotation
26   plt.text(xc-5,yc-3,'c')
27
28   #————————————————————————define rotation matrix Rz
29   def rotz(xp,yp,rz):
30       c11=np.cos(rz)
31       c12=-np.sin(rz)
32       c21=np.sin(rz)
33       c22=np.cos(rz)
34       xpp=xp*c11+yp*c12 #--rotated coordinates relative to xc,yc
35       ypp=xp*c21+yp*c22
36       xg=xc+xpp #--rotated coordinates relative to xg,yg
37       yg=yc+ypp
38       return [xg,yg]
39
40   #————————————————————————————————plot circles
41   xcc=25 #-xcc,ycc=center of starting circle in local X,Y system
42   ycc=0
43   r=10 #-radius
44
45   p1=0 #---p1,p2=angles around circle center
46   p2=2*np.pi
47   dp=(p2-p1)/100
```

```
48
49   alpha1=0 #--angles around xc,yc
50   alpha2=2*np.pi
51   dalpha=(alpha2-alpha1)/5
52
53   for alpha in np.arange(alpha1,alpha2,dalpha):
54       for p in np.arange(p1,p2,dp):
55           xp=xcc+r*np.cos(p) #—xp,yp=coordinates relative to local
                 X,Y system
56           yp=ycc+r*np.sin(p)
57           [xg,yg]=rotz(xp,yp,alpha)
58           if p < np.pi:
59               plt.scatter(xg,yg,s=1,color='r') #—plot lower half red
60           else:
61               plt.scatter(xg,yg,s=1,color='g') #—plot upper half green
62           xp1=xcc+r #—plot diameter bars and bar end points
63           yp1=0
64           [xg1,yg1]=rotz(xp1,yp1,alpha)
65           xp2=xcc-r
66           yp2=0
67           [xg2,yg2]=rotz(xp2,yp2,alpha)
68           plt.plot([xg1,xg2],[yg1,yg2],color='b')
69           plt.scatter(xg1,yg1,s=10,color='b')
70           plt.scatter(xg2,yg2,s=10,color='b')
71
72   plt.text(xc+31,yc-13,'starting circle')
73   plt.arrow(xc+31,yc-13,-3,2,head_length=2,head_width=1)
74
75   plt.show()
```

As shown in Figure 2-20, Listing 2-13 rotates the starting circle through increments of angle **dalpha** while keeping the orientation of each circle unchanged. The program is similar to the preceding one, with the exception that only the local center of each circle is rotated about point c while the circumferential points, as defined by the starting circle, remain unrotated. The program should be self-explanatory.

Note the difference between Listings 2-12 and 2-13. In Listing 2-12, the rotation takes place in lines 53-70. At each angle **alpha**, the coordinates of each point around the circle's circumference are determined in lines 55 and 56. These are then transformed in line 57 using the function **rotz(xp,yp,alpha)**. That is, each point around the circumference is rotated by the angle **alpha**. This has the effect of rotating the entire circle, as shown in Figure 2-18. In Listing 2-13, however, the plotting is done in lines 41-68. Here only the circle's center is rotated in lines 50 and 51. In line 55, **rotz(xp,yp,0)** uses the angle p=0 in its argument. This has the effect of not rotating the circle itself, only its center, as shown in Figure 2-20.

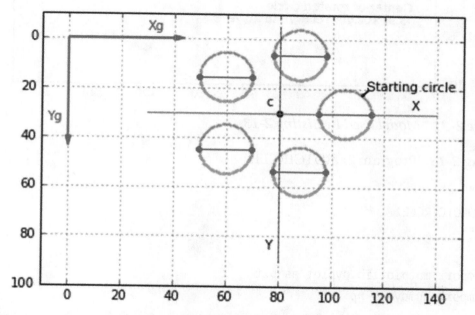

Figure 2-20. *Circles with centers rotated about point c from Listing 2-13*

Which method of rotation should you use: that shown in Figure 2-18 or 2-20? It depends on your application. In one you may want the entire object, including the points that comprise it, to rotate about a center whereas in another you may want only the center of the object to rotate while the object retains its original orientation. See Figure 2-21.

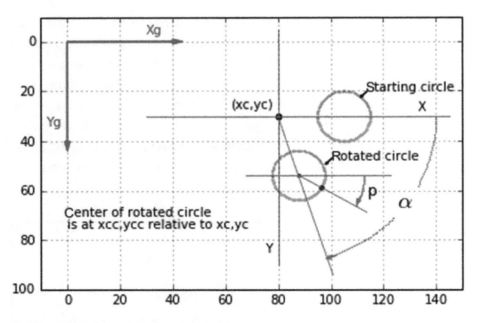

Figure 2-21. *Model used by Listing 2-13*

Listing 2-13. Program 2DROTCIRCLE2

```
1     """
2     2DROTCIRCLE2
3     """
4
5     import matplotlib.pyplot as plt
6     import numpy as np
7
8     plt.axis([-10,150,100,-10])
9     plt.axis('on')
10    plt.grid(True)
11
12    #------------------------------------------axes
13    plt.arrow(0,0,40,0,head_length=4,head_width=2,color='b')
14    plt.arrow(0,0,0,40,head_length=4,head_width=2,color='b')
15    plt.text(30,-3,'Xg',color='b')
16    plt.text(-8,34,'Yg',color='b')
17
18    xc=80 #---------------------center of rotation
```

```
19   yc=30
20   plt.plot([xc-50,xc+60],[yc,yc],linewidth=1,color='grey') #--X
21   plt.plot([xc,xc],[yc-35,yc+60],linewidth=1,color='grey') #--Y
22   plt.text(xc+50,yc-2,'X')
23   plt.text(xc-5,yc+55,'Y')
24
25   plt.scatter(xc,yc,s=20,color='k') #-plot center of rotation
26   plt.text(xc-5,yc-3,'c')
27
28   #------------------------------------------------define rotation matrix Rz
29   def rotz(xp,yp,rz):
30       c11=np.cos(rz)
31       c12=-np.sin(rz)
32       c21=np.sin(rz)
33       c22=np.cos(rz)
34       xpp=xp*c11+yp*c12 #--relative to xc,yc
35       ypp=xp*c21+yp*c22
36       xg=xc+xpp #--relative to xg,yg
37       yg=yc+ypp
38       return [xg,yg]
39
40   #------------------------------------------------plot circles
41   p1=0
42   p2=2*np.pi
43   dp=(p2-p1)/100
44
45   alpha1=0
46   alpha2=2*np.pi
47   dalpha=(alpha2-alpha1)/5
48
49   for alpha in np.arange(alpha1,alpha2,dalpha):
50       xcc=25*np.cos(alpha)
51       ycc=25*np.sin(alpha)
52       for p in np.arange(p1,p2,dp):
53           xp=xcc+r*np.cos(p)
54           yp=ycc+r*np.sin(p)
```

```
55              [xg,yg]=rotz(xp,yp,0)
56              if p < np.pi:
57                  plt.scatter(xg,yg,s=1,color='r')
58              else:
59                  plt.scatter(xg,yg,s=1,color='g')
60              xp1=xcc+r
61              yp1=ycc+0
62              [xg1,yg1]=rotz(xp1,yp1,0)
63              xp2=xcc-r
64              yp2=ycc+0
65              [xg2,yg2]=rotz(xp2,yp2,0)
66              plt.plot([xg1,xg2],[yg1,yg2],color='b')
67              plt.scatter(xg1,yg1,s=10,color='b')
68              plt.scatter(xg2,yg2,s=10,color='b')
69
70  plt.text(xc+34,yc-10,'starting circle')
71  plt.arrow(xc+34,yc-10,-2,2,head_length=1,head_ width=1)
72
73  plt.show()
```

2.10   Summary

In this chapter, you saw how to use dots and lines to construct shapes in two dimensions. You learned the concept of relative coordinates, specifically the *local system*, which is used to construct an image with coordinate values relative to a center, which in the case of rotation may be used as the center of rotation, and the *global system* which is used for plotting. You saw how local coordinates must be transformed into the global system for plotting, the origin of the global system being defined through the **plt.axes()** function. You saw how to construct lines from dots; arrange colored dots in artistic patterns; and draw arcs, discs, circles, and ellipses using dots and line segments. Then you learned about the concepts of translation (easy) and rotation (not so easy). You applied all this to points, rectangles, and circles. In the next chapter, you will extend these ideas to three dimensions.

CHAPTER 3

Graphics in Three Dimensions

In this chapter, you will learn how to create, translate, and rotate three-dimensional objects in a three-dimensional space. You will also learn how to project and display them on the two-dimensional surface of your computer screen. General movement of an object implies both translation and rotation. I discussed this in two dimensions in the previous chapter. You saw that translation in two dimensions is trivial. Just add or subtract a quantity from the x coordinates to translate in the x direction, similarly for the y direction. In three dimensions, it is still trivial, although you are able now to translate in the third dimension, the z direction, simply by adding or subtracting an amount to an object's z coordinates. Rotation is another matter, however. The analysis follows the method you used in two dimensions but is complicated by the fact that you now are able to rotate an object around three coordinate directions. In this chapter, I will not discuss 3D translation any further but will concentrate instead on 3D rotation.

3.1 The Three-Dimensional Coordinate System

In the previous discussion of two-dimensional rotation, you rotated two-dimensional objects in the two-dimensional x,y plane. You now extend those concepts to three dimensions by introducing a third axis, the z axis, as shown in Figure 3-1. Notice that the z axis points into the screen, not out. This is not an arbitrary choice. We are following the *right-hand rule* convention where the direction of positive z is found by rotating the x axis toward the y axis through the smaller angle between them. The positive z axis will then point in the direction that would be followed by a right-handed screw when turned in this fashion. In this case, the screw would progress into the screen; that is then the direction of the positive z axis. We could construct an entire mathematical

© B.J. Korites 2018
B.J. Korites, *Python Graphics*, https://doi.org/10.1007/978-1-4842-3378-8_3

theory based on a left-handed screw but the convention used most everywhere is that of a right-handed system. Some books and papers label the coordinate axes as x1,x2,x3. Following the right-hand rule, the direction of x3 would be found by rotating x1 into x2, as described above. In this work, we will stay with the x,y,z notation for the directions.

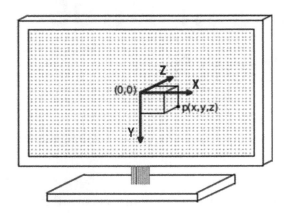

Figure 3-1. *Three-dimensional coordinate axes with point P at coordinates (x,y,z)*

It should be apparent now why I used the nomenclature Rz in the previous discussion of two-dimensional rotation; it refers to rotation about the z axis. This appears as a clockwise rotation in the x-y plane when x goes to the right and y goes down. If x went to the right and y were to go up, z would point out of the screen and a positive rotation about the z axis would appear to go counterclockwise.

Following the methods used in this analysis of two-dimensional rotation, in the remainder of this chapter I will discuss separate rotations around the x,y, and z axes and then combined rotations around all three axes. Incidentally, when I say "rotation around the x axis", for example, I am implying that this is equivalent to "rotation around the x *direction*" and vice versa. While rotation around an imaginary axis that is parallel to the x axis is not precisely the same as rotation around the x axis, the difference is only a matter of translation. I will use both terms interchangeably except when confusion may result.

Figure 3-2 shows the right-hand x,y,z system. Imagine you're standing at the origin, looking out in the direction of the x axis. If you were to turn a right-handed screw clockwise, it would progress in the direction of the positive x axis. The double-headed arrow is the conventional way of indicating the direction of a right-hand rotation, Rx; similarly for Ry and Rz.

Why have I chosen to orient the coordinate system as shown in Figure 3-2? Standard **matplotlib** uses a different orientation as shown, for example, in `https://matplotlin.org/mpl_toolkits/mplot3d/tutorial.html#scatter-plots`.

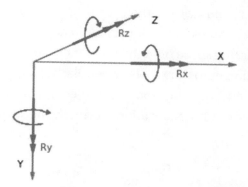

Figure 3-2. *Three-dimensional coordinate axes showing right-hand rotation around each coordinate direction*

As explained earlier, the orientation in Figure 3-2 is somewhat more intuitive. The object being constructed is inside a space defined by the x,y,z axes. In this situation, the observer is outside the space looking in. The object may be translated and rotated at will to give any view desired. You can look straight in at an object or view it from above or below, as shown in the images of Saturn in Chapter 10. The **matplotlib** orientation, on the other hand, is the one commonly used for data plotting and is the one you'll use for that purpose in Chapter 9; look at Figures 9-1 through 9-5. If you prefer the standard **matplotlib** system, it is easy to change to that orientation; just rotate the axes to any orientation you want, as is done in Chapter 9 where, to get z pointing up, you rotate around the global x direction by -100 degrees (tilts z slightly forward), the global y axis by -135 degrees, and the global z direction by +8 degrees (see lines 191-193 in Listing 9-1). You can fine-tune the orientation by small rotations about the global axes. After you complete this chapter, you should find it easy to shade the background planes, as shown in **matplotlib**, if you want. You can orient the axes any way you want as long as they follow the right-hand rule.

3.2 Projections onto the Coordinate Planes

How do we display a three-dimensional object on a two-dimensional computer monitor? We do so by projecting the object onto either of the three two-dimensional coordinate planes (x,y; x,z; and y,z) and then plotting either of those images on the monitor. Figure 3-3 show a three-dimensional line (black) running from A to B. Looking down from above the plotting space onto the x,z plane, you see it as the red line, which is the black line's projection onto the x,z plane. Similarly, the green line shows its projection onto the y,z plane; the blue line is its projection onto the x,y plane. I will use only one of these projections for visualization, normally the x,y projection.

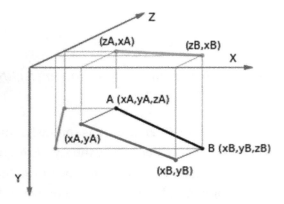

Figure 3-3. *Projection of a three-dimensional line (black) onto the three coordinate planes: red=x,z projection, green=y,z projection, and blue=x,y projection*

The x,y projection is obtained by plotting a point's x and y coordinates in the x,y plane; for a line, you plot a line between the x and y coordinates of the line's endpoints. In the case of the black line, which runs from spatial coordinates (xA,yA,zA) to (xB,yB,zB), you plot a line between xA,yA and xB,yB:

```
plt.plot([xA,xB],[yA,yB],color='b')
```

This gives you the blue line, which is the projection onto the x,y plane as shown in Figure 3-4. If you want to obtain the top view, you plot the black line's z,x coordinates. If plotting with your normal coordinate axes with x running from left to right and y running down on the left, the y axis replaces the z axis. This is equivalent to a -90 degree rotation about the x axis. You then plot between the line's z and x coordinates of

```
plt.plot([zA,zB],[xA,xB],color='r')
```

to get the red line. To get the green y, z projection, you plot the z and y coordinates using the command

```
plt.plot([zA,zB],[yA,yB],color='g')
```

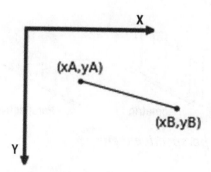

Figure 3-4. *Projection of a three-dimensional line onto the x, y plane*

In this case, you must reorient the screen coordinate axes such that +z runs from left to right across the top of the screen with the y axis running down the right side. This will give a z, y view from *outside* of the x,y,z coordinate system.

Note that in the case of a projection onto the x,y plane, you do not use the object's z coordinates. But you still need them in order to carry out rotations. Similarly for the other projections, one coordinate is not needed for the projection but is needed for rotations so it must be included in the analysis.

To simplify everything, you will use the x,y projection in most of the work that follows. As you will see, rotating an object around the three coordinate directions and projecting the object's (x,y) coordinates onto the x,y plane will produce a three-dimensional view.

The projections of three-dimensional objects onto two-dimensional coordinate planes are called *isometric projections*. They are commonly used in engineering and drafting. These images do not appear as they would to the human eye or as they would in a photograph because of the absence of what artists call *foreshortening*, more commonly known as *perspective*. As an example of foreshortening, if you look down a line of telephone poles that are running off into the distance alongside railroad tracks, the pole closest to you would look taller than those further away and the rails would appear to merge as they near the horizon. What causes foreshortening? It happens simply because there is more area for the eye to cover in the far distance than close up. In the case of telephone poles, it's because there is more vertical space in the distance so the poles, which are of fixed height, occupy a smaller percentage of it; for the railroad tracks, it's the expanding horizontal space. Isometric projections do not take foreshortening into account, but I will in Chapter 4 when I discuss perspective transformations.

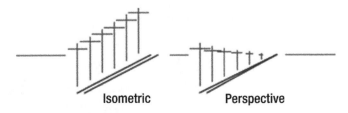

Figure 3-5. *Isometric vs. perspective views*

While you have seen how to project a simple three-dimensional line and its end points onto the three coordinate planes, you could have worked with a more complicated object consisting of many points and lines. As you have seen, even a circle can be constructed from just points (dots) or lines with any degree of refinement desired.

While a simple example, the three-dimensional line illustrates the method you will use in the following work: define a shape within the three-dimensional x,y,z space in terms of points and lines having coordinates (x,y,z); operate on them by rotating and translating; project them onto the x,y plane; and then plot them using their x and y coordinates. Thus you are able to project a 3D object onto your computer monitor's screen.

To rotate a point in three dimensions implies rotating it around the x,y, and z directions. You saw how to carry out two-dimensional rotation around the z direction, Rz, in the previous chapter. Here, you will derive transformations in three dimensions for rotation around the y,x, and z directions.

3.3 Rotation Around the y Direction

Figure 3-6 shows the unit vector geometry for rotation around the y direction, Ry. This is the view that would be seen by looking down onto the top of the x,y,z system. The y axis runs into the plane of the paper.

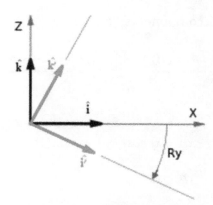

Figure 3-6. *Unit vectors for rotation about the y direction. This is a view looking down on the plotting space. The y axis runs into the plane of the paper.*

Following the method used in Chapter 2, a point whose position is initially defined by the vector **P** is rotated to **P**′. Vectors defining the location of P and P′ in the x,y,z (unrotated) and x′,y′,z′ (rotated) systems are

$$\mathbf{P} = xp\hat{\mathbf{i}} + yp\hat{\mathbf{j}} + zp\hat{\mathbf{k}} \tag{3-1}$$

$$\mathbf{P}' = xp'\hat{\mathbf{i}} + yp'\hat{\mathbf{j}} + zp'\hat{\mathbf{k}} \tag{3-2}$$

$$\mathbf{P}' = xp\hat{\mathbf{i}}' + yp\hat{\mathbf{j}}' + zp\hat{\mathbf{k}}' \tag{3-3}$$

where $\hat{\mathbf{i}}$, $\hat{\mathbf{j}}$, and $\hat{\mathbf{k}}$ are unit vector in the x,y, and z directions and $\hat{\mathbf{i}}'$, $\hat{\mathbf{j}}'$, and $\hat{\mathbf{k}}'$ are unit vectors in the x′,y′, and z′ directions. From Figure 3-6, you can see that

$$\hat{\mathbf{i}}' = cos(Ry)\hat{\mathbf{i}} + (0)\hat{\mathbf{j}} - sin(Ry)\hat{\mathbf{k}} \tag{3-4}$$

$$\hat{\mathbf{j}}' = (0)\hat{\mathbf{i}} + (1)\hat{\mathbf{j}} - (0)\hat{\mathbf{k}} \tag{3-5}$$

$$\hat{\mathbf{k}}' = sin(Ry)\hat{\mathbf{i}} + (0)\hat{\mathbf{j}} - cos(Ry)\hat{\mathbf{k}} \tag{3-6}$$

Plugging them into Equation 3-3 yields

$$\mathbf{P}' = xp\left[cos(Ry)\hat{\mathbf{i}} - sin(Ry)\hat{\mathbf{k}} \right] + yp\hat{\mathbf{j}} + zp\left[sin(Ry)\hat{\mathbf{i}} + cos(Ry)\hat{\mathbf{k}} \right] \tag{3-7}$$

Separating into $\hat{\mathbf{i}}$, $\hat{\mathbf{j}}$, and $\hat{\mathbf{k}}$ components, you get

$$\mathbf{P}' = \underbrace{\left[xp\cos(Ry) + zp\sin(Ry)\right]}_{xp'}\hat{\mathbf{i}} + \underbrace{\left[yp\right]}_{yp'}\hat{\mathbf{j}} + \underbrace{\left[-xp\sin(Ry) + zp\cos(Ry)\right]}_{zp'}\hat{\mathbf{k}} \qquad (3\text{-}8))$$

With Equation 3-2,

$$xp' = xp\cos(Ry) + zp\sin(Ry) \qquad (3\text{-}9)$$

$$yp' = yp \qquad (3\text{-}10)$$

$$zp' = -xp\sin(Ry) + zp\cos(Ry) \qquad (3\text{-}11)$$

Equations 3-9 through 3-11 give the coordinates of the rotated point in the local x,y,z system. Of course, yp'=yp in Equation 3-10 since the y coordinate doesn't change with rotation about the y axis.

Equations 3-9, 3-10, and 3-11 can be expressed in matrix form, as shown in Equation 3-12:

$$\begin{bmatrix} xp' \\ yp' \\ zp' \end{bmatrix} = \begin{bmatrix} \cos(Ry) & 0 & \sin(Ry) \\ 0 & 1 & 0 \\ -\sin(Ry) & 0 & \cos(Ry) \end{bmatrix} \begin{bmatrix} xp \\ yp \\ zp \end{bmatrix} \qquad (3\text{-}12)$$

It can be abbreviated as

$$[P'] = [Ry][P] \qquad (3\text{-}13)$$

[Ry], the transformation matrix for y axis rotation, is

$$[Ry] = \begin{bmatrix} Cy(1,1) & Cy(1,2) & Cy(1,3) \\ Cy(2,1) & Cy(2,2) & Cy(2,3) \\ Cy(3,1) & Cy(3,2) & Cy(3,3) \end{bmatrix} \qquad (3\text{-}14)$$

$$Cy(1,1) = \cos(Ry) \qquad (3\text{-}15)$$

$$Cy(1,2) = 0 \qquad (3\text{-}16)$$

$$Cy(1,3) = \sin(Ry) \qquad (3\text{-}17)$$

$$Cy(2,1) = 0 \qquad (3\text{-}18)$$

$$Cy(2,2) = 0 \qquad (3\text{-}19)$$

$$Cy(2,3) = 0 \qquad (3\text{-}20)$$

$$Cy(3,1) = -sin(Ry) \qquad (3\text{-}21)$$

$$Cy(3,2) = 0 \qquad (3\text{-}22)$$

$$Cy(3,3) = cos(Ry) \qquad (3\text{-}23)$$

These elements will be used in the programs that follow.

3.4 Rotation Around the x Direction

Figure 3-7 shows the unit vector geometry for rotation around the x direction.

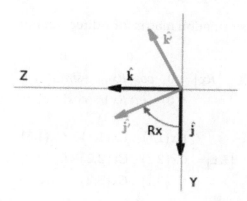

Figure 3-7. *Unit vectors for rotation around the x direction. The x axis runs into the plane of the paper.*

You see that

$$\hat{\mathbf{i}}' = (1)\hat{\mathbf{i}} + (0)\hat{\mathbf{j}} + (0)\hat{\mathbf{k}} \qquad (3\text{-}24)$$

$$\hat{\mathbf{j}}' = (0)\hat{\mathbf{i}} + cos(Rx)\hat{\mathbf{j}} + sin(Rx)\hat{\mathbf{k}} \qquad (3\text{-}25)$$

$$\hat{\mathbf{k}}' = (0)\hat{\mathbf{i}} - sin(Rx)\hat{\mathbf{j}} + cos(Rx)\hat{\mathbf{k}} \qquad (3\text{-}26)$$

Following the methods in the previous section,

$$\mathbf{P} = xp\hat{\mathbf{i}} + yp\hat{\mathbf{j}} + zp\hat{\mathbf{k}} \tag{3-27}$$

$$\mathbf{P}' = xp\hat{\mathbf{i}} + yp\left[\cos(Rx)\hat{\mathbf{j}} + \sin(Rx)\hat{\mathbf{k}}\right] + zp\left[-\sin(Rx)\hat{\mathbf{j}} + \cos(Rx)\hat{\mathbf{k}}\right] \tag{3-28}$$

$$= \underbrace{xp\hat{\mathbf{i}}}_{xp'} + \underbrace{\left[yp\cos(Rx) - zp\sin(Rx)\right]\hat{\mathbf{j}}}_{yp'} + \underbrace{\left[yp\sin(Rx) + zp\cos(Rx)\right]\hat{\mathbf{k}}}_{zp'} \tag{3-29}$$

In matrix form, it's

$$\begin{bmatrix} xp' \\ yp' \\ zp' \end{bmatrix} = \begin{bmatrix} 1 & 0 & 0 \\ 0 & \cos(Rx) & -\sin(Rx) \\ 0 & \sin(Rx) & \cos(Rx) \end{bmatrix} \begin{bmatrix} xp \\ yp \\ zp \end{bmatrix} \tag{3-30}$$

which can be abbreviated as

$$[P'] = [Rx][P] \tag{3-31}$$

This leads to the transformation matrix for x direction rotation of

$$[Rx] = \begin{bmatrix} 1 & 0 & 0 \\ 0 & \cos(Rx) & -\sin(Rx) \\ 0 & \sin(Rx) & \cos(Rx) \end{bmatrix} \tag{3-32}$$

$$[Rx] = \begin{bmatrix} Cx(1,1) & Cx(1,2) & Cx(1,3) \\ Cx(2,1) & Cx(2,2) & Cx(2,3) \\ Cx(3,1) & Cx(3,2) & Cx(3,3) \end{bmatrix} \tag{3-33}$$

$$Cx(1,1) = 1 \tag{3-34}$$

$$Cx(1,2) = 0 \tag{3-35}$$

$$Cx(1,3) = 0 \tag{3-36}$$

$$Cx(2,1) = 0 \tag{3-37}$$

$$Cx(2,2) = \cos(Rx) \tag{3-38}$$

$$Cx(2,3) = -sin(Rx)$$

$$(3-39)$$

$$Cx(3,1) = 0$$

$$(3-40)$$

$$Cx(3,2) = sin(Rx)$$

$$(3-41)$$

$$Cx(3,3) = cos(Rx)$$

$$(3-42)$$

3.5 Rotation Around the z Direction

In Chapter 2, you derived the transformation matrix for two-dimensional rotation around the z direction. You will now do it in three dimensions. Repeating the two-dimensional Rz matrix (Equation 3-43) from Chapter 2:

$$\begin{bmatrix} xp' \\ yp' \end{bmatrix} = \begin{bmatrix} cos(Rz) & -sin(Rz) \\ sin(Rz) & cos(Rz) \end{bmatrix} \begin{bmatrix} xp \\ yp \end{bmatrix}$$

$$(3-43)$$

In three dimensions, you have the following:

$$\begin{bmatrix} xp' \\ yp' \\ zp' \end{bmatrix} = \begin{bmatrix} cos(Rz) & -sin(Rz) & 0 \\ sin(Rz) & cos(Rz) & 0 \\ 0 & 0 & 1 \end{bmatrix} \begin{bmatrix} xp \\ yp \\ zp \end{bmatrix}$$

$$(3-44)$$

$$[Rz] = \begin{bmatrix} Cz(1,1) & Cz(1,2) & Cz(1,3) \\ Cz(2,1) & Cz(2,2) & Cz(2,3) \\ Cz(3,1) & Cz(3,2) & Cz(3,3) \end{bmatrix}$$

$$(3-45)$$

$$Cz(1,1) = cos(Rz)$$

$$(3-46)$$

$$Cz(1,2) = -sin(Rz)$$

$$(3-47)$$

$$Cz(1,3) = 0$$

$$(3-48)$$

$$Cz(2,1) = sin(Rz)$$

$$(3-49)$$

$$Cz(2,2) = cos(Rz)$$

$$(3-50)$$

$$Cz(2,3) = 0 \tag{3-51}$$

$$Cz(3,1) = 0 \tag{3-52}$$

$$Cz(3,2) = 0 \tag{3-53}$$

$$Cz(3,3) = 1 \tag{3-54}$$

You can extend the two-dimensional matrix equation to three-dimensions in Equation 3-44 by simply observing that in the first row xp' does not depend on zp, hence C(1,3)=0; in the second row, yp' also does not depend on zp, hence c(2,3)=0; in the third row, zp' does not depend on either xp' or yp', hence C(3,1) and C(3,2) both equal 0. C(3,3)=1 since the z coordinate remains unchanged after rotation about the z axis.

The three transformations are summarized as follows:

$$[Rx] = \begin{bmatrix} 1 & 0 & 0 \\ 0 & cos(Rx) & -sin(Rx) \\ 0 & sin(Rx) & cos(Rx) \end{bmatrix} \tag{3-55}$$

$$[Ry] = \begin{bmatrix} cos(Ry) & 0 & sin(Ry) \\ 0 & 1 & 0 \\ -sin(Ry) & 0 & cos(Ry) \end{bmatrix} \tag{3-56}$$

$$[Rz] = \begin{bmatrix} cos(Rz) & -sin(Rz) & 0 \\ sin(Rz) & cos(Rz) & 0 \\ 0 & 0 & 1 \end{bmatrix} \tag{3-57}$$

3.6 Separate Rotations Around the Coordinate Directions

Figure 3-8 shows *separate* rotations of a box (a) about the x,y, and z directions. The figure was created using Listing 3-1. The rotations are separate, not sequential. That is, box (b) is box (a) rotated by Rx; box (c) is (a) rotated by Ry; and box (d) is (a) rotated by Rz. The rotations are not additive, which means Ry is *not* added to the results of Rx and Rz is not added to the results of Rx and Ry; they are each separate rotations of the original box (a). The rotations take place around the center of the box.

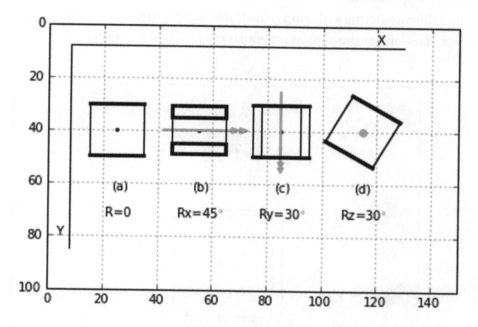

Figure 3-8. *Output from Listing 3-1. Projection (a) of an unrotated box on the x,y plane, (b) rotated around the x direction by Rx=45°, (c) around the y direction by Ry=30°, and (d) around the z direction by Rz=30°. Double-headed red arrows show the direction of rotation using the right-hand rule convention. Heavy lines indicate the top and bottom. The boxes are rotated about their center, which is indicated by a black dot.*

Listing 3-1 makes use of functions and lists. Without them, the program would more than double in size. Using them reduces the program size considerably. It could be shortened even further by the use of arrays but the savings would be minimal and tends to obscure the methodology.

Figure 3-9 shows the corner numbering scheme used by Listing 3-1. The corner numbers are in blue. They are Python list numberings and start at 0. Normally we number the corners from 1 to 8. However, in Python, the first element in a list is always 0. In the case of an eight-cornered box, the last, the eighth, is element 7 in the list. For example, the x coordinate of the first point is x[0], the second is x[1], and so on. It's like numbering the first rung of a ladder as the zeroth rung. Confusing? Yes. Blame it on the C programming language, from which this trap is a carryover. Perhaps the best way to avoid problems is to get in the habit of numbering things from 0 instead of 1, which is what I have done in Figure 3-9. I could have used a different arrangement of numbering in Figure 3-9 but starting with the top left corner and proceeding clockwise seems logical (e.g. I could have started the numbering at the top right-front corner instead of the top upper-left). It doesn't matter as long as the chosen scheme is consistent with the program.

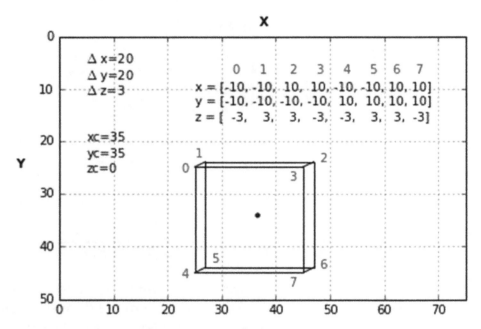

Figure 3-9. *Numbering scheme for the box's corners in Lsiting 3-1. Lists at the upper right contain the coordinate values. They are the same as the lists in Listing 3-1, lines 14, 15, and 16. The center coordinates xc,yc,zc are not the same as used in Listing 3-1. The z axis is not shown.*

The lists shown in the figure define the corner coordinates. There are eight elements in each list because there are eight corners in the box. Corner 2, which is the *third* element in the list, has coordinates x[3]=10,y[3]=-10,z[3]=3. These are *local* coordinates; in other words, they are relative to the box's center, which is the center of rotation.

114

Listing 3-1 starts off by defining lists for [x],[y], and [z] in lines 14-16. These lines hold the coordinates of the box's corners relative to its center. [xg],[yg], and [zg] in lines 18-20 will hold the global plotting coordinates after transformations have been done. Space is reserved for eight in each list since there are eight corners in the box.

Next are the definitions of the rotation functions **rotx**, **roty**, and **rotz**. They rotate a point's coordinates xp,yp,zp around the x,y, and z directions, respectively. Each function returns a new set of coordinates: xg,yg, and zg, which are the global coordinates of the rotated point. These coordinates will be used for plotting.

Looking at the definition of **rotx**, which begins in line 23, when invoked to do a transformation about the x direction **rotx** receives the box's center coordinates xc,yc,zc, which, in this case is the center of rotation, plus the point's unrotated coordinates xp,yp,zp and the angle of rotation about the x direction, Rx. The list **a=[xp,yp,zp]** in line 24 contains the coordinates of the unrotated point. This is, in effect, a vector to point xp,yp,zp. In line 25, **b=[1,0,0]** is a list of the first row of the Rx transformation matrix shown in Equation 3-55. Line 26, **xpp=np.inner(a,b)**, forms the dot or scalar product of these lists. There is also an **np.dot(a,b)** function that could be used. For simple non-complex vectors, **np.inner(a,b)** and **np.dot(a,b)** give the same results. But for higher dimensional arrays the results may differ.

To illustrate the calculation of ypp for rotation around the x direction, you have seen that vector **p**′ is related to **p** by

$$
\begin{bmatrix} xpp \\ ypp \\ zpp \end{bmatrix} = \begin{bmatrix} 1 & 0 & 0 \\ 0 & cos(Rx) & -sin(Rx) \\ 0 & sin(Rx) & cos(Rx) \end{bmatrix} \begin{bmatrix} xp \\ yp \\ zp \end{bmatrix}
\tag{3-58}
$$

where ypp (i.e. yp′) is the y coordinate of the rotated point. Line 27 in the program is the second row of Equation 3-57. The scalar product of a and b is formed in line 28 producing ypp (yp′). That is,

$$
a = [xp,yp,zp]
\tag{3-59}
$$

$$
b = \begin{bmatrix} 0,cos(Rx),-sin(Rx) \end{bmatrix}
\tag{3-60}
$$

$$ypp = \text{np.inner}(a,b) \tag{3-61}$$

$$= xp(0) + yp(\cos(Rx)) + zp(-\sin(Rx)) \tag{3-62}$$

$$= yp\cos(Rx) - zp\sin(Rx) \tag{3-63}$$

which is line 28. Lines 29 and 30 repeat the process using the third row of Equation 3-57, producing zpp (zp′). Line 31 adds xc,yc,zc, the coordinates of the box's center, to xpp,ypp,zpp, thus translating the rotated points relative to the origin of the global coordinate system producing [xg,yg,zg] which are the global plotting coordinates. **roty** and **rotz** follow the same structure using the rows of [Ry] and [Rz] in their b lists.

Next is the function **plotbox** in line 56. This plots the box using its global corner coordinates xg,yg, and zg. The loop starting in line 57 plots the top by connecting the first three corners with lines. Line 60 closes the top by plotting a line between corners 3 and 0. This has not been included in the loop, which was set up to plot one corner with the next. The problem comes when you try to connect corner 3 with 0; the algorithm in the loop doesn't work. It could be modified to handle it, but it's easier to just add line 60 rather than complicate the loop. The rest of **plotbox** up to line 68 completes the box. Line 70 plots a dot at its center.

Line 72 starts function **plotboxx**. This transforms the corner coordinates to get them ready for plotting by **plotbox**. The loop from line 73 to 74 rotates all eight corners around the x direction by invoking **rotx**. Line 76 invokes function **plotbox**, which does the plotting. **plotboxy** and **plotboxz** do the same for rotations about the y and z directions.

Up to this point, you have been defining functions. You use functions in this program since many of the operations are repetitive. If you tried to write this program using single statements, it would be at least twice as long.

Control of the program lies between lines 91 and 116. Lines 91-95 plot the first box (a). Since this first box (a) is unrotated, you specify Rx=0 in line 91. You use function **plotboxx** with the Rx=0 parameter to do the plotting. You could use Ry=0 with **plotboxy** or Rz=0 with **plotboxz**. It doesn't matter since the angle of rotation is 0. Lines 92-94 specify the box's center coordinates. Line 95 invokes **plotboxx**. The result is shown in Figure 3-8 as (a). Lines 98-116 produce the rotated boxes (b), (c), and (d).

To summarize the procedure using box (b) as an example, the angle of rotation is set in line 98; the box's center coordinates in lines 99-101. Then, in line 102, function **plotboxx** is invoked. The center coordinates and the angle Rx are passed as arguments. **plotboxx**, which begins in line 72, rotates the eight corners by invoking **rotx. plotboxx** doesn't use xc,yc, and zc, but it passes them onto **rotx**, which needs them. **rotx** rotates and translates the coordinates producing xg,yg,zg. Line 76 invokes function **plotbox**, which does the plotting.

In lines 91, 98, 105, and 112 you use the function **radians()**, which was imported from the **math** library in line 7. (Note that you could have used **numpy** for this). It converts an argument in degrees to one in radians, which are required by **sin()** and **cos()**. In earlier programs, you did the conversion with **np.pi/180**.

Listing 3-1. Program 4BOXES

```
1    """
2    4BOXES
3    """
4
5    import numpy as np
6    import matplotlib.pyplot as plt
7    from math import sin, cos, radians #-or use numpy
8
9    plt.axis([0,150,100,0])
10   plt.axis('on')
11   plt.grid(True)
12
13   #————————————————————-lists
14   x=[-10,-10,10,10,-10,-10,10,10] #-un-rotated corner coordinates
15   y=[-10,-10,-10,-10,10,10,10,10] #-relative to box's center
16   z=[ -3, 3, 3, -3,-3, 3, 3,-3]
17
18   xg=[0,1,2,3,4,5,6,7] #-define global coordinates
19   yg=[0,1,2,3,4,5,6,7]
20   zg=[0,1,2,3,4,5,6,7]
21
22   #————————————————-function definitions
23   def rotx(xc,yc,zc,xp,yp,zp,Rx):
24       a=[xp,yp,zp]
25       b=[1,0,0] #—————————-[cx11,cx12,cx13]
```

```
26        xpp=np.inner(a,b) #—scalar product of a,b=xp*cx11+yp*cx12+ zp*cx13
27        b=[0,cos(Rx),-sin(Rx)] #———[cx21,cx22,cx23]
28        ypp=np.inner(a,b)
29        b=[0,sin(Rx),cos(Rx)] #———[cx31,cx32,cx33]
30        zpp=np.inner(a,b)
31        [xg,yg,zg]=[xpp+xc,ypp+yc,zpp+zc]
32        return[xg,yg,zg]
33
34    def roty(xc,yc,zc,xp,yp,zp,Ry):
35        a=[xp,yp,zp]
36        b=[cos(Ry),0,sin(Ry)] #———-[cx11,cx12,cx13]
37        xpp=np.inner(a,  b)
38        b=[0,1,0] #———[cx21,cx22,cx23]
39        ypp=np.inner(a,b) #———-scalar product of a,b
40        b=[-sin(Ry),0,cos(Ry)] #———[cx31,cx32,cx33]
41        zpp=np.inner(a,b)
42        [xg,yg,zg]=[xpp+xc,ypp+yc,zpp+zc]
43        return[xg,yg,zg]
44
45    def rotz(xc,yc,zc,xp,yp,zp,Rz):
46        a=[xp,yp,zp]
47        b=[cos(Rz),-sin(Rz),0] #———-[cx11,cx12,cx13]
48        xpp=np.inner(a,  b)
49        b=[sin(Rz),cos(Rz),0] #———[cx21,cx22,cx23]
50        ypp=np.inner(a,b)
51        b=[0,0,1] #———[cx31,cx32,cx33]
52        zpp=np.inner(a,b) #———scalar product of a,b
53        [xg,yg,zg]=[xpp+xc,ypp+yc,zpp+zc]
54        return[xg,yg,zg]
55
56    def plotbox(xg,yg,zg): # -plots the box using its rotated
                                    coordinates xg,yg,zg
57        for i in (0,1,2): #———————-plot top
58            plt.plot([xg[i],xg[i+1]],[yg[i],yg[i+1]],linewidth=3,
                color='k')
```

```
59
60          plt.plot([xg[3],xg[0]],[yg[3],yg[0]],linewidth=3,color='k')
            #-close top

61
62          for i in (4,5,6): #————————-plot bottom
63              plt.plot([xg[i],xg[i+1]],[yg[i],yg[i+1]],linewidth=3,
                color='k')

64
65          plt.plot([xg[7],xg[4]],[yg[7],yg[4]],linewidth=3,color='k')
            #-close bottom

66
67          for i in (0,1,2,3): #————————plot sides
68              plt.plot([xg[i],xg[i-4]],[yg[i],yg[i-4]],linewidth=1,
                color='k')

69
70          plt.scatter(xc,yc,s=5) #-plot a dot at the center

71
72      def plotboxx(xc,yc,zc,Rx):
73          for i in (0,1,2,3,4,5,6,7): #————————-rotate eight corners
74              [xg[i],yg[i],zg[i]]=rotx(xc,yc,zc,x[i],y[i],z[i],Rx)

75
76          plotbox(xg,yg,zg)

77
78      def plotboxy(xc,yc,zc,Ry):
79          for i in (0,1,2,3,4,5,6,7): #————————-rotate eight corners
80              [xg[i],yg[i],zg[i]]=roty(xc,yc,zc,x[i],y[i],z[i],Ry)

81
82          plotbox(xg,yg,zg)

83
84      def plotboxz(xc,yc,zc,Rz):
85          for i in (0,1,2,3,4,5,6,7): #————————-rotate eight corners
86              [xg[i],yg[i],zg[i]]=rotz(xc,yc,zc,x[i],y[i],z[i],Rz)

87
88          plotbox(xg,yg,zg)

89
```

```
90   #——————————————————R=0 box(a)
91   Rx=radians(0)
92   xc=25 #————box (a) center coordinates
93   yc=40
94   zc=20
95   plotboxx(xc,yc,zc,Rx) #-since Rx=0 we could use plotboxy or plotboxz
96
97   #——————————————————Rx box(b)
98   Rx=radians(45)
99   xc=55
100  yc=40
101  zc=20
102  plotboxx(xc,yc,zc,Rx)
103
104  #——————————————————Ry box (c)
105  Ry=radians(30)
106  xc=85
107  yc=40
108  zc=20
109  plotboxy(xc,yc,zc,Ry)
110
111  #——————————————————Rz box (d)
112  Rz=radians(30)
113  xc=115
114  yc=40
115  zc=20
116  plotboxz(xc,yc,zc,Rz)
117
118  #————————————————————-notes
119  plt.text(23,63,'(a)')
120  plt.text(53,63,'(b)')
121  plt.text(83,63,'(c)')
122  plt.text(112,63,'(d)')
123  plt.text(21,73,'R=0')
124  plt.text(47,73,'Rx=45°')
```

```
125    plt.text(77,73,'Ry=30°')
126    plt.text(107,73,'Rz=30°')
127    plt.arrow(42,40,25,0,head_width=2,head_length=3,color='r')
       #-red arrows
128    plt.arrow(42,40,28,0,head_width=2,head_length=3,color='r')
129    plt.arrow(85,25,0,27,head_width=2,head_length=2,color='r')
130    plt.arrow(85,25,0,29,head_width=2,head_length=2,color='r')
131    plt.plot([8,130],[8,8],color='k') #-axes
132    plt.plot([8,8],[8,85],color='k')
133    plt.text(120,6,'X')
134    plt.text(3,80,'Y')
135    plt.scatter(115,40,s=30,color='r') #——-red dot center of box (d)
136
137    plt.show()
```

3.7 Sequential Rotations Around the Coordinate Directions

In Listing 3-1, you operated on a box's initial corner coordinates defined by the lists in lines 14, 15, and 16. The program produced *separate* rotations around the x,y, and z coordinate directions. In this section, you begin with the same set of corner coordinates but you rotate *sequentially*. That is, after a rotation Rx about the x direction (b), rotation Ry is *added* to the results of Rx (c). Rz is then *added* to the results of Ry (d). The rotations are thus not independent as before but are additive. You do this by replacing the x,y, and z definitions in lines 14, 15, and 16 with a new set of coordinates following each rotation. That is, the box's corner coordinates are updated after each rotation so that the next rotation starts with the updates coordinates. This is accomplished by simply modifying functions **plotboxx**, **plotboxy**, and **plotboxz** between lines 72-88 in Listing 3-1. In Listing 3-2, lines 74b, 80b, and 86b are added. They do the updating by replacing the initial corner coordinates x,y,z with the transformed ones xg,yg,zg after each rotation. The code replaces lines 72-88 in Listing 3-1.

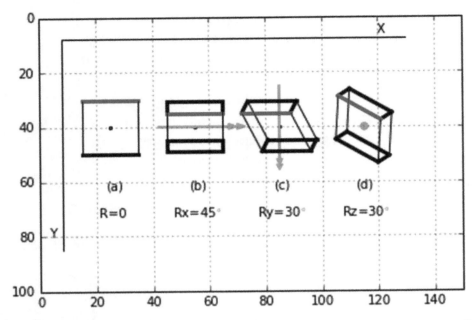

Figure 3-10. *Sequential rotations of a box. Box (a) is rotated by Rx=30° to (b),*
then by an additional *rotation of Ry=30° to (c), and then by an* additional *rotation*
of Rz=15° to (d). x and y axes show direction only. Coordinate values are indicated
by the grid.

Listing 3-2. Program 4BOXESUPDATE

```
71
72     def plotboxx(xc,yc,zc,Rx):
73             for i in (0,1,2,3,4,5,6,7): #————————rotate eight corners
74                     [xg[i],yg[i],zg[i]]=rotx(xc,yc,zc,x[i],y[i],z[i],Rx)
74b                    [x[i],y[i],z[i]]=[xg[i]-xc,yg[i]-yc,zg[i]-zc]
75
76             plotbox(xg,yg,zg)
77
78     def plotboxy(xc,yc,zc,Ry):
79             for i in (0,1,2,3,4,5,6,7): #————————rotate eight corners
80                     [xg[i],yg[i],zg[i]]=roty(xc,yc,zc,x[i],y[i],z[i],Ry)
80b                    [x[i],y[i],z[i]]=[xg[i]-xc,yg[i]-yc,zg[i]-zc]
81
82             plotbox(xg,yg,zg)
```

```
83
84    def plotboxz(xc,yc,zc,Rz):
85          for i in (0,1,2,3,4,5,6,7): #————————rotate eight corners
86              [xg[i],yg[i],zg[i]]=rotz(xc,yc,zc,x[i],y[i],z[i],Rz)
86b             [x[i],y[i],z[i]]=[xg[i]-xc,yg[i]-yc,zg[i]-zc]
87
88          plotbox(xg,yg,zg)
89
```

The transformation parameters are set in lines 91-116 by the values of rotations Rx, Ry, and Rz and the box center coordinates xc, yc, zc.

The sequence of rotations in this program is hard-wired to produce Figure 3-10 with (a) first, followed by (b), (c), and (d). In a general program, the sequence and values of rotations and center coordinates could be set to anything suitable by moving sections of code around or by entering the sequences through the keyboard. You will do both shortly. But first, you will do sequential rotations of a circle.

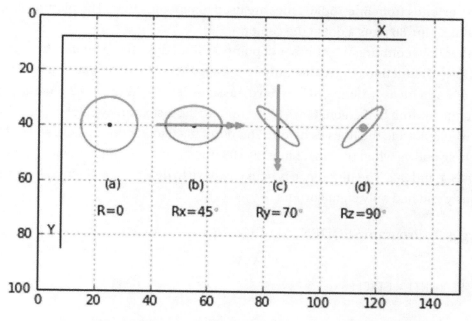

Figure 3-11. *Sequential rotations of a circle created by Listing 3-3. Circle (a) is rotated by Rx=45° to (b), then by an additional rotation of Ry=70° to (c), and then by an additional rotation of Rz=90° to (d). Red indicates the upper half of circle. x and y axes show direction only, not coordinate values, which are indicated by the grid.*

Listing 3-3 is similar to the preceding modified version of Listings 3-1 and 3-2 where you did sequential rotations of a box. In that program, the box had eight corners, which had to be transformed and updated with every rotation. Here you have a circle, which has many more points, to transform and update.

In lines 23-38, you fill lists between lines 33 and 38 with starting values of local and global coordinates of points around the circumference of the circle. They are spaced dphi=5° apart as shown in line 25. The circle's radius is 10 as shown in line 27. The empty lists were previously defined in lines 14-20. As the loop starting at line 29 advances around the circle with angle phi, lines 30 to 32 calculate the local coordinates of each point. Lines 33-38 add the coordinates to the list using the **append()** function, which adds elements to a list. For example, with each cycle through the loop line 33 appends (adds) the local value of xp at the current angle phi to the x list. Since you are just filling the list at this point, you can use xp,yp,zp to also fill the xg, yg, and zg lists in lines 36-38. Note that zp=0 (program line 32) in this initial definition of the circle. That is, the circle starts off flat in the x,y plane. Subsequent rotations will be around that initial orientation.

Lines 41-72 define the transformation functions as before. The circle plotting function extends from line 75-86. Lines are used to plot the circle. The plotting loop runs from 78-82. Line 86 plots a dot at the center.

Rather than counting the number of points around the circle, you use the **range(len(x))** function to give the number of elements in the lists. You can use the length of x as a measure since all lists have the same length. Lines 79-82 plot the top half red and the bottom half green. Lines 83-84 update the last xg any yg global coordinates to use when plotting the lines as before. You don't need to include zg here since you use only xg and yg when plotting. Lines 89-108 transform coordinates as was done in Listings 3-1 and 3-2. The difference is here you have to deal with lists len(x) long whereas previously you had only eight corners.

Listing 3-3. Program SEQUENTIALCIRCLES

```
1    """
2    SEQUENTIALCIRCLES
3    """
4
5    import numpy as np
6    import matplotlib.pyplot as plt
```

```
7    from math import sin, cos, radians

8

9    plt.axis([0,150,100,0])

10   plt.axis('on')

11   plt.grid(True)

12

13   #────────────────────────define lists

14   x=[]

15   y=[]

16   z=[]

17

18   xg=[]

19   yg=[]

20   zg=[]

21

22   #──────────────fill lists with starting coordinates

23   phi1=radians(0)

24   phi2=radians(360)

25   dphi=radians(5) #-circumferential points spaced 5 degrees

26

27   r=10 #-circle's radius

28

29   for phi in np.arange(phi1,phi2+dphi,dphi): #-establish coordinates of
                                                circumferential points

30       xp=r*cos(phi)

31       yp=r*sin(phi)

32   zp=0

33   x.append(xp)    #-fill lists

34   y.append(yp)

35   z.append(zp)

36   xg.append(xp)

37   yg.append(yp)

38   zg.append(zp)

39
```

```
40     #————————————define rotation functions
41     def rotx(xc,yc,zc,xp,yp,zp,Rx):
42          a=[xp,yp,zp]
43          b=[1,0,0] #——————————-[cx11,cx12,cx13]
44          xpp=np.inner(a,b) #--scalar product of a,b=xp*cx11+yp*cx12+ zp*cx13
45          b=[0,cos(Rx),-sin(Rx)] #————[cx21,cx22,cx23]
46          ypp=np.inner(a,b)
47          b=[0,sin(Rx),cos(Rx)] #————[cx31,cx32,cx33]
48          zpp=np.inner(a,b)
49          [xg,yg,zg]=[xpp+xc,ypp+yc,zpp+zc]
50          return[xg,yg,zg]
51
52     def roty(xc,yc,zc,xp,yp,zp,Ry):
53          a=[xp,yp,zp]
54          b=[cos(Ry),0,sin(Ry)] #————-[cx11,cx12,cx13]
55          xpp=np.inner(a, b)
56          b=[0,1,0] #————[cx21,cx22,cx23]
57          ypp=np.inner(a,b) #————-scalar product of a,b
58          b=[-sin(Ry),0,cos(Ry)] #————[cx31,cx32,cx33]
59          zpp=np.inner(a,b)
60          [xg,yg,zg]=[xpp+xc,ypp+yc,zpp+zc]
61          return[xg,yg,zg]
62
63     def rotz(xc,yc,zc,xp,yp,zp,Rz):
64          a=[xp,yp,zp]
65          b=[cos(Rz),-sin(Rz),0] #————-[cx11,cx12,cx13]
66          xpp=np.inner(a, b)
67          b=[sin(Rz),cos(Rz),0] #————[cx21,cx22,cx23]
68          ypp=np.inner(a,b)
69          b=[0,0,1] #————[cx31,cx32,cx33]
70          zpp=np.inner(a,b) #————scalar product of a,b
71          [xg,yg,zg]=[xpp+xc,ypp+yc,zpp+zc]
72          return[xg,yg,zg]
73
```

```
74     #————————————define circle plotting function
75     def plotcircle(xg,yg,zg):
76         lastxg=xg[0]
77         lastyg=yg[0]
78         for i in range(len(x)): #--len(x)=length of all lists
79             if i < len(x)/2: #--half green
80                     plt.plot([lastxg,xg[i]],[lastyg,yg[i]],
                        linewidth=1,color='g')
81             else:
82                     plt.plot([lastxg,xg[i]],[lastyg,yg[i]],
                        linewidth=1,color='r')
83         lastxg=xg[i]
84         lastyg=yg[i]
85
86         plt.scatter(xc,yc,s=5) #-plot a dot at the center
87
88     #————————————transform coordinates and plot
89     def plotcirclex(xc,yc,zc,Rx): #————-transform & plot Rx circle
90         for i in range(len(x)): #-for i in range(len(x)): ok too
91             [xg[i],yg[i],zg[i]]=rotx(xc,yc,zc,x[i],y[i],z[i],Rx)
92             [x[i],y[i],z[i]]=[xg[i]-xc,yg[i]-yc,zg[i]-zc]
93
94         plotcircle(xg,yg,zg) #————plot
95
96     def plotcircley(xc,yc,zc,Ry):
97         for i in range(len(x)): #————-transform & plot Ry circle
98             [xg[i],yg[i],zg[i]]=roty(xc,yc,zc,x[i],y[i],z[i],Ry)
99             [x[i],y[i],z[i]]=[xg[i]-xc,yg[i]-yc,zg[i]-zc]
100
101        plotcircle(xg,yg,zg)
102
```

```
103    def plotcirclez(xc,yc,zc,Rz):
104        for i in range(len(x)): #———-transform &  plot Rz circle
105            [xg[i],yg[i],zg[i]]=rotz(xc,yc,zc,x[i],y[i],z[i],Rz)
106            [x[i],y[i],z[i]]=[xg[i]-xc,yg[i]-yc,zg[i]-zc]
107
108        plotcircle(xg,yg,zg)
109
110    #———————————————plot circles
111    Rx=radians(0)
112    xc=25 #———circle (a) center coordinates
113    yc=40
114    zc=20
115    plotcirclex(xc,yc,zc,Rx) #-since R=0 we could use plotcircley or
       plotcirclez
116
117    #————————————-Rx circle (b)
118    Rx=radians(45)
119    xc=55
120    yc=40
121    zc=20
122    plotcirclex(xc,yc,zc,Rx)
123
124    #————————————-Ry circle (c)
125    Ry=radians(70)
126    xc=85
127    yc=40
128    zc=20
129    plotcircley(xc,yc,zc,Ry)
130
131    #————————————-Rz circle (d)
132    Rz=radians(90)
133    xc=115
134    yc=40
135    zc=20
136    plotcirclez(xc,yc,zc,Rz)
```

```
137
138    #————————————————-notes
139    plt.text(23,63,'(a)')
140    plt.text(53,63,'(b)')
141    plt.text(83,63,'(c)')
142    plt.text(112,63,'(d)')
143    plt.text(21,73,'R=0')
144    plt.text(47,73,'Rx=45°')
145    plt.text(77,73,'Ry=70°')
146    plt.text(107,73,'Rz=90°')
147    plt.arrow(42,40,25,0,head_width=2,head_length=3,color='r') #-red
       arrows
148    plt.arrow(42,40,28,0,head_width=2,head_length=3,color='r')
149    plt.arrow(85,25,0,27,head_width=2,head_length=2,color='r')
150    plt.arrow(85,25,0,29,head_width=2,head_length=2,color='r')
151    plt.plot([8,130],[8,8],color='k') #-axes
152    plt.plot([8,8],[8,85],color='k')
153    plt.text(120,6,'X')
154    plt.text(3,80,'Y')
155    plt.scatter(115,40,s=30,color='r') #————red dot center of box (d)
156
157    plt.show()
```

3.8 Matrix Concatenation

Comparing Figure 3-12 with 3-11, you can see that, although Rx,Ry, and Rz have the same values in both figures, the resulting orientations of the circle in (c) and (d) are different. This is because the order of the rotation in Figure 3-11 is Rx,Ry,Rz while in Figure 3-12 it is Rx,Rz,Ry. Clearly the order of rotations is important.

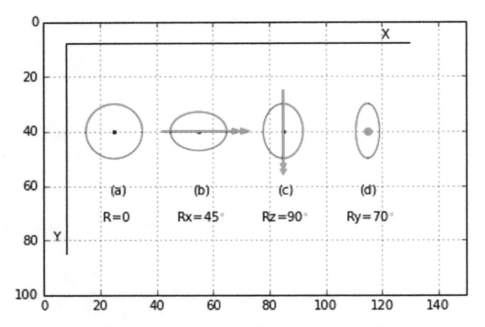

Figure 3-12. *Circle (a) is rotated sequentially by Rx=45° to (b), then by an additional rotation of Rz=90° to (c), followed by an additional rotation of Ry=70 to (d). Red indicates the lower half of circle. x and y axes show direction only, not coordinate values, which are indicated by the grid.*

You can demonstrate this yourself. Take a book and place it on the edge of your desk front side up, top facing to the right. Imagine the desk's edge is the x direction going from left to right. Next, rotate it 90 degrees around the x direction, followed by 90 degrees around the z direction. This is RxRz. The book will be upside down with the front facing you. Then reverse the order by rotating around the z direction first followed by the x direction. This is RzRx. As you can see, you get a different final orientation of the book in the two cases.

While you have carried out sequential rotations by ordering them and updating rotated coordinates in the program's code, mathematically it amounts to a multiplication of matrices. For example, the following equation produces a rotation Rx of vector [P] followed by a rotation Rz. The two rotations produce the vector [P'].

$$[P']=[Rz][Rx][P]$$ (3-64)

[Rx] operates on the vector [P], [Rz] then operates on the result of [Rx][P]. To rotate by Rz followed by Rx,

$$[P'] = [Rx][Rz][P] \tag{3-65}$$

In general,

$$[Rx][Rz] \neq [Rz][Rx] \tag{3-66}$$

You can show this by a simple example using two-dimensional matrices. Consider two matrices, A and B, where

$$[A] = \begin{bmatrix} a & b \\ c & d \end{bmatrix} \tag{3-67}$$

$$[B] = \begin{bmatrix} e & f \\ g & h \end{bmatrix} \tag{3-68}$$

$$AB = \begin{bmatrix} a & b \\ c & d \end{bmatrix}\begin{bmatrix} e & f \\ g & h \end{bmatrix} = \begin{bmatrix} ae+bg & af+bh \\ ce+dg & cf+dh \end{bmatrix} \tag{3-69}$$

$$BA = \begin{bmatrix} e & f \\ g & h \end{bmatrix}\begin{bmatrix} a & b \\ c & d \end{bmatrix} = \begin{bmatrix} ae+cf & be+df \\ ag+ch & bg+dh \end{bmatrix} \tag{3-70}$$

$$\therefore AB \neq BA \tag{3-71}$$

For only three rotations around three different coordinate directions, there are six combinations of possible transformation sequences:

$$RxRyRz \tag{3-72}$$

$$RxRzRy \tag{3-73}$$

$$RyRxRz \tag{3-74}$$

$$RyRzRx \tag{3-75}$$

$$RzRxRy \tag{3-76}$$

$$RzRyRx \tag{3-77}$$

Each of these combinations involves three separate rotations. You could multiply the three transformation matrices shown in Equations 3-55, 3-56, and 3-57 to get a single transformation matrix for each of these combinations. You could then write a program that would execute each of these combinations: select one combination, input the three angles, and then get the final rotation. But what if you wanted more than three rotations, such as RyRzRxRyRz? That would require a lot of matrix multiplying! Clearly it's much easier to incorporate the sequencing by coding it into the Python program and updating coordinates after each transformation, as you have learned how to do here.

To produce Figure 3-12, lines 110-136 of Listing 3-3 were replaced with the code in Listing 3-4.

Listing 3-4. Program SEQUENTIALCIRCLESUPDATE

```
109
110    #————————————————plot circles
111    Rx=radians(0)
112    xc=25 #————circle (a) center coordinates
113    yc=40
114    zc=20
115    plotcirclex(xc,yc,zc,Rx) #-since R=0 we could use plotcircley or
                                            plotcirclez
116
117    #————————————————-Rx circle (b)
118    Rx=radians(45)
119    xc=55
120    yc=40
121    zc=20
122    plotcirclex(xc,yc,zc,Rx)
123
124    #————————————————-Rz circle (d)
125    Rz=radians(90)
126    xc=85
127    yc=40
128    zc=20
129    plotcirclez(xc,yc,zc,Rz)
130
```

```
131    #————————————————Ry circle (c)
132    Ry=radians(70)
133    xc=115
134    yc=40
135    zc=20
136    plotcircley(xc,yc,zc,Ry)
137
```

Here you have performed the operation RxRzRy, reversing the order of the last two transformations. Circle (a) is plotted as before with Rx=0 in line 111. Also as before, circle (b) is plotted next with Rx=45 degrees in line 118. The difference is in lines 124-136 where the rotations Ry and Rz are reversed and Rz is plotted *before* Ry. The angles have the same values as before. Rearranging the order of plotting is easy; just cut and paste sections of the code. But be sure to update the center coordinates xc, yc, and zc. You could make the program a lot more user-friendly by introducing the **input()** function, which will give you the ability to input the order of transformations through the keyboard. You could then enter the rotations Rx,Ry, or Rz and the amount and the center coordinates in any order. You will do that next.

3.9 Keyboard Data Entry with Functional Program Structure

As you saw in the discussion of matrix concatenation, rearranging the order of rotations in a program can be a useful option. However, as you will see in this section, entering data via the keyboard is much more satisfactory. You will also use a functional programming structure where a few lines of code control various predefined functions that carry out the various operations. This will give you great flexibility in controlling the program.

Listing 3-5 produced the results shown in Figures 3-13 through 3-16. The first figure shows a circle rotated around the x direction by 0°; the second around the y direction by 60°; the third around the x direction by 45°; and the fourth around the z direction by 90°. All rotations are added to the previous orientation of the circle. The axis of rotation and the amount were entered through the keyboard. The sequence of rotation directions did not matter, nor did the number of rotations.

Referring to Listing 3-5, lines 111-113 specify the circle's center coordinates. All circles have the same center coordinates. The **while True:** statement in line 115 keeps the data entry loop running so you can do an unlimited number of sequential rotations. Line 116 asks you to specify the axis of rotation in the Spyder output pane. Enter x,y, or z in lower case letters. To exit the loop, press the Enter key. (**Important**: If you are using the Spyder console, be sure to click the mouse with the cursor in the output pane before entering anything. If you forget and leave it in the program pane, you are liable to get an unwanted x,y, or z imbedded somewhere in the program. If this happens, go to the top of the screen and open a new console. This essentially starts the program over.). If you enter x (lower case), line 118 asks for the angle of rotation Rx. Enter it as a positive or negative angle in degrees. The **input()** function returns a string. The **float** command converts it to a float. Line 119 then invokes function **plotcirclex()**, which plots the rotated circle. Ry and Rz rotations are carried out in a similar way. Note there is no restriction on the sequence or the number of rotations. Line 126 checks to see if you entered a blank for **axis**, in which case line 127 exits the program. All circles are rotated around the same center, xc,yc,zc. If you want to be able to move the centers of each circle, just add **input()** lines for the center coordinates between lines 115 and 116.

Lines 89-108 rotate and update the coordinates of the circle's circumferential points as was done in Listing 3-3. In function **plotcircle()**, lines 71-86 do the plotting. Each time this function is invoked, the axes and grid are replotted. Line 86 shows the latest plot.

This program is an important illustration of program control. Just the few lines between 115 and 127 control the entire operation of the program and give great flexibility in controlling the sequence of operations and the data used. In other programming languages, such as Basic and Fortran, this is referred to as *top-down programming*. In those languages *subroutines*, which are the equivalents of Python functions, are generally placed at the bottom, while the controlling code is put at the top. In Python, you normally put the functions at the top with the control at the bottom, a style called *bottom-up programming*. Whether control is at the top or the bottom, this program structure is called *functional programming* since the controlling code uses functions to carry out the various operations. Since controlling data is input through the keyboard, it offers considerable flexibility.

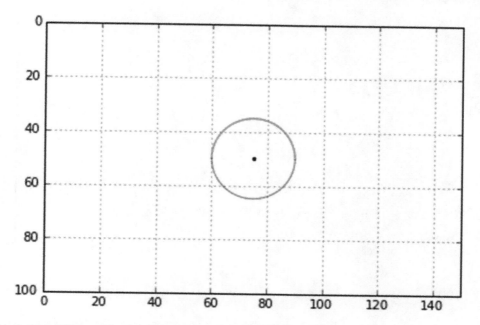

Figure 3-13. *The circle is rotated around the x axis by 0°*

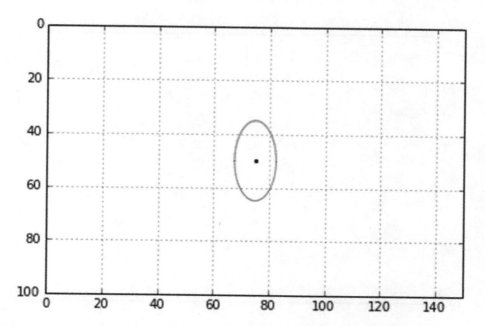

Figure 3-14. *The previous circle is rotated around the y axis by 60°*

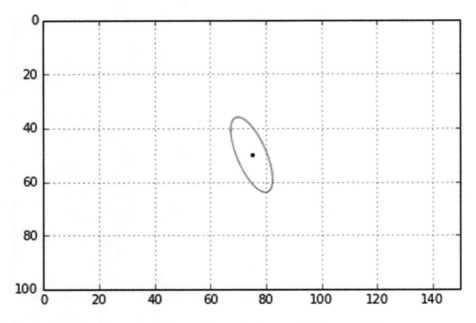

Figure 3-15. *The previous circle is rotated around the y axis by 45°*

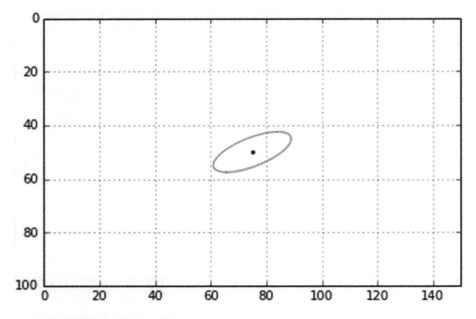

Figure 3-16. *The previous circle is rotated around the z axis by 90°*

Listing 3-5. Program KEYBOARDDATAENTRY

```
1    """
2    KEYBOARDDATAENTRY
3    """
4
5    import numpy as np
6    import matplotlib.pyplot as plt
7    from math import sin, cos, radians
8
9    #———————————————-define  lists
10   x=[]
11   y=[]
12   z=[]
13
14   xg=[]
15   yg=[]
16   zg=[]
17
18   #———————————fill lists with starting coordinates
19   phi1=radians(0)
20   phi2=radians(360)
21   dphi=radians(5) #-circumferential points spaced 5 degrees
22
23   radius=15 #-circle's radius
24
25   for phi in np.arange(phi1,phi2+dphi,dphi): #-establish coordinates of
                                               circumferential points
26           xp=radius*cos(phi)
27           yp=radius*sin(phi)
28           zp=0
29           x.append(xp) #-fill lists
30           y.append(yp)
31           z.append(zp)
32           xg.append(xp)
```

```
33          yg.append(yp)
34          zg.append(zp)
35
36     #—————————————-define rotation functions
37     def rotx(xc,yc,zc,xp,yp,zp,Rx):
38          a=[xp,yp,zp]
39          b=[1,0,0] #—————————-[cx11,cx12,cx13]
40          xpp=np.inner(a,b) #—scalar product of a,b=xp*cx11+yp*cx12+ zp*cx13
41          b=[0,cos(Rx),-sin(Rx)] #————[cx21,cx22,cx23]
42          ypp=np.inner(a,b)
43          b=[0,sin(Rx),cos(Rx)] #————[cx31,cx32,cx33]
44          zpp=np.inner(a,b)
45          [xg,yg,zg]=[xpp+xc,ypp+yc,zpp+zc]
46          return[xg,yg,zg]
47
48     def roty(xc,yc,zc,xp,yp,zp,Ry):
49          a=[xp,yp,zp]
50          b=[cos(Ry),0,sin(Ry)] #————-[cx11,cx12,cx13]
51          xpp=np.inner(a, b)
52          b=[0,1,0] #————[cx21,cx22,cx23]
53          ypp=np.inner(a,b) #————————scalar product of a,b
54          b=[-sin(Ry),0,cos(Ry)] #————[cx31,cx32,cx33]
55          zpp=np.inner(a,b)
56          [xg,yg,zg]=[xpp+xc,ypp+yc,zpp+zc]
57          return[xg,yg,zg]
58
59     def rotz(xc,yc,zc,xp,yp,zp,Rz):
60          a=[xp,yp,zp]
61          b=[cos(Rz),-sin(Rz),0] #————-[cx11,cx12,cx13]
62          xpp=np.inner(a, b)
63          b=[sin(Rz),cos(Rz),0] #————[cx21,cx22,cx23]
64          ypp=np.inner(a,b)
65          b=[0,0,1] #————[cx31,cx32,cx33]
66          zpp=np.inner(a,b) #————————scalar product of a,b
```

```
67          [xg,yg,zg]=[xpp+xc,ypp+yc,zpp+zc]
68          return[xg,yg,zg]
69
70      #——————————-define circle plotting function
71      def plotcircle(xg,yg,zg):
72          lastxg=xg[0]
73          lastyg=yg[0]
74          for i in range(len(x)): #-for i in range(len(x)): ok too
75                  if i < len(x)/2: #--half green
76                          plt.plot([lastxg,xg[i]],[lastyg,yg[i]],
                               linewidth=1   ,color='g')
77                  else:
78                          plt.plot([lastxg,xg[i]],[lastyg,yg[i]],
                               linewidth=1   ,color='r')
79          lastxg=xg[i]
80          lastyg=yg[i]
81
82          plt.scatter(xc,yc,s=5,color='k') #-plot a dot at the center
83          plt.axis([0,150,100,0]) #-replot axes and grid
84          plt.axis('on')
85          plt.grid(True)
86          plt.show() #-plot latest rotation
87
88      #——————————transform coordinates and plot
89      def plotcirclex(xc,yc,zc,Rx): #——-transform and plot Rx circle
90          for i in range(len(x)):
91                  [xg[i],yg[i],zg[i]]=rotx(xc,yc,zc,x[i],y[i],z[i],Rx)
92                  [x[i],y[i],z[i]]=[xg[i]-xc,yg[i]-yc,zg[i]-zc]
93
94          plotcircle(xg,yg,zg) #——plot
95
```

```
96    def plotcircley(xc,yc,zc,Ry):
97          for i in range(len(x)): #————-transform and plot Ry circle
98                [xg[i],yg[i],zg[i]]=roty(xc,yc,zc,x[i],y[i],z[i],Ry)
99                [x[i],y[i],z[i]]=[xg[i]-xc,yg[i]-yc,zg[i]-zc]
100
101        plotcircle(xg,yg,zg)
102
103   def plotcirclez(xc,yc,zc,Rz):
104         for i in range(len(x)): #————-transform and plot Rz circle
105               [xg[i],yg[i],zg[i]]=rotz(xc,yc,zc,x[i],y[i],z[i],Rz)
106               [x[i],y[i],z[i]]=[xg[i]-xc,yg[i]-yc,zg[i]-zc]
107
108        plotcircle(xg,yg,zg)
109
110   #————————————plot circles
111   xc=75 #-center coordinates
112   yc=50
113   zc=50
114
115   while True:
116        axis=input('x, y or z?: ') #-input axis of rotation (lower case)
117        if axis == 'x': #-if x axis
118               Rx=radians(float(input('Rx degrees?: ')))
119               plotcirclex(xc,yc,zc,Rx) #-call function plotcirclex
120        if axis == 'y':
121               Ry=radians(float(input('Ry degrees?: ')))
122               plotcircley(xc,yc,zc,Ry)
123        if axis == 'z':
124               Rz=radians(float(input('Rz degrees?: ')))
125               plotcirclez(xc,yc,zc,Rz)
126        if axis == '':
127               break
```

3.10 Summary

In this chapter, you learned how to construct three-dimensional coordinate axes and three-dimensional shapes and rotate them around the three coordinate directions. This involved derivation of rotation transformations around the three coordinate directions. You saw the difference between rotating an object once from its original orientation and rotating it in sequential steps where each subsequent rotation uses the object's coordinates from the prior rotation as the starting point. You explored the idea that the sequence of rotations is important; Rx,Ry,Rz does not produce the same results as Rx,Rz,Ry. This was shown by matrix concatenation. Finally, you developed a program where sequential rotations could be entered through the keyboard as opposed to specifying them in the program. All of this work involved the use of lists.

CHAPTER 4

Perspective

I discussed isometric vs. perspective views in the previous chapter. Now you will develop a transformation that will automatically produce a perspective view. It operates much like a camera where rays are traced from the various points that comprise an object onto a plane that you might think of as a film plane. Figure 4-1 shows the geometry. It's a three-dimensional box in the x,y,z space. The x,y plane represents the film plane. There's also a *focal point* that is outside the x,y,z space in front of the x,y plane. Rays are traced from the box's corners to the focal point. By connecting the points where the rays hit the x,y plane, you can construct a perspective view of the box.

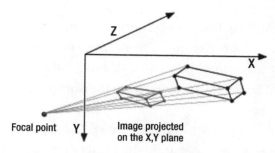

Figure 4-1. *Geometry used to project a perspective image of an object on the x,y plane*

As shown in Figure 4-2, a primitive camera can be constructed by putting a small hole in an opaque sheet. Rays from an object passing through this hole will produce a photographic-like perspective image on a "film plane." The perspective transformation you will be producing in this chapter will operate in a somewhat similar manner, except you will be tracing the image on your computer screen. The geometry is geometrically similar, except that the pinhole geometry produces a reversed image. If the focal point is moved far back in the -z direction, the rays from the object become almost parallel and the perspective effect is lost; the image becomes flattened. This phenomenon is well known to photographers when shooting with a long focal length lens.

© B.J. Korites 2018
B.J. Korites, *Python Graphics*, https://doi.org/10.1007/978-1-4842-3378-8_4

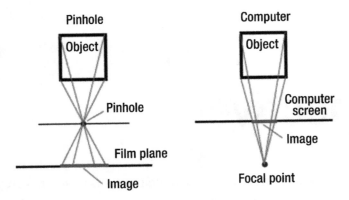

Figure 4-2. *Pinhole camera vs. computer projection geometry*

Figures 4-3 and 4-4 show the geometry you will use to construct your transformation. Figure 4-3 shows a three-dimensional object inside the x,y,z space. The focal point is outside the space at global coordinates (xfp,yfp,zfp). It can be anywhere in front of (-z direction) the x,y plane. Different locations will produce different views of the object, much as a camera will produce different images when photographing an object from different locations.

Imaginary rays emanating from the corners of the box pass through the x,y plane, which you can imagine is your computer screen. Each ray hits the x,y plane at a *hit point* (xh,yh,zh=0) on its way to the focal point of zh=0 since the x,y plane is at z=0. Connecting the hit points produced by the rays coming from the points comprising the object will produce a perspective image.

A typical point on the object is located at (x,y,z). The distance between the point and the focal point is Q. Qh is the distance from the focal point to the hit point. |zfp|+z is the horizontal distance from the focal point to the object point. |z| is the horizontal distance from the focal point to the hit point. û is a unit vector pointing from the focal point toward the object point. Using this geometry, you can derive the following relations:

$$a = x - xfp \qquad\qquad\qquad (4\text{-}1)$$

$$b = y - yfp \qquad\qquad\qquad (4\text{-}2)$$

$$c = z + |zfp| \qquad\qquad\qquad (4\text{-}3)$$

Since, in Equation 4-3 zfp is negative (it lies in front of the x,y plane), you use its absolute value of |zfp| because it adds to z to give the total z-direction distance between the focal point and the object point. You could, of course, write Equation 4-3 as c=z-zfp, which is equivalent, but the use of the absolute value |zfp| makes the following analysis more understandable. Also, it won't matter if you forget and enter a positive z value for zfp.

$$Q = \sqrt{a^2 + b^2 + c^2} \tag{4-4}$$

$$ux = a / Q \tag{4-5}$$

$$uy = b / Q \tag{4-6}$$

$$uz = c / Q \tag{4-7}$$

$$\hat{\mathbf{u}} = ux\hat{\mathbf{i}} + uy\hat{\mathbf{j}} + uz\hat{\mathbf{k}} \tag{4-8}$$

$$Qh = \frac{Q|zfp|}{z + |zfp|} \tag{4-9}$$

$$xh = uxQh + xfp \tag{4-10}$$

$$yh = uyQh + yfp \tag{4-11}$$

$$zh = 0 \tag{4-12}$$

You can show zh=0 (i.e. the hit point lies on the x,y plane, as it should), by the following:

$$|zh = uzQh - |zfp| \tag{4-13}$$

$$= \frac{c}{Q}Qh - |zfp| \tag{4-14}$$

$$= \left(z + |zfp|\right)\frac{Qh}{Q} - |zfp| \tag{4-15}$$

$$= \frac{\left(z + |zfp|\right)}{Q}\frac{Q|zfp|}{\left(z + |zfp|\right)} - |zfp| \tag{4-16}$$

$$= |zfp| - |zfp| \tag{4-17}$$

$$= 0 \tag{4-18}$$

The negative sign in Equation 4-13 is because |zfp| is always positive while you know that the focal point is always in the -z position.

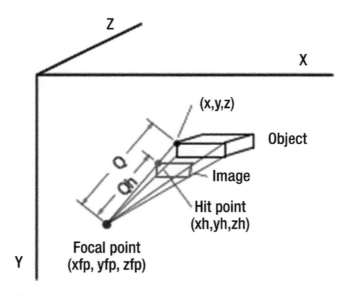

Figure 4-3. *Perspective image projection geometry*

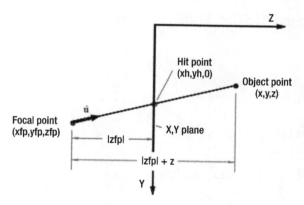

Figure 4-4. *Perspective image projection geometry side view*

Listing 4-1 illustrates the use of the above model. It enables you to construct an object, rotate it, and then view it in perspective. The object, in this case a house, is defined in lines 14-29. Lines 14-16 establish corner coordinates x,y,z in local coordinates; that is, in relation to a point xc,yc,zc, which is set in lines 18-20. This is at the center of the house and it will be the center of rotation. Lines 22-29 convert x,y,z to global coordinates xg,yg,zg by adding elements to the empty lists set in lines 22-24. Lines 31-47 plot the house by connecting the corner points with lines.

Lines 50-63 define a function that rotates the local coordinates about xc,yc,zc, saving the results as xg,yg,zg. It uses function **roty**, which is defined in lines 54-63. This function was used in prior programs. It is the only rotation function in this program, which means you can only rotate around the y direction. Next is the perspective transformation **perspective(xfp,yfp,zfp)**; it implements Equations 4-1 through 4-12, developed above. The loop beginning in line 67 calculates the coordinates of the hit point for rays that go to the focal point from each of the object's corner points. The hit points, in terms of global coordinates, are saved in lines 79-81.

Control of the program takes place in lines 83-95. Lines 83-85 define the location of the focal point; lines 87-89 the house's center point. Ry in line 91 specifies the angle of rotation about the y direction. Line 93 then invokes function **plothouse(xc,yc,zc,Ry)**, which rotates the house. Line 94 invokes **perspective(xfp,yfp,zfp)**, which performs the perspective transformation. Line 95 plots the house. This could have been incorporated in the function **perspective** but it has been placed here to illustrate the sequence of operations.

Listing 4-1. Program PERSPECTIVE

```
1    """
2    PERSPECTIVE
3    """
4
5    import matplotlib.pyplot as plt
6    import numpy as np
7    from math import sin, cos, radians
8
9    plt.axis([0,150,100,0])
10
11   plt.axis('on')
12   plt.grid(True)
13
14   x=[-20,-20,20,20,-20,-20,20,20,-20,20] #---object local corner coordinates
15   y=[-10,-10,-10,-10,10,10,10,10,-20,-20]
16   z=[5,-5,-5,5,5,-5,-5,5,0,0]
17
18   xc=30 #---------------object center coordinates
19   yc=50
20   zc=10
21
22   xg=[ ] #---------------object global coordinates
23   yg=[ ]
24   zg=[ ]
25
26   for i in np.arange(len(x)):
27        xg.append(x[i]+xc)
28        yg.append(y[i]+yc)
29        zg.append(z[i]+zc)
30
31   #-------------plot object
32   def plothouse(xg,yg,zg):
33        plt.plot([xg[0],xg[3]],[yg[0],yg[3]],color='k')
34        plt.plot([xg[1],xg[2]],[yg[1],yg[2]],color='k')
```

```
35      plt.plot([xg[4],xg[7]],[yg[4],yg[7]],color='k')
36      plt.plot([xg[5],xg[6]],[yg[5],yg[6]],color='k')
37      plt.plot([xg[8],xg[9]],[yg[8],yg[9]],color='k')
38      plt.plot([xg[4],xg[0]],[yg[4],yg[0]],color='k')
39      plt.plot([xg[5],xg[1]],[yg[5],yg[1]],color='k')
40      plt.plot([xg[6],xg[2]],[yg[6],yg[2]],color='r')
41      plt.plot([xg[7],xg[3]],[yg[7],yg[3]],color='r')
42      plt.plot([xg[0],xg[8]],[yg[0],yg[8]],color='k')
43      plt.plot([xg[1],xg[8]],[yg[1],yg[8]],color='k')
44      plt.plot([xg[2],xg[9]],[yg[2],yg[9]],color='r')
45      plt.plot([xg[3],xg[9]],[yg[3],yg[9]],color='r')
46      plt.plot([xg[4],xg[5]],[yg[4],yg[5]],color='k')
47      plt.plot([xg[6],xg[7]],[yg[6],yg[7]],color='r')
48
49  #————————————rotate object about the Y direction
40  def plothousey(xc,yc,zc,Ry):
51      for i in range(len(x)): #————rotate 10 corners
52          [xg[i],yg[i],zg[i]]=roty(xc,yc,zc,x[i],y[i],z[i],Ry)
53
54  def roty(xc,yc,zc,x,y,z,Ry):
55      a=[x,y,z]
56      b=[cos(Ry),0,sin(Ry)]
57      xpp=np.inner(a,b)
58      b=[0,1,0]
59      ypp=np.inner(a,b)
60      b=[-sin(Ry),0,cos(Ry)]
61      zpp=np.inner(a,b)
62      [xg,yg,zg]=[xpp+xc,ypp+yc,zpp+zc]
63      return [xg,yg,zg]
64
65  #————————————————————————————perspective transformation
66  def perspective(xfp,yfp,zfp):
67      for i in range(len(x)):
68          a=xg[i]-xfp
69          b=yg[i]-yfp
```

```
70                    c=zg[i]+abs(zfp)
71                    q=np.sqrt(a*a+b*b+c*c)
72                    ux=a/q
73                    uy=b/q
74                    uz=c/q
75                    qh=q*abs(zfp)/(zg[i]+abs(zfp))
76                    xh=ux*qh+xfp
77                    yh=uy*qh+yfp
78                    zh=0
79                    xg[i]=xh
80                    yg[i]=yh
81                    zg[i]=zh
82
83    xfp=80 #────────────────────focal point coordinates
84    yfp=50
85    zfp=-100
86
87    xc=80 #───────────redefine center coordinates
88    yc=50
89    zc=50
90
91    Ry=radians(45)   #────────────────angle of rotation
92
93    plothousey(xc,yc,zc,Ry)          #--rotate
94    perspective(xfp,yfp,zfp)         #--transform
95    plothouse(xg,yg,zg)              #--rotate
96
97    plt.show()
```

Figures 4-5 through 4-8 show output from Listing 4-1. Figure 4-5 shows the house in its unrotated (Ry=0) orientation. The right side is red. The focal point is at xc=80,yc=50,-100. This is in line with the house's center but 100 in front of the x,y plane. Figure 4-6 shows the house rotated 45 degrees around the y direction. The perspective effect is apparent. Figure 4-7 shows the house with the same settings but with the focal point moved back from zfp=-100 to zfp=-600. You can see how the image is flattened and the perspective effect is mostly lost. Figure 4-8 shows the house with some random settings. By following the procedure in Listing 4-1, you should be able to create a more elaborate scene quite easily.

Figure 4-5. *Perspective image with Ry=0, zfp=-100*

Figure 4-6. *Perspective image with Ry=45, zfp=-100*

Figure 4-7. *Perspective image with Ry=45, zfp=-600*

Figure 4-8. *Perspective image with Ry=-60, zfp=-100, xc=40, yc=70, xfp=100, zfp=-80*

The question is, where to place the focal point. If you're projecting the image onto the x,y plane, clearly it should be in front of that plane (i.e. i the -z direction). But what about the x,y coordinates of the focal point? The best results, most like what would be seen by the human eye, would be to place it at the same x,y coordinates as the house's center. Of course, if there are many objects in the model, such as more houses and trees, it is not obvious where to place the focal point. The best results will be obtained by situating it in front of the x,y plane at the coordinates that correspond to the approximate center of the model. This is akin to aiming a camera at the center of a scene to be photographed. The painter Vermeer chose this structure in many of his paintings. In fact, in some of his canvases art historians have found a nail hole at the vanishing point where all parallel lines such as room corners and floor tiles converge. The nail hole is in the approximate center of the scene. It is believed he tied a string to a nail and used it to trace the converging lines, much as you have used lines in your algorithm. You can see this structure in many of Vermeer's interior paintings.

4.1 Summary

In this chapter, you learned how to construct a perspective view. The geometry is based on the simple box camera. You had the perspective image projected onto the x,y plane. You could have used any of the other coordinate planes, for example the x,z plane; the geometry would be similar. You explored the question of where to place the focal point, which corresponds to the observation point of a viewer or a camera. The answer is, unless you are looking for an unusual image, at the approximate center of the model. This was the structure used by Vermeer in many of his paintings.

CHAPTER 5

Intersections

In this chapter, you will develop algorithms that will tell you where lines and planes intersect a variety of objects. The techniques you develop will be useful later when you remove hidden lines and trace shadows cast by objects. You will also learn how to show the intersection of lines and planes with a sphere. As you will see, there is no one magic algorithm that will satisfy all situations; each requires its own methodology. While you may never need some of these algorithms, such as a line intersecting a circular sector, the procedures, which rely on vector-based geometry, are interesting and should give you the tools you will need when you encounter different situations.

Instead of using vectors, many of these solutions could be derived analytically. For example, the solution for a line intersecting a sphere can be obtained by combining the equation of a line with that of a sphere. The result is a quadratic equation that, when solved, yields the entrance and exit points. Such an approach can be fast and simple provided you are dealing with objects that can be represented by simple equations. However, the vector-based procedures, while they may seem more complex, are actually quite simple and intuitive. They can also be much more versatile and adaptable to unusual situations. They are the ones you will use here.

5.1 Line Intersecting a Rectangular Plane

Figure 5-1 shows a line intersecting a rectangular plane. You will develop the algorithm and a program to find the point of intersection, called the *hit point*. Here you are stipulating that the plane is finite, but it doesn't have to be. After going through the analysis, you will see there is nothing here that requires the plane be finite. You also start off by assuming the plane is rectangular. It doesn't have to be rectangular but, for now, it is easier to keep it finite and rectangular.

153

© B.J. Korites 2018
B.J. Korites, *Python Graphics*, https://doi.org/10.1007/978-1-4842-3378-8_5

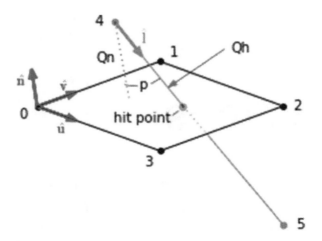

Figure 5-1. *Geometry of a line intersecting a rectangular plane*

The plane has corners at 0, 1, 2, and 3. These have local coordinates of (x0,y0,z0) - (x3,y3,z3) relative to the center of rotation at (xc,yc,zc). The line starts at x[4],y[4],z[4] and ends at x[5],y[5],z[5]. It intersects the plane at the hit point.

There are three unit vectors at corner 0; $\hat{u}$, $\hat{v}$, and $\hat{n}$. Unit vector $\hat{v}$ points from corner 0 to 1; $\hat{u}$ from 0 to 3. $\hat{n}$ is normal to the plane. $\hat{l}$ is a unit vector pointing along the line from 4 to 5. Q_{45} is the distance from 4 to 5. Q_h is the distance from 4 to the hit point. Q_n is the perpendicular distance from 4 to the plane. Your quest is to determine the location of the hit point (xh,yh,zh). Using vector geometry, you can write the following relations:

Distance 4 → 5:

$$a = x[5] - x[4] \tag{5-1}$$

$$b = y[5] - y[4] \tag{5-2}$$

$$c = z[5] - z[4] \tag{5-3}$$

$$Q_{45} = \sqrt{a^2 + b^2 + c^2} \tag{5-4}$$

Unit vector 4 → 5:

$$lx = \frac{a}{Q_{45}} \tag{5-5}$$

$$ly = \frac{b}{Q_{45}} \tag{5-6}$$

$$lz = \frac{c}{Q_{45}} \tag{5-7}$$

$$\hat{\mathbf{l}} = lx\hat{\mathbf{i}} + ly\hat{\mathbf{j}} + lz\hat{\mathbf{k}} \tag{5-8}$$

Distance $0 \rightarrow 3$:

$$a = x[3] - x[0] \tag{5-9}$$

$$b = y[3] - y[0] \tag{5-10}$$

$$c = z[3] - z[0] \tag{5-11}$$

$$Q_{03} = \sqrt{a^2 + b^2 + c^2} \tag{5-12}$$

Unit vector $0 \rightarrow 3$:

$$ux = \frac{a}{Q_{03}} \tag{5-13}$$

$$uy = \frac{b}{Q_{03}} \tag{5-14}$$

$$uz = \frac{c}{Q_{03}} \tag{5-15}$$

$$\hat{\mathbf{u}} = ux\hat{\mathbf{i}} + uy\hat{\mathbf{j}} + uz\hat{\mathbf{k}} \tag{5-16}$$

Distance $0 \rightarrow 1$:

$$a = x[1] - x[0] \tag{5-17}$$

$$b = y[1] - y[0] \tag{5-18}$$

$$c = z[1] - z[0] \tag{5-19}$$

$$Q_{01} = \sqrt{a^2 + b^2 + c^2} \tag{5-20}$$

Unit vector $0 \rightarrow 1$:

$$vx = \frac{a}{Q_{01}} \tag{5-21}$$

$$vy = \frac{b}{Q_{01}} \tag{5-22}$$

$$vz = \frac{c}{Q_{01}} \tag{5-23}$$

$$\hat{\mathbf{v}} = vx\hat{\mathbf{i}} + vy\hat{\mathbf{j}} + vz\hat{\mathbf{k}} \tag{5-24}$$

Unit vector $\hat{\mathbf{n}}$:

$$\hat{\mathbf{n}} = \hat{\mathbf{u}} \times \hat{\mathbf{v}} \tag{5-25}$$

$$= \begin{bmatrix} \hat{\mathbf{i}} & \hat{\mathbf{j}} & \hat{\mathbf{k}} \\ ux & uy & uz \\ vx & vy & vz \end{bmatrix} \tag{5-26}$$

$$\hat{\mathbf{n}} = \hat{\mathbf{i}}\underbrace{\left(uy{\cdot}vz - uz{\cdot}vy\right)}_{nx} + \hat{\mathbf{j}}\underbrace{\left(uz{\cdot}vx - ux{\cdot}vz\right)}_{ny} + \hat{\mathbf{k}}\underbrace{\left(ux{\cdot}vy - uy{\cdot}vx\right)}_{nz} \tag{5-27}$$

$$\hat{\mathbf{n}} = nx\hat{\mathbf{i}} + ny\hat{\mathbf{j}} + nz\hat{\mathbf{k}} \tag{5-28}$$

$$nx = uy{\cdot}vz - uz{\cdot}vy \tag{5-29}$$

$$ny = uz{\cdot}vx - ux{\cdot}vz \tag{5-30}$$

$$nz = ux{\cdot}vy - uy{\cdot}vx \tag{5-31}$$

Vector $0 \rightarrow 4$:

$$\mathbf{V}_{04} = vx_{04}\hat{\mathbf{i}} + vy_{04}\hat{\mathbf{j}} + vz_{04}\hat{\mathbf{k}} \tag{5-32}$$

$$vx_{04} = x[4] - x[0] \tag{5-33}$$

$$vy_{04} = y[4] - y[0] \tag{5-34}$$

$$vz_{04} = z[4] - z[0] \tag{5-35}$$

Perpendicular distance 4 to plane:

$$Q_n = \left| \mathbf{V}_{04} \cdot \hat{\mathbf{n}} \right| \qquad (5\text{-}36)$$

Hit point:

$$Q_n = Q_h \, cos(p) \qquad (5\text{-}37)$$

$$Q_h = \frac{Q_n}{cos(p)} \qquad (5\text{-}38)$$

$$cos(p) = \hat{\mathbf{l}} \cdot \hat{\mathbf{n}} \qquad (5\text{-}39)$$

$$= lx \cdot nx + ly \cdot ny + lz \cdot nz \qquad (5\text{-}40)$$

$$xh = x[4] + Q_h lx \qquad (5\text{-}41)$$

$$yh = y[4] + Q_h ly \qquad (5\text{-}42)$$

$$zh = z[4] + Q_h lz \qquad (5\text{-}43)$$

You can test to see if the hit point lies within the boundaries of the plane. Figure 5-2 shows the geometry. Vector **V0h** runs from corner 0 to the hit point h. up and vp are the projections of **V0h** on the 03 and 01 directions, respectively. To test for an in-bound or out-of-bound hit,

if up < 0 or up > Q03   hit is out of bounds
if vp < 0 or vp > Q01   hit is out of bounds

With xh,yh, and zh being the coordinates of the hit point h, you can calculate up and vp as follows:

$$a = xh - x[0] \qquad (5\text{-}44)$$

$$b = yh - y[0] \qquad (5\text{-}45)$$

$$c = zh - z[0] \qquad (5\text{-}46)$$

$$\mathbf{V0h} = a\hat{\mathbf{i}} + b\hat{\mathbf{j}} + c\hat{\mathbf{k}} \qquad (5\text{-}47)$$

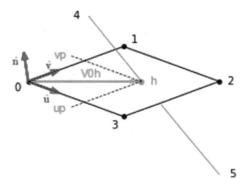

Figure 5-2. *Out-of-bounds geometry*

To find up, you project **V0h** onto the 03 direction. To do that, you take the dot product of **V0h** with **û**:

$$up = a \cdot ux + b \cdot uy + c \cdot uz \qquad (5\text{-}48)$$

To find vp, you take the dot product of **V0h** with $\hat{v}$:

$$vp = a \cdot vx + b \cdot vy + c \cdot vz \qquad (5\text{-}49)$$

If you regard the line from 4 to 5 as being finite, you can test to see if it is long enough to reach the plane. From Figure 5-1,

$$a = xh - x[4] \qquad (5\text{-}50)$$

$$b = yh - y[4] \qquad (5\text{-}51)$$

$$c = zh - z[4] \qquad (5\text{-}52)$$

$$Q4h = \sqrt{a^2 + b^2 + c^2} \qquad (5\text{-}53)$$

if Q45 < Qh   LINE TOO SHORT, NO HIT

All of this has been incorporated in Listing 5-1, which has the same structure as Listing 3-5 in Chapter 3, although some of the functions and operations have been altered. As in that program, rotation directions and amounts are entered through the keyboard. Rotations are additive; for example, if the system is rotated first by Rx=40 degrees, followed by Rx=10, the total angle will be 50 degrees. Ry and Rz operate similarly.

Some data is hard-wired in Listing 5-1, such as definitions of the rectangular plane and the line intersecting it. They are shown in the lists in lines 18–20. There are six elements in each list numbered [0]-[5]: [0]-[3] are the four corners of the plane while [4] and [5] are the beginning and end of the line. They are coordinated with the diagrams in Figures 5-1 and 5-2. To modify the plane and line, just put new numbers in the lists. For example, item [5] is the end of the line. To drop it down in the +y direction, increase y[5]. The numbers in the lists are in local coordinates relative to the center of rotation (xc,yc,zc), which is at the center of the plane. The values are shown in Lines 14-16.

It takes only three points to define a plane. Here you have a four-corner rectangular plane. If you alter the plane's corner coordinates, be sure they lie in the same plane. The easiest way to do so is to start off with a plane that lies in or is parallel to one of the coordinate planes. It can be rotated out of that coordinate plane later. In line 19, the first four elements of the y list are all zero. That describes a flat plane parallel to the x,z plane at y=0. Also, if altering the [x] or [z] lists, be sure the plane remains rectangular since the calculations of the hit point in this analysis assume that is the case.

Rotation functions **rotx**, **roty**, and **rotz**, which rotate coordinates around the coordinate directions, are included in lines 28-35. They are the same as used in prior programs so they have not been listed.

Line 45 plots a dot at the hit point (xhg,yhg) where the line intersects the plane. If the hit point lies within the plane's boundaries, the color of the dot is red; if it's outside, it is blue. If the line from [4] to [5] is too short and never reaches the plane, the color is changed to green and a dot is placed at [5], the end of the line. This is illustrated in Figure 5-5. The calculation of the hit point is carried out by function **hitpoint(x,y,z)**, which begins in line 53. The program follows the analysis above in Equations 5-1 through 5-49 and should be self-explanatory.

Data input takes place in lines 154-166. This is similar to Listing 3-5. Samples of the output are shown in Figures 5-3, 5-4, and 5-5. Parameters are included in the captions.

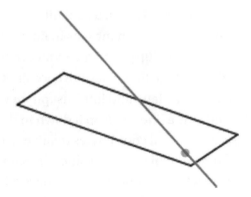

Figure 5-3. *Line intersecting the plane defined by a rectangle. The hit point lies within the plane's boundaries: y[5]=+5, Rx=45°, Ry=45°, Rz°=20*

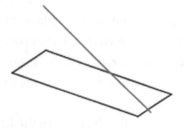

Figure 5-4. *Line intersecting the plane defined by a rectangle. The hit point lies outside the rectangle's boundaries: y[5]=-5, Rx=45°, Ry=45°, Rz°=20.*

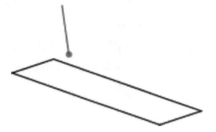

Figure 5-5. *Example of a line too short, in which case a green dot appears at coordinate [5]: x[4]=-40, y[4]=-20, z[4]=15, x[5]=-20, y[5]=-10, z[5]=0, Rx=30°, Ry=45°, Rz°=20*

Listing 5-1. Program LRP

```
1    """
2    LRP
3    """
4
5    import numpy as np
6    import matplotlib.pyplot as plt
7    from math import sin, cos, radians,sqrt
8
9    #───────────────fill lists with starting coordinates
10   xg=[ ]
11   yg=[ ]
12   zg=[ ]
13
14   xc=80 #─────────center coordinates
15   yc=40
16   zc=40
17
18   x=[-40,-40,40,40,-40,50] #─system (plane and line geometry)
19   y=[0,0,0,0,-20,3]
20   z=[-10,10,10,-10,15,-10]
21
22   for i in range(len(x)):
23        xg.append(x[i]+xc)
24        yg.append(y[i]+yc)
25        zg.append(z[i]+zc)
26
27   #─────────────────define  rotation  functions
28   def rotx(xc,yc,zc,xp,yp,zp,Rx):
29        (same as in prior programs)
30
31   def  roty(xc,yc,zc,xp,yp,zp,Ry):
32        (same as in prior programs)
33
```

```
34  def rotz(xc,yc,zc,xp,yp,zp,Rz):
35      (same as in prior programs)
36
37  #───────────────-plot  plane, line and hit point
38  def plotsystem(xg,yg,zg,xh,yh,xhg,yhg,hitcolor):
39      plt.plot([xg[0],xg[1]],[yg[0],yg[1]],color='k')  #────plot plane
40      plt.plot([xg[1],xg[2]],[yg[1],yg[2]],color='k')
41      plt.plot([xg[2],xg[3]],[yg[2],yg[3]],color='k')
42      plt.plot([xg[3],xg[0]],[yg[3],yg[0]],color='k')
43      plt.plot([xg[4],xg[5]],[yg[4],yg[5]],color='b') #──plot line
44
45      if hitcolor='g': #────plot hit point at [5]
46          plot.scatter(xg[5],yg[5],s=20,color=hitcolor)
47      else: #────plot hit point at h
48          plt.scatter(xhg,yhg,s=20,color=hitcolor)
49
50      plt.axis([0,150,100,0]) #──replot axes and grid
51      plt.axis('on')
52      plt.grid(False)
53      plt.show() #──plot latest rotation
54
55  #──────────────find hit point coordinates and color
56  def hitpoint(x,y,z):
57      a=x[5]-x[4]
58      b=y[5]-y[4]
59      c=z[5]-z[4]
60      Q45=sqrt(a*a+b*b+c*c)  #──distance  point  4  to  5
61
62      lx=a/Q45 #──unit vector components point 4 to 5
63      ly=b/Q45
64      lz=c/Q45
65
66      a=x[3]-x[0]
67      b=y[3]-y[0]
68      c=z[3]-z[0]
69      Q03=sqrt(a*a+b*b+c*c) #──distance 0 to 3
```

```
70
71        ux=a/Q03 #——unit vector 0 to 3
72        uy=b/Q03
73        uz=c/Q03
74
75        a=x[1]-x[0]
76        b=y[1]-y[0]
77        c=z[1]-z[0]
78        Q01=sqrt(a*a+b*b+c*c) #——distance 0 to 1
79
80        vx=a/Q01 #——unit vector 0 to 1
81        vy=b/Q01
82        vz=c/Q01
83
84        nx=uy*vz-uz*vy #——normal unit vector
85        ny=uz*vx-ux*vz
86        nz=ux*vy-uy*vx
87
88        vx1b=x[4]-x[0] #——vector components 0 to 4
89        vy1b=y[4]-y[0]
90        vz1b=z[4]-z[0]
91
92        Qn=(vx1b*nx+vy1b*ny+vz1b*nz) #——perpendicular distance 4 to plane
93
94        cosp=lx*nx+ly*ny+lz*nz #——cos of angle p
95        Qh=abs(Qn/cosp) #——distance 4 to hit point
96
97        xh=x[4]+Qh*lx  #——hit  point  coordinates
98        yh=y[4]+Qh*ly
99        zh=z[4]+Qh*lz
100
101       xhg=xh+xc #——global hit point coordinates
102       yhg=yh+yc
103       zhg=zh+zc
104
```

```
105  #————————————out of bounds check
106      a=xh-x[0] #——components of vector V0h
107      b=yh-y[0]
108      c=zh-z[0]
109
110      up=a*ux+b*uy+c*uz #——dot products
111      vp=a*vx+b*vy+c*vz
112
113      hitcolor='r' #——if inbounds plot red hit point
114      if up<0: #——change color to blue if hit point out of bounds
115          hitcolor='b'
116
117      if up>Q03:
118          hitcolor='b'
119
120      if vp<0:
121          hitcolor='b'
122
123      if vp>Q01:
124          hitcolor='b'
125
126      a=x[5]-x[4]
127      b=y[5]-y[4]
128      c=z[5]-z[4]
129      Q45=sqrt(a*a+b*b+c*c)
130
131      if Q45 < Qh:
132          hitcolor='g'
133
134      return xh,yh,xhg,yhg,hitcolor
135
136  #————————————transform  coordinates  and  plot
137  def  plotx(xc,yc,zc,Rx):  #——transform  &  plot  Rx  system
138      for i in range(len(x)):
```

```
139              [xg[i],yg[i],zg[i]]=rotx(xc,yc,zc,x[i],y[i],z[i],Rx)
140              [x[i],y[i],z[i]]=[xg[i]-xc,yg[i]-yc,zg[i]-zc]
141
142         xh,yh,xhg,yhg,hitcolor=hitpoint(x,y,z) #——returns xh,yh,xhg,yhg
143
144         plotsystem(xg,yg,zg,xh,yh,xhg,yhg,hitcolor) #——plot
145
146 def ploty(xc,yc,zc,Ry):  #——transform & plot Ry system
147      for i in range(len(x)):
148              [xg[i],yg[i],zg[i]]=roty(xc,yc,zc,x[i],y[i],z[i],Ry)
149              [x[i],y[i],z[i]]=[xg[i]-xc,yg[i]-yc,zg[i]-zc]
150
151      xh,yh,xhg,yhg,hitcolor=hitpoint(x,y,z)
152
153      plotsystem(xg,yg,zg,xh,yh,xhg,yhg,hitcolor)
154
155 def plotz(xc,yc,zc,Rz):   #——transform  &  plot  Rz  system
156      for i in range(len(x)):
157              [xg[i],yg[i],zg[i]]=rotz(xc,yc,zc,x[i],y[i],z[i],Rz)
158              [x[i],y[i],z[i]]=[xg[i]-xc,yg[i]-yc,zg[i]-zc]
159
160      xh,yh,xhg,yhg,hitcolor=hitpoint(x,y,z)
161
162      plotsystem(xg,yg,zg,xh,yh,xhg,yhg,hitcolor)
163
164 #————————————-input data and plot system
165 while True:
166      axis=input('x, y or z?: ') #——input axis of rotation (lower case)
167      if axis == 'x': #-if x axis
168              Rx=radians(float(input('Rx Degrees?: '))) #——input degrees
169              plotx(xc,yc,zc,Rx) #-call function plotx
```

```
170        if axis == 'y':
171            Ry=radians(float(input('Ry Degrees?: '))) #——input degrees
172            ploty(xc,yc,zc,Ry)
173        if axis == 'z':
174            Rz=radians(float(input('Rz Degrees?: '))) #——input degrees
175            plotz(xc,yc,zc,Rz)
176        if axis == '':
177                break #—quit the program
```

5.2 Line Intersecting a Triangular Plane

Almost any flat surface can be formed by an array of triangular planes and a curved surface can be approximated by triangles, hence our interest in triangular planes.

Figure 5-6 shows the geometry for a line intersecting a triangular plane. The algorithms used in Listing 5-3 are mostly the same as in Listing 5-1. One difference is that the lengths of the list are, of course, shorter since the triangle has one less corner. Another is that the check on whether the hit point lies within the triangle or is out of bounds is different.

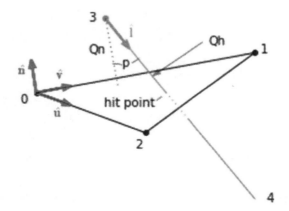

Figure 5-6. *Geometry of a line intersecting a triangular plane*

Before going on to Listing 5-3, you will develop a simple way to determine if a hit point lies within a triangle or outside of it. Figure 5-7 shows the geometry used for the out-of-bounds calculation. Listing 5-2 produces the output shown in Figure 5-8 and, with modification to the lists defining the coordinates of point 3, in Figure 5-9. In Figure 5-8, the hit is out of bounds; in Figure 5-9, it is within the triangle.

Figure 5-7 shows three triangles: the black one, defined by points 0, 1, and 2, is the base triangle, the one you are concerned with. It has area A. The triangle defined by points 0, 1, and 3 (the hit point) has area A1. The third triangle between point 0, 3, and 2 has area A2. It is easy to see that if A1+A2>A, the hit point is out of bounds; if A1+A2<A, it is in bounds. If you can calculate the areas of the three triangles, you will have an easy way to determine if the hit point is within or outside of the base triangle. To do so, you rely on a simple expression for determining the area of a triangle:

$$s = (a+b+c)/2 \tag{5-54}$$

$$A = \sqrt{s(s-a)(s-b)(s-c)} \tag{5-55}$$

where a, b, and c are the lengths of the three sides of the triangle and A is its area. This is known as Heron's formula, named after Hero of Alexandria, a Greek engineer and mathematician circa 10 AD - 70 AD.

This relation is put to use in Listing 5-2 and later in Listing 5-3. In Listing 5-2, most of the program is concerned with evaluating the lengths of the lines shown in Figure 5-7. Heron's formula is then used to calculate the three areas: A, A1, and A2. The decision whether the hit point is inside or outside of the base triangle is made in lines 114-117 of Listing 5-2. It produces Figure 5-8. Program THT2 (not shown) is the same as THT1 (Listing 5-2) but has the lists adjusted to put the hit point within the triangle. It produces Figure 5-9. The adjusted lists are

x=[40,30,80,55]

y=[60,10,60,45]

z=[0,0,0,0]

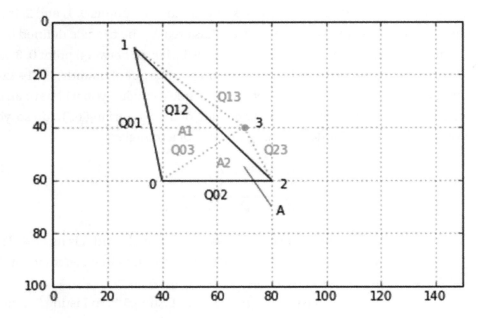

Figure 5-7. *Model for out-of-bounds test*

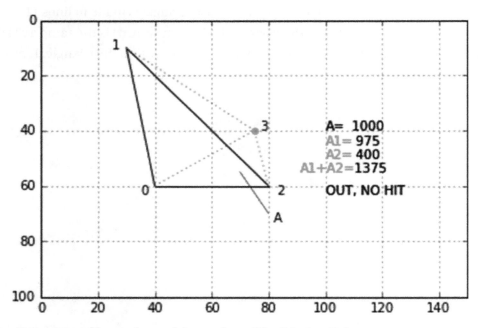

Figure 5-8. *Out of bounds, no hit produced by Listing 5-2*

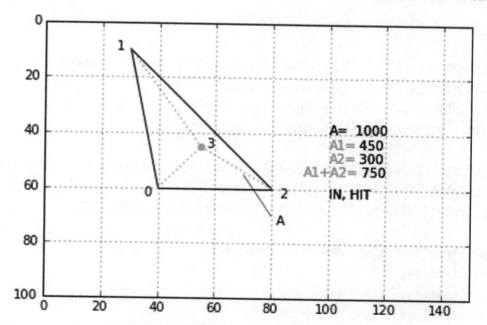

Figure 5-9. *In bounds, hit produced by modified Listing 5-2*

As you can see from these lists, the hit point has been moved to (55,45,0).

Listing 5-2. Program THT1

```
1    """
2    THT1
3    """
4
5    import matplotlib.pyplot as plt
6    import numpy as np
7    from math import sin, cos, radians, sqrt
8
9    plt.axis([0,150,100,0])
10
11   plt.axis('on')
12   plt.grid(True)
13
14   x=[40,30,80,75] #——plane
15   y=[60,10,60,40]
```

```
16   z=[0,0,0,0]
17
18   plt.plot([x[0],x[1]],[y[0],y[1]],color='k') #—plot plane A
19   plt.plot([x[1],x[2]],[y[1],y[2]],color='k')
20   plt.plot([x[2],x[0]],[y[2],y[0]],color='k')
21   plt.scatter(x[3],y[3],s=20,color='r')
22
23   plt.plot([x[0],x[3]],[y[0],y[3]],linestyle=':',color='r') #plot planes
24   plt.plot([x[1],x[3]],[y[1],y[3]],linestyle=':',color='r')
25   plt.plot([x[2],x[3]],[y[2],y[3]],linestyle=':',color='r')
26
27   plt.text(35,63,'0') #—label corners
28   plt.text(25,10,'1')
29   plt.text(83,63,'2')
30   plt.text(x[3]+2,y[3],'3')
31
32   a=x[1]-x[0] #—calculate dimensions
33   b=y[1]-y[0]
34   c=z[1]-z[0]
35   Q01=sqrt(a*a+b*b+c*c)
36
37   a=x[2]-x[1]
38   b=y[2]-y[1]
39   c=z[2]-z[1]
40   Q12=sqrt(a*a+b*b+c*c)
41
42   a=x[2]-x[0]
43   b=y[2]-y[0]
44   c=z[2]-z[0]
45   Q02=sqrt(a*a+b*b+c*c)
46
47   a=x[1]-x[3]
48   b=y[1]-y[3]
49   c=z[1]=z[3]
```

```
50   Q13=sqrt(a*a+b*b+c*c)

51

52   a=x[2]-x[3]
53   b=y[2]-y[3]
54   c=z[2]-z[3]
55   Q23=sqrt(a*a+b*b+c*c)

56

57   a=x[0]-x[3]
58   b=y[0]-y[3]
59   c=z[0]-z[3]
60   Q03=sqrt(a*a+b*b+c*c)

61

62   s=(Q01+Q12+Q02)/2 #—calculate areas A, A1 and A2
63   A=sqrt(s*(s-Q01)*(s-Q12)*(s-Q02))

64

65   s1=(Q01+Q03+Q13)/2
66   A1=sqrt(s1*(s1-Q01)*(s1-Q03)*(s1-Q13))

67

68   s2=(Q02+Q23+Q03)/2
69   A2=sqrt(s2*(s2-Q02 )*(s2-Q23)*(s2-Q03))

70

71   plt.arrow(70,55,10,15,linewidth=.5,color='grey') #—label area A
72   plt.text(82,73,'A',color='k')

73

74   plt.text(100,40,'A=') #—plot output
75   dle='%7.0f'%  (A)
76   dls=str(dle)
77   plt.text(105,40,dls)

78

79   plt.text(100,45,'A1=',color='r')
80   dle='%7.0f'% (A1)
81   dls=str(dle)
82   plt.text(105,45,dls)

83

84   plt.text(100,50,'A2=',color='r')
```

```
85   dle='%7.0f'% (A2)
86   dls=str(dle)
87   plt.text(105,50,dls)
88
89   plt.text(91,55,'A1+A2=',color='r')
90   dle='%7.0f'%  (A1+A2)
91   dls=str(dle)
92   plt.text(106,55,dls)
93
94   plt.text(100,40,'A=')
95   dle='%7.0f'%  (A)
96   dls=str(dle)
97   plt.text(105,40,dls)
98
99   plt.text(100,45,'A1=',color='r')
100  dle='%7.0f'% (A1)
101  dls=str(dle)
102  plt.text(105,45,dls)
103
104  plt.text(100,50,'A2=',color='r')
105  dle='%7.0f'% (A2)
106  dls=str(dle)
107  plt.text(105,50,dls)
108
109  plt.text(91,55,'A1+A2=',color='r')
110  dle="%7.0f'% (A1+A2)
111  dls=str(dle)
112  plt.text(106,55,dls)
113
114  if A1+A2 > A:
115      plt.text(100,63,'OUT, NO HIT')
116  else:
117      plt.text(100,63,'IN, HIT')
118
119  plt.show()
```

Listing 5-3 plots the hit point between a line and a triangle. It is similar to Listing 5-1 except it uses the inside or outside test developed above. Examples of output are shown in Figures 5-10, 5-11, and 5-12. One difference worth noting is in the calculation of the unit vector $\hat{\mathbf{n}}$, which is perpendicular to the plane of the triangle. In Listing 5-1, this was found by taking the cross product of $\hat{\mathbf{u}}$ with $\hat{\mathbf{v}}$. Since the angle between $\hat{\mathbf{u}}$ and $\hat{\mathbf{v}}$ was 90°, this produced a unit vector that was normal to both of them, which implies normal to the plane, and of magnitude 1. This is because $|\hat{\mathbf{u}} \times \hat{\mathbf{v}}| = |\hat{\mathbf{u}}||\hat{\mathbf{v}}|\sin(\alpha)$ where α is the angle between $\hat{\mathbf{u}}$ and $\hat{\mathbf{v}}$. When α equals 90°, $|\hat{\mathbf{u}} \times \hat{\mathbf{v}}| = (1)(1)(1) = 1$.

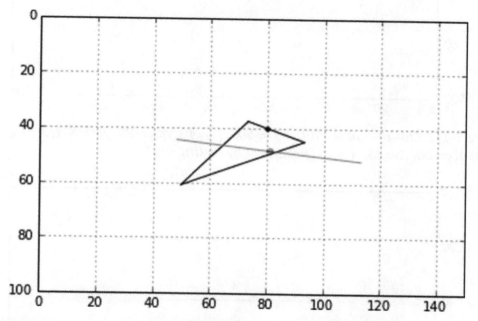

Figure 5-10. *In-bounds hit. x[3]=-60, x[4]=70, y[3]=-20, y[4]=20, z[3]=15, z[4]=0, Rx=-90, Ry=45, Rz=20 (produced by Listing 5-3)*

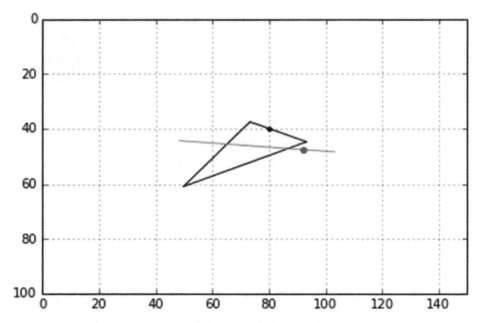

Figure 5-11. *Out-of-bounds hit. x[3]=-60, x[4]=40, y[3]=-20, y[4]=5, z[3]=15, z[4]=0, Rx=-90, Ry=45, Rz=20 (produced by Listing 5-3)*

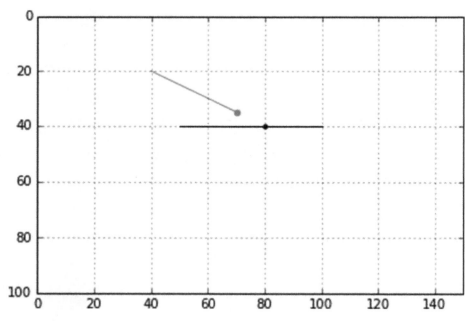

Figure 5-12. *Line too short, no hit. x[3]=-40, x[4]=-10, y[3]=-20, y[4]=-5, z[3]=15, z[4]=0, Rx=0, Ry=0, Rz=0 (produced by Listing 5-3)*

174

However, with a general non-right triangle, the angle is not 90° so the vector resulting from the cross product, while normal to the plane, does not have a value of 1; in other words, it is not a *unit* vector. The algorithm between lines 88 and 91 makes the correction by normalizing $\hat{\mathbf{n}}$'s components. It does this by dividing each of them by the magnitude of $\hat{\mathbf{n}}$. In line 88, magn is the magnitude of $\hat{\mathbf{n}}$ *before* normalization of the vector's components. Depending on the angle α, its value will be somewhere between 0 and 1. Dividing each component of $\hat{\mathbf{n}}$ by magn makes $\hat{\mathbf{n}}$ a unit vector.

Listing 5-3. Program LTP

```
1    """
2    LTP
3    """
4
5    import numpy as np
6    import matplotlib.pyplot as plt
7    from math import sin, cos, radians,sqrt
8
9    #—————————————fill lists with starting coordinates
10   xg=[ ]
11   yg=[ ]
12   zg=[ ]
13
14   xc=80 #—————————center coordinates
15   yc=40
16   zc=40
17
18   x=[-10,-30,20,-40,-10]
19   y=[0,0,0,-20,-5]
20   z=[0,30,0,15,0]
21
22   for i in range(len(x)):
23         xg.append(x[i]+xc)
24         yg.append(y[i]+yc)
25         zg.append(z[i]+zc)
26
```

```
27   #————————————-define  rotation  functions
28   def rotx(xc,yc,zc,xp,yp,zp,Rx):
29       (same as in prior programs)
30
31   def  roty(xc,yc,zc,xp,yp,zp,Ry):
32       (same as in prior programs)
33
34   def rotz(xc,yc,zc,xp,yp,zp,Rz):
35       (same as in prior programs)
36
37   #————————————-define  system  plotting  functions
38   def plotsystem(xg,yg,zg,xh,yh,xhg,yhg,hitcolor):
39       plt.plot([xg[0],xg[1]],[yg[0],yg[1]],color='k')  #————plot plane
40       plt.plot([xg[1],xg[2]],[yg[1],yg[2]],color='k')
41       plt.plot([xg[2],xg[0]],[yg[2],yg[0]],color='k')
42       plt.plot([xg[3],xg[4]],[yg[3],yg[4]],color='g') #——plot line
43       plt.scatter(xc,yc,s=10,color='k') #——plot center of rotation
44
45       if hitcolor=='g':
46           plt.scatter(xg[4],yg[4],s=20,color=hitcolor)
47       else:
48           plt.scatter(xhg,yhg,s=20,color=hitcolor) #————plot hit point
49
50       plt.axis([0,150,100,0]) #——replot axes and grid
51       plt.axis('on')
52       plt.grid(True)
53       plt.show() #——plot latest rotation
54
55   #————————-calculate hit point coordinates and color
56   def hitpoint(x,y,z):
57       a=x[4]-x[3]
58       b=y[4]-y[3]
59       c=z[4]-z[3]
60       Q34=sqrt(a*a+b*b+c*c)  #——distance point 3 to 4
61
62       lx=a/Q34 #——unit vector components point 3 to 4
```

```
63          ly=b/Q34
64          lz=c/Q34
65
66          a=x[2]-x[0]
67          b=y[2]-y[0]
68          c=z[2]-z[0]
69          Q02=sqrt(a*a+b*b+c*c) #——distance 0 to 3
70
71          ux=a/Q02 #——unit vector 0 to 3
72          uy=b/Q02
73          uz=c/Q02
74
75          a=x[1]-x[0]
76          b=y[1]-y[0]
77          c=z[1]-z[0]
78          Q01=sqrt(a*a+b*b+c*c) #——distance 0 to 1
79
80          vx=a/Q01 #——unit vector 0 to 1
81          vy=b/Q01
82          vz=c/Q01
83
84          nx=uy*vz-uz*vy #——normal unit vector
85          ny=uz*vx-ux*vz
86          nz=ux*vy-uy*vx
87  #——————————-correct magnitude of unit vector n̂
88          magn=sqrt(nx*nx+ny*ny+nz*nz)
89          nx=nx/magn
90          ny=ny/magn
91          nz=nz/magn
92  #————————————————
93          a=x[3]-x[0] #——vector components 0 to 3
94          b=y[3]-y[0]
95          c=z[3]-z[0]
96
97          Qn=(a*nx+b*ny+c*nz) #——perpendicular distance 3 to plane
98
```

```
99         cosp=lx*nx+ly*ny+lz*nz #——cos of angle p
100        Qh=abs(Qn/cosp) #——distance 4 to hit point
101
102        xh=x[3]+Qh*lx #——hit point coordinates
103        yh=y[3]+Qh*ly
104        zh=z[3]+Qh*lz
105
106        xhg=xh+xc #——global hit point coordinates
107        yhg=yh+yc
108        zhg=zh+zc
109
110 #—————————————————out of bounds check
111        a=x[1]-x[2]
112        b=y[1]-y[2]
113        c=z[1]-z[2]
114        Q12=sqrt(a*a+b*b+c*c)
115
116        a=x[1]-xh
117        b=y[1]-yh
118        c=z[1]-zh
119        Q1h=sqrt(a*a+b*b+c*c)
120
121        a=x[2]-xh
122        b=y[2]-yh
123        c=z[2]-zh
124        Q2h=sqrt(a*a+b*b+c*c)
125
126        a=x[0]-xh
127        b=y[0]-yh
128        c=z[0]-zh
129        Q0h=sqrt(a*a+b*b+c*c)
130
131        s=(Q01+Q12+Q02)/2 #—area A
132        A=sqrt(s*(s-Q01)*(s-Q12)*(s-Q02))
133
```

```
134        s1=(Q01+Q0h+Q1h)/2 #——area A1
135        A1=sqrt(s1*(s1-Q01)*(s1-Q0h)*(s1-Q1h))
136
137        s2=(Q02+Q2h+Q0h)/2 #—area A2
138        A2=sqrt(s2*(s2-Q02)*(s2-Q2h)*(s2-Q0h))
139
140        hitcolor='r' #——if within bounds plot red hit point
141
142        if A1+A2 > A: #——if out of bounds plot blue hit point
143            hitcolor='b'
144
145        a=x[4]-x[3]
146        b=y[4]-y[3]
147        c=z[4]-z[3]
148        Q34=sqrt(a*a+b*b+c*c)
149
150        if Q34 < Qh: #——if line too short plot green at end of line
151            hitcolor='g'
152
153        return xh,yh,xhg,yhg,hitcolor
154
155 #————————————transform coordinates and plot
156 def plotx(xc,yc,zc,Rx):    #——transform & plot Rx system
157        for i in range(len(x)):
158            [xg[i],yg[i],zg[i]]=rotx(xc,yc,zc,x[i],y[i],z[i],Rx)
159            [x[i],y[i],z[i]]=[xg[i]-xc,yg[i]-yc,zg[i]-zc]
160
161     xh,yh,xhg,yhg,hitcolor=hitpoint(x,y,z) #——returns xh,yh,xhg,yhg
162
163     plotsystem(xg,yg,zg,xh,yh,xhg,yhg,hitcolor) #——plot plane, line,
        hit point
164
165        def ploty(xc,yc,zc,Ry):   #——transform & plot Ry system
166        for i in range(len(x)):
```

```
167          [xg[i],yg[i],zg[i]]=roty(xc,yc,zc,x[i],y[i],z[i],Ry)
168          [x[i],y[i],z[i]]=[xg[i]-xc,yg[i]-yc,zg[i]-zc]
169
170      xh,yh,xhg,yhg,hitcolor=hitpoint(x,y,z)
171
172      plotsystem(xg,yg,zg,xh,yh,xhg,yhg,hitcolor)
173
174 def plotz(xc,yc,zc,Rz):   #——transform & plot Rz  system
175      for i in range(len(x)):
176          [xg[i],yg[i],zg[i]]=rotz(xc,yc,zc,x[i],y[i],z[i],Rz)
177          [x[i],y[i],z[i]]=[xg[i]-xc,yg[i]-yc,zg[i]-zc]
178
179      xh,yh,xhg,yhg,hitcolor=hitpoint(x,y,z)
180
181      plotsystem(xg,yg,zg,xh,yh,xhg,yhg,hitcolor)
182
183 #——————————————input data and plot system
184      while True:
185          axis=input('x, y or z?: ') #——input axis of rotation (lower
                 case)
186          if axis == 'x': #–if x axis
187                  Rx=radians(float(input('Rx Degrees?: '))) #——input
                     degrees of rotation
188                  plotx(xc,yc,zc,Rx) #-call function plotx
189          if axis == 'y':
190                  Ry=radians(float(input('Ry Degrees?: '))) #——input
                     degrees of rotation
191                  ploty(xc,yc,zc,Ry)
192          if axis == 'z':
193                  Rz=radians(float(input('Rz Degrees?: '))) #——input
                     degrees of rotation
194                  plotz(xc,yc,zc,Rz)
195          if axis == '':
196                  break #——quit the program
```

5.3 Line Intersecting a Circle

The determination of whether the hit point of a line intersecting the plane of a circle is within the circle is trivial. As shown in Figure 5-13, if the distance from the circle's center to the hit point is greater than the circle's radius, it lies outside the circle:

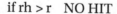

if rh > r   NO HIT

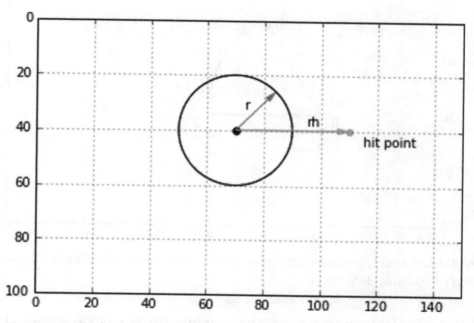

Figure 5-13. *Model for out-of-bounds test for a circle*

We won't bother writing a separate program to demonstrate this. You should be able to do that yourself by modifying Listing 5-1 or Listing 5-3. Simply fill the x[ ],y[ ], and z[ ] lists with the points defining the circle's perimeter and the line coordinates and modify the functions **plotsystem** and **hitpoint**.

5.4 Line Intersecting a Circular Sector

In this section, you develop a procedure to determine if the hit point of a line intersecting the plane of a sector of a circle is inside or outside the sector. Figure 5-14 shows the sector. It has a center at point 0 and a radius r. The hit point is at 3. rh is the distance from 0 to the hit point. Your goal is to determine if the hit point lies inside or outside the sector. (We will not be developing a full three-dimensional program here; you'll just see how the inside or outside algorithm works.) It could be easily incorporated into any of the preceding programs, such as Listing 5-3.

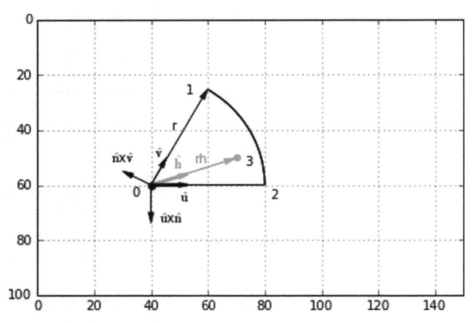

Figure 5-14. *Model for determining whether a line intersecting a circular sector is in or out of bounds. 3=hit point.*

There are five unit vectors at point 0: $\hat{u}$ points from 0 to 2; $\hat{v}$ points from 0 to 1; and $\hat{h}$ from 0 to the hit point at 3. $\hat{n}$ is a unit vector normal to the plane of the sector. It is not shown since it points up and out of the plane. $\hat{u} \times \hat{n}$ is the result of the cross product of $\hat{u}$ with $\hat{n}$; $\hat{n} \times \hat{v}$ is from the cross product of $\hat{n}$ with $\hat{v}$.

Your strategy is to first determine if Rh>r, in which case the hit point is outside the sector in the radial direction. Then you take the dot product of $\hat{h}$ with $\hat{u} \times \hat{n}$. If the result is positive, the hit point is outside the sector on the 0-2 side. Then you take the dot product of $\hat{h}$ with $\hat{n} \times \hat{v}$. If it is positive, the hit point is out of bounds on the 0-1 side.

In Listing 5-4, the local coordinates (relative to point 0) are defined in the lists in lines 14-16. The last element in the lists defines the coordinates of the hit point, point 3. xc,yc, and zc in lines 18-20 are the global coordinates of point 0. The hit test algorithm begins in line 23. Most of it should be self-explanatory based on the previous discussion.

Attention is called to lines 52-58. This is where the normal vector $\hat{\mathbf{n}}$ is evaluated by taking the cross product of $\hat{\mathbf{u}}$ with $\hat{\mathbf{v}}$. As explained earlier, this produces a unit vector (magnitude 1) only if $\hat{\mathbf{u}}$ and $\hat{\mathbf{v}}$ are perpendicular to one another. Since the angle between them in a general sector will not necessarily be 90 degrees, the vector must be normalized. That takes place in lines 55-58. The dot product of $\hat{\mathbf{u}} \times \hat{\mathbf{n}}$ with $\hat{\mathbf{h}}$ takes place in line 64, $\hat{\mathbf{n}} \times \hat{\mathbf{v}}$ with $\hat{\mathbf{h}}$ in line 70. Line 72 assumes the hit color is red, which means the hit is within the sector. If A is positive, it lies outside the sector, in which case the hit color is changed to blue in line 74. Lines 76 and 77 perform the same test for the other side of the sector. Lines 79 and 80 check for the hit point lying outside the sector in the radial direction. Figures 5-15 and 5-16 show two sample runs. You can move the hit point around yourself by changing the coordinates of point 3 in the lists in lines 14-15. You change only the x and y coordinates of the hit point since it is assumed to lie in the z=0 plane, as does the sector.

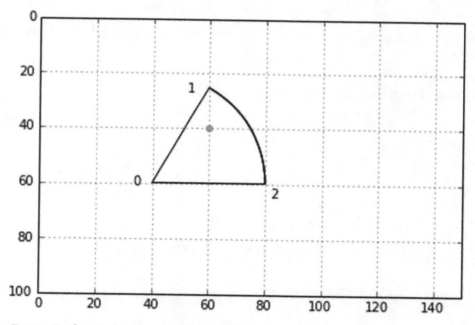

Figure 5-15. *In-bounds or out-of-bounds test produced by Listing 5-4: red=in, blue=out*

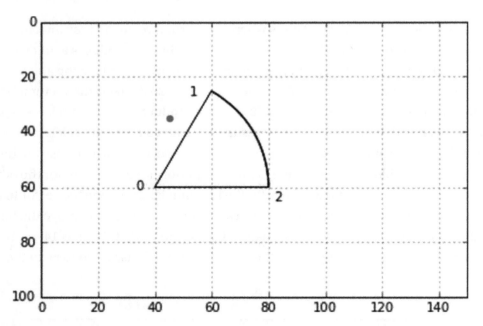

Figure 5-16. *In-bounds or out-of-bounds test produced by Listing 5-4: red=in, blue=out*

Listing 5-4. Program LCSTEST

```
1    """
2      LCSTEST
3    """
4
5    import matplotlib.pyplot as plt
6    import numpy as np
7    from math import sin, cos, radians, degrees, sqrt, acos
8
9    plt.axis([0,150,100,0])
10
11   plt.axis('on')
12   plt.grid(True)
13
14   x=[0,20,40,5]
15   y=[0,-35,0,-25]
16   z=[0,0,0,0]
```

```
17
18   xc=40
19   yc=60
20   zc=0
21
22   #——————————hit test
23   a=x[3]-x[0]
24   b=y[3]-y[0]
25   c=z[3]-z[0]
26   rh=sqrt(a*a+b*b+c*c)
27
28   a=x[3]-x[0]
29   b=y[3]-y[0]
30   c=z[3]-z[0]
31   Q0h=sqrt(a*a+b*b+c*c)
32   hx=a/Q0h #——unit vector 0 to hit point
33   hy=b/Q0h
34   hz=c/Q0h
35
36   a=x[2]-x[0]
37   b=y[2]-y[0]
38   c=z[2]-z[0]
39   Q02=sqrt(a*a+b*b+c*c)
40   ux=a/Q02 #——unit vector 0 to 3
41   uy=b/Q02
42   uz=c/Q02
43
44   a=x[1]-x[0]
45   b=y[1]-y[0]
46   c=z[1]-z[0]
47   Q01=sqrt(a*a+b*b+c*c)
48   vx=a/Q01 #——unit vector 0 to 1
49   vy=b/Q01
50   vz=c/Q01
51
```

```
52   a=uy*vz-uz*vy #——vector ûxv̂ normal to plane
53   b=uz*vx-ux*vz
54   c=ux*vy-uy*vx
55   Quxv=sqrt(a*a*b*b+c*c) #——normalize ûxv̂
56   nx=a/Quxv
57   ny=b/Quxv
58   nz=c/Quxv
59
60   uxnx=uy*nz-uz*ny #——unit vector ûxv̂
61   uxny=uz*nx-ux*nz
62   uxnz=ux*ny-uy*nx
63
64   A=uxnx*hx+uxny*hy+uxnz*hz #——dot product ûxv̂ with ĥ
65
66   nxvx=ny*vz-nz*vy #——unit vector ûxv̂
67   nxvy=nz*vx-nx*vz
68   nxvz=nx*vy-ny*vx
69
70   B=nxvx*hx+nxvy*hy+nxvz*hz #——dot product ûxv̂ with ĥ
71
72   hitcolor='r'
73   if A>0:   #—out
74       hitcolor='b'
75
76   if B>0: #—out
77       hitcolor='b'
78
79   if rh>r: #—out
80      hitcolor='b'
81
82   plt.scatter(x[3]+xc,y[3]+yc,s=20,color=hitcolor)
83
```

```
84  #——————-plot    arc
85  r=40
86  phi1=0
87  phi2=-radians(60)
88  dphi=(phi2-phi1)/180
89  xlast=xc+r
90  ylast=yc+0
91  for phi in np.arange(phi1,phi2,dphi):
92      x=xc+r*cos(phi)
93      y=yc+r*sin(phi)
94      plt.plot([xlast,x],[ylast,y],color='k')
95      xlast=x
96      ylast=y
97
98
99  #——————-labels
100 print('rh=',rh)
101 print('r=',r)
102 plt.arrow(xc,yc,40,0)
103 plt.arrow(xc,yc,20,-35,linewidth=.5,color='k')
103 plt.text(33,61,'0')
104 plt.text(52,27,'1')
105 plt.text(82,65,'2')
106
107  plt.show()
```

5.5 Line Intersecting a Sphere

Figure 5-17, output from Listing 5-5, shows a line intersecting a sphere. The entrance and exit points are shown in red. Figure 5-18 shows the model used by Listing 5-5. The line begins at B and ends at E.

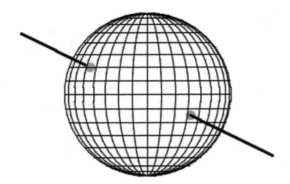

Figure 5-17. *Line intersecting a sphere, produced by Listing 5-5*

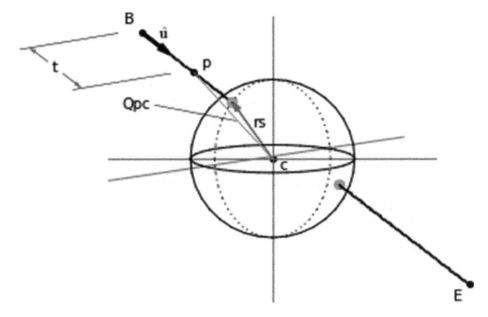

Figure 5-18. *Model for a line intersecting a sphere*

To find the entrance hit point, you start at B and move a point p incrementally along the line toward E. At each step, you calculate Qpc, the distance between p and c. If it is less than or equal to the sphere's radius rs, you have made contact with the sphere and a red dot is plotted. You continue moving p along the line inside the sphere without plotting anything (you could plot a dotted line), calculating Qpc as you go, until Qpc becomes equal to or greater than rs. At that point, p leaves the sphere and another red dot is plotted. p continues moving along the line to E, plotting black dots along the way. Instead of plotting the line with dots, you could have used short line segments as was done in prior programs.

To move p along the line, you use parameter t, which is the distance from B to p. To get the coordinates of p, you construct unit vector $\hat{\mathbf{u}}$, which points along the line

$$a = xe - xb \tag{5-56}$$

$$b = ye - yb \tag{5-57}$$

$$c = ze - zb \tag{5-58}$$

$$Qbe = \sqrt{a^2 + b^2 + c^2} \tag{5-59}$$

$$ux = a / Qbe \tag{5-60}$$

$$uy = b / Qbe \tag{5-61}$$

$$uz = c / Qbe \tag{5-62}$$

where Qbe is the distance along the line from B to E and ux, uy, and uz are the components of $\hat{\mathbf{u}}$. The coordinates of p are thus

$$xp = xb + uxt \tag{5-63}$$

$$yp = yb + uyt \tag{5-64}$$

$$zp = zb + uzt \tag{5-65}$$

Qpc is easy to determine:

$$a = xc - xp \tag{5-66}$$

$$b = yc - yp \tag{5-67}$$

$$c = zc - zp \tag{5-68}$$

$$Qpc = \sqrt{a^2 + b^2 + c^2} \tag{5-69}$$

In Listing 5-5, the sphere's center coordinates are set in lines 18-20. The sphere is composed of longitude (vertical) lines and latitude (horizontal) lines. The lists in lines 10-16 contain the local and global coordinates of the longitudes. The initial filling of these lists takes place in lines 25-38, which create a half circle in the z=0 plane. As shown in Figure 5-19, point p lies on the circumference at coordinates xp,yp,zp where

$$xp = rscos(\phi) \tag{5-70}$$

$$yp = rssin(\phi) \tag{5-71}$$

$$zp = 0 \tag{5-72}$$

They are set in lines 30-32. ϕ is the angle around the z direction. It runs from -90° to +90°. You don't need the back half of the longitudes so they are not plotted. This half circle will be rotated around the y direction to create the oval longitudes. They are 10° apart as set in line 74. Since they are rotated around the y direction only, the program contains just the rotation function **roty**: **rotx** and **rotz** are not needed in this model. Plotting of the longitudes takes place in lines 72-77.

The latitudes are plotted in lines 80-97. Figure 5-21 shows a front view of the sphere looking into the x,y plane. Each latitude is essentially a circle having radius rl where

$$xl = rscos(\phi) \tag{5-73}$$

This is calculated in line 89 of the program. When viewed from the front, the latitude appears as a straight line since you are not rotating the sphere in this program.

The ϕ loop beginning at line 88 ranges ϕ from -90° to +90° in 10° increments. At each increment a new latitude is plotted. It will have a radius given by Equation 5-73 above. The α loop beginning at line 92 sweeps across the front of the circular latitude from α=0° to 180° in 10° increments. This is illustrated in Figure 5-22, which shows the top view looking down on the x,z plane.

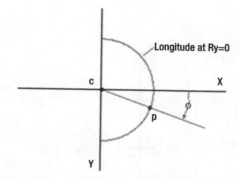

Figure 5-19. *x,y view of sphere longitude shown at starting position Ry=0. Rotation around the y direction in 10° increments will produce longitudes.*

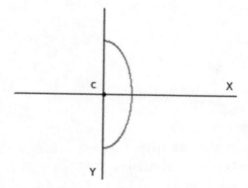

Figure 5-20. *x,y view of sphere longitude rotated by Ry=60°*

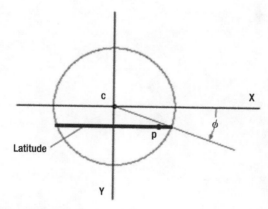

Figure 5-21. *Sphere latitude - x,y view*

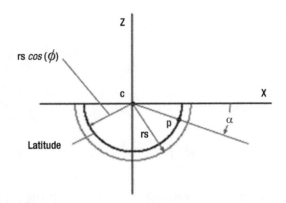

Figure 5-22. *Sphere latitude - x,z view*

Listing 5-5. Program LS

```
1    """
2    LS
3    """
4
5    import numpy as np
6    import matplotlib.pyplot as plt
7    from math import sin, cos, radians, sqrt
8
9    #————————————————lists
10   x=[ ]
11   y=[ ]
12   z=[ ]
13
14   xg=[ ]
15   yg=[ ]
16   zg=[ ]
17
18   xc=80 #——sphere center
19   yc=50
20   zc=0
21
```

```
22    rs=40 #——sphere radius
23
24    #————————————fill longitude lists
25    phi1=radians(-90)
26    phi2=radians(90)
27    dphi=radians(10)
28
29    for phi in np.arange(phi1,phi2,dphi):
30         xp=rs*cos(phi)
31         yp=rs*sin(phi)
32         zp=0
33         x.append(xp)
34         y.append(yp)
35         z.append(zp)
36         xg.append(xp)
37         yg.append(yp)
38         zg.append(zp)
39
40    #=================================================define rotation function
41    def roty(xc,yc,zc,xp,yp,zp,Ry):
42         a=[xp,yp,zp]
43         b=[cos(Ry),0,sin(Ry)] #————[cx11,cx12,cx13]
44         xpp=np.inner(a, b)
45         b=[0,1,0] #————[cx21,cx22,cx23]
46         ypp=np.inner(a,b) #————scalar product of a,b
47         b=[-sin(Ry),0,cos(Ry)] #————[cx31,cx32,cx33]
48         zpp=np.inner(a,b)
49         [xg,yg,zg]=[xpp+xc,ypp+yc,zpp+zc]
50         return[xg,yg,zg]
51
52    #=========================================================
53    def plotsphere(xg,yg,zg):
54         lastxg=xg[0]
55         lastyg=yg[0]
56         for i in range(len(x)):
```

```
57              if i < len(x)/2:
58                      plt.plot([lastxg,xg[i]],[lastyg,yg[i]],linewidth=1,
                        color='k')
59              else:
60                      plt.plot([lastxg,xg[i]],[lastyg,yg[i]],linewidth=1,
                        color='k')
61       lastxg=xg[i]
62       lastyg=yg[i]
63
64   #=================================================transform coordinates
65   def plotspherey(xc,yc,zc,Ry):
66       for i in range(len(x)): #————transform and plot Ry sphere
67            [xg[i],yg[i],zg[i]]=roty(xc,yc,zc,x[i],y[i],z[i],Ry)
68
69   plotsphere(xg,yg,zg)  #——plot rotated coordinates
70
71   #——————————plot longitudes
72   Ry1=radians(0)
73   Ry2=radians(180)
74   dRy=radians(10)
75
76   for Ry in np.arange(Ry1,Ry2,dRy):
77       plotspherey(xc,yc,zc,Ry)
78
79   #——————————plot latitudes
80   alpha1=radians(0)
81   alpha2=radians(180)
82   dalpha=radians(10)
83
84   phi1=radians(-90)
85   phi2=radians(90)
86   dphi=radians(10)
87
```

```
88   for phi in np.arange(phi1,phi2,dphi):
89        r=rs*cos(phi) #————————latitude radius
90        xplast=xc+r
91        yplast=yc+rs*sin(phi)
92        for  alpha  in  np.arange(alpha1,alpha2,dalpha):
93             xp=xc+r*cos(alpha)
94             yp=yplast
95             plt.plot([xplast,xp],[yplast,yp],color='k')
96             xplast=xp
97             yplast=yp
98
99   #————————————————line and hit points
100  xb=-60 #—line beginning
101  yb=-30
102  zb=-20
103
104  xe=60 #——line end
105  ye=30
106  ze=-40
107
108  a=xe-xb
109  b=ye-yb
110  c=ze-zb
111  Qbe=sqrt(a*a+b*b+c*c)  #——line length
112  ux=a/Qbe #—unit vector û
113  uy=b/Qbe
114  uz=c/Qbe
115
116  dt=1
117  for t in np.arange(0,Qbe,dt):
118       xp=xb+ux*t
119       yp=yb+uy*t
120       zp=zb+uz*t
121       Qpc=sqrt(xp*xp+yp*yp+zp*zp)
122       if Qpc > rs:
```

```
123              plt.scatter(xp+xc,yp+yc,s=5,color='k')
124       if Qpc <= rs:
125              plt.scatter(xp+xc,yp+yc,s=80,color='r')
126       tlast=t
127       break
128
129 for t in np.arange(tlast,Qbe,dt):
130       xp=xb+ux*t
131       yp=yb+uy*t
132       zp=zb+uz*t
133       Qpc=sqrt(xp*xp+yp*yp+zp*zp)
134       if Qpc >= rs:
135              plt.scatter(xp+xc,yp+yc,s=80,color='r')
136       tlast=t
137       break
138
139 for t in np.arange(tlast,Qbe,dt):
140       xp=xb+ux*t
141       yp=yb+uy*t
142       zp=zb+uz*t
143       Qpc=sqrt(xp*xp+yp*yp+zp*zp)
144       if Qpc >= rs:
145              plt.scatter(xp+xc,yp+yc,s=5,color='k')
146
147 plt.axis([0,150,100,0]) #-plot axes and grid
148 plt.axis('off')
149 plt.grid(False)
150
151  plt.show()
```

5.6 Plane Intersecting a Sphere

In this section, you will work out a technique for plotting a flat rectangular plane intersecting a sphere. Figure 5-23 shows the output of Listing 5-6; Figure 5-24 shows the model used by that listing.

The strategy here is to use the algorithms developed in the previous section for a line intersecting a sphere as your basic element. By representing the plane as a series of parallel lines, you can easily find the intersection of a plane with a sphere. Figure 5-23 shows unit vector $\hat{\mathbf{u}}$ at corner 1. As before, this points from the beginning to end of the first line. There is also unit vector $\hat{\mathbf{v}}$ at corner 1. This points to corner 3. By advancing along the line from 1 to 3 in small steps, you can construct lines running parallel to the first one from 1 to 2. Advancing down each of these lines in small increments of t, you can find the coordinates of points across the plane. To advance in the $\hat{\mathbf{v}}$ direction, you introduce parameter s, which is the distance from corner 1 to the beginning of the new line. To get the coordinates of the end of that line, you perform the same operation starting at point 2 using $\hat{\mathbf{v}}$ and s, as in

$$xe = x2 + vx \cdot s \qquad\qquad (5\text{-}74)$$

$$ye = yr + vy \cdot s \qquad\qquad (5\text{-}75)$$

$$ze = z2 + vz \cdot s \qquad\qquad (5\text{-}76)$$

where xe, ye, and ze are the coordinates of the end of the line; x2,y2, and z2 are the coordinates of point 2; and vx,vy, and vz are the components of unit vector $\hat{\mathbf{v}}$.

Incrementing down and across the plane with parameters t and s allows you to sweep across the surface of the plane. At each point p you calculate the distance from p to the center of the sphere. If it is equal to or less than the sphere's radius, you have a hit.

I won't list the entire program that produced Figure 5-23 since it is mostly similar to Listing 5-5, except for the addition of an s loop that sweeps in the $\hat{\mathbf{v}}$ direction. Control of the program begins at line 27. Lines 27-37 define the coordinates of plane corners 1, 2, and 3. The unit vectors $\hat{\mathbf{u}}$ and $\hat{\mathbf{v}}$ are established in lines 39-53. Lines 55 and 56 set the scan increments in dt and ds. The loop 57-64 scans in the $\hat{\mathbf{v}}$ direction, establishing the beginning and end coordinates of each line. Function **plane**, which begins at line 1, determines if there is a hit with each line and the sphere. For each s, the loop beginning at line 3 advances down the line in the $\hat{\mathbf{u}}$ direction, calculating the coordinates xp,yp,zp of each point p along the line. Line 10 calculates the distance of p from the sphere's center. Line 11 says, if the distance is greater than the sphere's radius, plot a black dot. If it is less than or equal to the radius, line 18 plots a colorless dot. The rest of the logic up to line 24 determines if the line has emerged from the sphere, in which case plotting of black dots resumes. Results are shown in Figure 5-23.

Figure 5-23. *Plane intersecting a sphere produced by Listing 5-6*

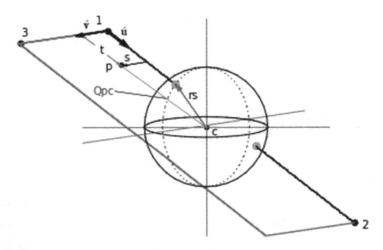

Figure 5-24. *Model for Listing 5-6*

Listing 5-6. Program PS

```
"""
PS
"""
import numpy as np
import matplotlib.pyplot as plt
from math import sin, cos, radians, sqrt
.
(similar to Program LS)
.
```

```
     #==========================================================plane
1    def plane(xb,yb,zb,xe,ye,ze,Q12,dt):
2        hit='off'
3        for t in np.arange(0,Q12,dt): #——B to hit
4                xp=xb+ux*t
5                yp=yb+uy*t
6                zp=zb+uz*t
7                xpg=xc+xp
8                ypg=yc+yp
9                zpg=zc+zp
10               Qpc=sqrt(xp*xp+yp*yp+zp*zp)
11               if Qpc>=rs:
12                       plt.scatter(xpg,ypg,s=.5,color='k')
13               if Qpc<=rs:
14                   if hit=='off':
15                           hit='on'
16               if Qpc<rs:
17                   if hit=='on':
18                           plt.scatter(xpg,ypg,s=10,color='')
19               if Qpc>=rs:
20                   if hit=='on':
21                           hit='off'
22               if Qpc>rs:
23                   if hit=='off':
24                           plt.scatter(xpg,ypg,s=.5,color='k')
25
26   #————————————scan   across   plane
27   x1=-40
28   y1=-30
29   z1=-20
30
31   x2=60
32   y2=25
33   z2=-35
34
```

```
35   x3=-65
36   y3=-20
37   z3=-50
38
39   a=x2-x1
40   b=y2-y1
41   c=z2-z1
42   Q12=sqrt(a*a+b*b+c*c)
43   ux=a/Q12
44   uy=b/Q12
45   uz=c/Q12
46
47   a=x3-x1
48   b=y3-y1
49   c=z3-z1
50   Q13=sqrt(a*a+b*b+c*c)
51   vx=a/Q13
52   vy=b/Q13
53   vz=c/Q13
54
55   dt=.7 #————————scan increment
56   ds=.7
57   for s in np.arange(0,Q13,ds):
58       sbx=x1+s*vx
59       sby=y1+s*vy
60       sbz=z1+s*vz
61       sex=x2+s*vx
62       sey=y2+s*vy
63       sez=z2+s*vz
64       plane(sbx,sby,sbz,sex,sey,sez,Q12,dt)
65
66   plt.axis([0,150,100,0]) #-replot axes and grid
67   plt.axis('off')
68   plt.grid(False)
69
70   plt.show() #-plot latest rotation
```

5.7 Summary

In this chapter, you learned how to predict whether a three-dimensional line or plane will intersect a three-dimensional surface or solid object. Why bother with this? Because it is fundamental to removing hidden lines, you will see in Chapter 6. When plotting surface A, which may be behind another surface or object B, you do so in small steps, plotting a scatter dot (or a short line segment) at each step. If the point on A is hidden by B, you do not plot it. To determine if it is hidden from view by an observer, you draw an imaginary line from the point on A to the observer (i.e. in the -z direction). If you can determine if that line from A intersects a surface or object B in front of it, then you will know whether or not it is hidden. While you cannot develop hidden line algorithms for every conceivable situation (you did rectangular planes, triangular planes, circular sectors, circles, and spheres here), by understanding how it is done for these objects you should, with a bit of creativity, be able to develop your own hidden line algorithms for other surfaces and objects. Perhaps the line-triangular plane is most useful since complex surfaces and objects can often by approximated by an assembly of triangles. You will see more about this in Chapter 6.

CHAPTER 6

Hidden Line Removal

Most of the models used in the previous chapters were essentially stick figures constructed of dots and lines. When such objects are viewed in three dimensions, it is possible to see the lines on the back side, as if the objects were transparent. This chapter is concerned with removing the lines, which would normally be hidden, from objects so they appear solid.

This chapter will cover two types of situations. The first is called *intra-object* hidden line removal. This refers to removing hidden lines from a single object. We assume that most objects are constructed of flat planes; the examples are a box, a pyramid, and a spherical surface that is approximated by planes. The technique you will use relies on determining whether a particular plane faces toward the viewer, in which case it is visible and is plotted, or away from the viewer, in which case it is not visible and is not plotted.

Inter-object hidden line removal, on the other hand, refers to a system of more than one object, such as two planes, one behind the other. Here the general approach is to use some of the ray tracing techniques that were developed in the previous chapter to find intersections between lines and surfaces. You start by drawing the back object using dots or short line segments. At each point you construct a line (ray) going toward the observer, who is in the -z direction, and see if it intersects with the front object. If it does, that point on the back object is hidden and is not plotted.

6.1 Box

As an example of intra-object hidden line removal, let's start off with a simple box, as shown in Figures 6-1 and 6-2. They were drawn by Listing 6-1. Figures 6-3, 6-4, and 6-5 show the model used by the program.

In Figure 6-3, you see that the box has eight corners, numbered 0 to 7. At corner 0, there are two vectors: **V01**, which goes from corner 0 to 1, and **V03**, which goes from 0 to 3. Looking at the 0,1,2,3 face first, as the box is rotated, the strategy is to determine if it is tilted toward or away from an observer who is in the -z direction. If it is facing toward the

© B.J. Korites 2018
B.J. Korites, *Python Graphics*, https://doi.org/10.1007/978-1-4842-3378-8_6

observer, the edges of the face are plotted. If it is facing away from the observer, they are not plotted. How do you determine if the face is facing the observer? The cross (vector) product **V03**×**V01** gives a vector **N**, which is normal to the 0,1,2,3 face, so

$$\mathbf{V03} = V03x\hat{\mathbf{i}} + V03y\hat{\mathbf{j}} + V03z\hat{\mathbf{k}} \tag{6-1}$$

$$\mathbf{V01} = V01x\hat{\mathbf{i}} + V01y\hat{\mathbf{j}} + V01z\hat{\mathbf{k}} \tag{6-2}$$

$$V03x = x[3] - x[0] \tag{6-3}$$

$$V03y = y[3] - y[0] \tag{6-4}$$

$$V03z = z[3] - z[0] \tag{6-5}$$

$$V01x = x[1] - x[0] \tag{6-6}$$

$$V01y = y[1] - y[0] \tag{6-7}$$

$$V01z = z[1] - z[0] \tag{6-8}$$

$$\mathbf{N} = \mathbf{V03} \times \mathbf{V01} = \begin{bmatrix} \hat{\mathbf{i}} & \hat{\mathbf{j}} & \hat{\mathbf{k}} \\ V03x & V03y & V03z \\ V01x & V01y & V01z \end{bmatrix} \tag{6-9}$$

$$\mathbf{N} = Nx\hat{\mathbf{i}} + Ny\hat{\mathbf{j}} + Nz\hat{\mathbf{k}} \tag{6-10}$$

$$\mathbf{N} = \hat{\mathbf{i}}[V03y \cdot V01z - V03z \cdot V01y] + \hat{\mathbf{j}}[V03z \cdot V01x - V03x \cdot V01z]$$
$$+ \hat{\mathbf{k}}\underbrace{[V03x \cdot V01y - V03y \cdot V01x]}_{Nz} \tag{6-11}$$

You can determine if the plane is facing toward or away from the observer by the value of Nz, **N**'s z component. Figures 6-4 and 6-5 show a plane (blue) relative to an observer. This is the side view of one of the faces of the box shown in Figure 6-3. The observer is on the right side of the coordinate system looking in the +z direction. Referring to Figure 6-4, if the z component of **N**, Nz in Equation 6-11, is < 0 (i.e. pointing in the -z direction), the plane is facing the observer, it is visible to the observer, and it is plotted.

If Nz is positive (i.e. pointing in the +z direction), as shown in Figure 6-5, the face is tilted away from the observer, in which case it is not seen by the observer and is not plotted. Note that you can use the full vector **V** rather than a unit vector since you are only concerned with the sign of **V**.

What about the other faces? The 4,5,6,7 face is parallel to 0,1,2,3 so its outward pointing normal vector is opposite to that of face 0,1,2,3. You do a similar check on whether its normal vector is pointing in the +z (don't plot) or =z (plot) direction.

The remaining faces are handled in a similar fashion. The normal to 1,2,6,5 is opposite to that of 0,3,7,4; the normal to 3,2,6,7 is opposite to that of 0,1,5,4.

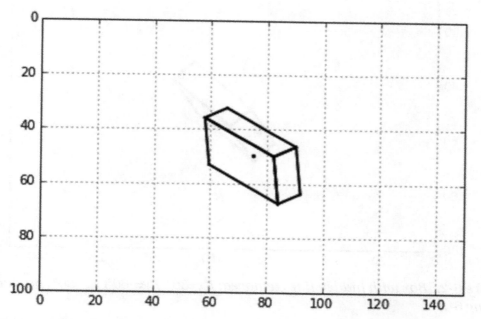

Figure 6-1. *Box with hidden lines removed: Rx=45°, Ry=45°, Rz=30° (produced by Listing 6-1)*

Listing 6-1 produced Figures 6-1 and 6-2. The lists in lines 9, 10, and 11 define the coordinates of the unrotated box relative to its center, which is set in lines 124-126. Lines 13-15 fill the global coordinate lists with zeroes. These lists have the same length as list x (also lists y and z) and are set by the **len(x)** function.

Lines 124-140 accept keyboard input as in previous programs. As an example of the sequence of operations, suppose you enter x in line 129 followed by an angle in degrees. Line 132 calls the function **plotboxx**, which begins at line 102. Lines 103-105 rotate the corner points and update the local and global coordinate lists. Line 107 calls function **plotbox**, which begins in line 40. This function plots the box in its new rotated orientation using the lists xg,yg, and zg. Starting with the 0,1,2,3 face, lines 41-47 calculate Nz, the z component of the normal vector N in line 47 using the above analysis. If Nz<=0, the 0,1,2,3 face is plotted in lines 49-52. If it is not visible (i.e. Nz>0), then you know the opposing face 4,5,6,7 must be visible and it is plotted in lines 54-57. The other faces are processed in a similar manner.

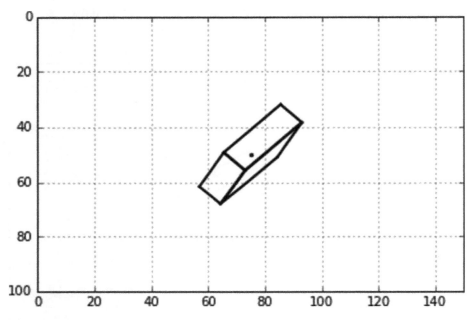

Figure 6-2. *Box with hidden lines removed: Rx=30°, Ry=-60°, Rz=30° (produced by Listing 6-1)*

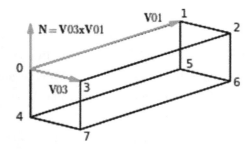

Figure 6-3. *Model for hidden line removal of a box used by Listing 6-1. N not to scale.*

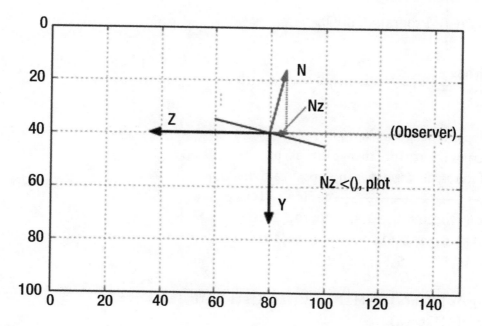

Figure 6-4. *Model for hidden line removal of a box used by Listing 6-1*

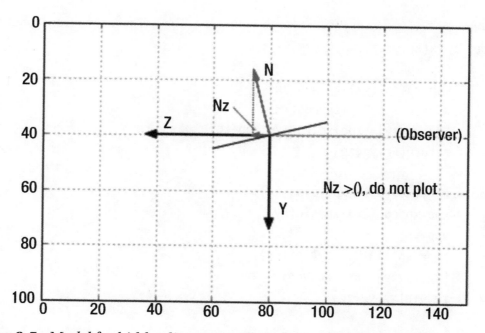

Figure 6-5. *Model for hidden line removal of a box used by Listing 6-1*

Listing 6-1. Program HLBOX

```
1    """
2    HLBOX
3    """
4
5    import numpy as np
6    import matplotlib.pyplot as plt
7    from math import sin, cos, radians
8    #————————————————define  lists
9    x=[-20,20,20,-20,-20,20,20,-20]
10   y=[-10,-10,-10,-10,10,10,10,10]
11   z=[5,5,-5,-5,5,5,-5,-5]
12
13   xg=[0]*len(x) #—fill xg,yg,zg lists with len(x) zeros
14   yg=[0]*len(x)
15   zg=[0]*len(x)
16
17   #====================================================rotation functions
18   def rotx(xc,yc,zc,xp,yp,zp,Rx):
19       xpp=xp
20       ypp=yp*cos(Rx)-zp*sin(Rx)
21       zpp=yp*sin(Rx)+zp*cos(Rx)
22       [xg,yg,zg]=[xpp+xc,ypp+yc,zpp+zc]
23       return[xg,yg,zg]
24
25   def  roty(xc,yc,zc,xp,yp,zp,Ry):
26       xpp=xp*cos(Ry)+zp*sin(Ry)
27       ypp=yp
28       zpp=-xp*sin(Ry)+zp*cos(Ry)
29       [xg,yg,zg]=[xpp+xc,ypp+yc,zpp+zc]
30       return[xg,yg,zg]
31
32   def rotz(xc,yc,zc,xp,yp,zp,Rz):
33       xpp=xp*cos(Rz)-yp*sin(Rz)
34       ypp=xp*sin(Rz)+yp*cos(Rz)
```

```
35        zpp=zp
36        [xg,yg,zg]=[xpp+xc,ypp+yc,zpp+zc]
37        return[xg,yg,zg]
38
39   #================================================box plotting function
40   def plotbox(xg,yg,zg):
41        v01x=x[1]-x[0] #——0,1,2,3 face
42        v01y=y[1]-y[0]
43        v01z=z[1]-z[0]
44        v03x=x[3]-x[0]
45        v03y=y[3]-y[0]
46        v03z=z[3]-z[0]
47        nz=v03x*v01y-v03y*v01x
48        if nz<=0 :
49             plt.plot([xg[0],xg[1]],[yg[0],yg[1]],color='k',linewidth=2)
50             plt.plot([xg[1],xg[2]],[yg[1],yg[2]],color='k',linewidth=2)
51             plt.plot([xg[2],xg[3]],[yg[2],yg[3]],color='k',linewidth=2)
52             plt.plot([xg[3],xg[0]],[yg[3],yg[0]],color='k',linewidth=2)
53        else: #--plot the other side
54             plt.plot([xg[4],xg[5]],[yg[4],yg[5]],color='k',linewidth=2)
55             plt.plot([xg[5],xg[6]],[yg[5],yg[6]],color='k',linewidth=2)
56             plt.plot([xg[6],xg[7]],[yg[6],yg[7]],color='k',linewidth=2)
57             plt.plot([xg[7],xg[4]],[yg[7],yg[4]],color='k',linewidth=2)
58
59        v04x=x[4]-x[0] #——0,3,7,4 face
60        v04y=y[4]-y[0]
61        v04z=z[4]-z[0]
62        v03x=x[3]-x[0]
63        v03y=y[3]-y[0]
64        v03z=z[3]-z[0]
65        nz=v04x*v03y-v04y*v03x
66        if nz<=0 :
67             plt.plot([xg[0],xg[3]],[yg[0],yg[3]],color='k',linewidth=2)
68             plt.plot([xg[3],xg[7]],[yg[3],yg[7]],color='k',linewidth=2)
69             plt.plot([xg[7],xg[4]],[yg[7],yg[4]],color='k',linewidth=2)
70             plt.plot([xg[4],xg[0]],[yg[4],yg[0]],color='k',linewidth=2)
```

```
71      else: #——plot the other side
72          plt.plot([xg[1],xg[2]],[yg[1],yg[2]],color='k',linewidth=2)
73          plt.plot([xg[2],xg[6]],[yg[2],yg[6]],color='k',linewidth=2)
74          plt.plot([xg[6],xg[5]],[yg[6],yg[5]],color='k',linewidth=2)
75          plt.plot([xg[5],xg[1]],[yg[5],yg[1]],color='k',linewidth=2)
76
77      v01x=x[1]-x[0] #-0,1,5,4 face
78      v01y=y[1]-y[0]
79      v01z=z[1]-z[0]
80      v04x=x[4]-x[0]
81      v04y=y[4]-y[0]
82      v04z=z[4]-z[0]
83      nz=v01x*v04y-v01y*v04x
84      if nz<=0 :
85          plt.plot([xg[0],xg[1]],[yg[0],yg[1]],color='k',linewidth=2)
86          plt.plot([xg[1],xg[5]],[yg[1],yg[5]],color='k',linewidth=2)
87          plt.plot([xg[5],xg[4]],[yg[5],yg[4]],color='k',linewidth=2)
88          plt.plot([xg[4],xg[0]],[yg[4],yg[0]],color='k',linewidth=2)
89      else: #——plot the other side
90          plt.plot([xg[3],xg[2]],[yg[3],yg[2]],color='k',linewidth=2)
91          plt.plot([xg[2],xg[6]],[yg[2],yg[6]],color='k',linewidth=2)
92          plt.plot([xg[6],xg[7]],[yg[6],yg[7]],color='k',linewidth=2)
93          plt.plot([xg[7],xg[3]],[yg[7],yg[3]],color='k',linewidth=2)
94
95      plt.scatter(xc,yc,s=5,color='k') #-plot a dot at the center
96      plt.axis([0,150,100,0]) #-replot axes and grid
97      plt.axis('on')
98      plt.grid(True)
99      plt.show() #-plot latest rotation
100
101 #===============================transform coordinates and plot functions
102 def plotboxx(xc,yc,zc,Rx): #———transform & plot Rx box
103     for i in range(len(x)):
104         [xg[i],yg[i],zg[i]]=rotx(xc,yc,zc,x[i],y[i],z[i],Rx)
```

```
105             [x[i],y[i],z[i]]=[xg[i]-xc,yg[i]-yc,zg[i]-zc]
106
107     plotbox(xg,yg,zg) #————plot
108
109 def plotboxy(xc,yc,zc,Ry):
110     for i in range(len(x)): #————transform & plot Ry box
111             [xg[i],yg[i],zg[i]]=roty(xc,yc,zc,x[i],y[i],z[i],Ry)
112             [x[i],y[i],z[i]]=[xg[i]-xc,yg[i]-yc,zg[i]-zc]
113
114     plotbox(xg,yg,zg)
115
116 def plotboxz(xc,yc,zc,Rz):
117     for i in range(len(x)): #————transform & plot Rz box
118             [xg[i],yg[i],zg[i]]=rotz(xc,yc,zc,x[i],y[i],z[i],Rz)
119             [x[i],y[i],z[i]]=[xg[i]-xc,yg[i]-yc,zg[i]-zc]
120
121     plotbox(xg,yg,zg)
122
123 #————————————————————plot  box
124 xc=75 #-center coordinates
125 yc=50
126 zc=50
127
128 while True:
129     axis=input('x, y or z?: ') #————input axis of rotation (lower case)
130     if axis == 'x': #-if x axis
131             Rx=radians(float(input('Rx Degrees?: '))) #————input degrees
                of rotation
132             plotboxx(xc,yc,zc,Rx) #————call function plotboxx
133     if axis == 'y':
134             Ry=radians(float(input('Ry Degrees?: '))) #————input degrees
                of rotation
135             plotboxy(xc,yc,zc,Ry)
```

```
136        if axis == 'z':
137                Rz=radians(float(input('Rz Degrees?: '))) #——input degrees
138                plotboxz(xc,yc,zc,Rz)
139        if axis == ":
104            break
```

6.2 Pyramid

Listing 6-2 was used to plot Figures 6-6 and 6-7. The model used is shown in Figure 6-8. The analysis is similar to that used for the box in the previous section. The difference is there are four faces to contend with and none of them are parallel, as they were with the box, so you must process each face independently to see if it is facing toward or away from an observer. The hidden lines are plotted as dots in program lines 54-56, 67-69, and 77-79. To remove the dots, replace ":" with " " in these lines. The code in Listing 6-2 should be self-explanatory.

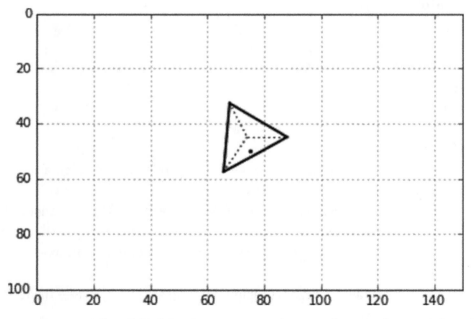

Figure 6-6. *Pyramid with hidden lines removed: Rx=30°, Ry=45°, Rz=0° (produced by Listing 6-2)*

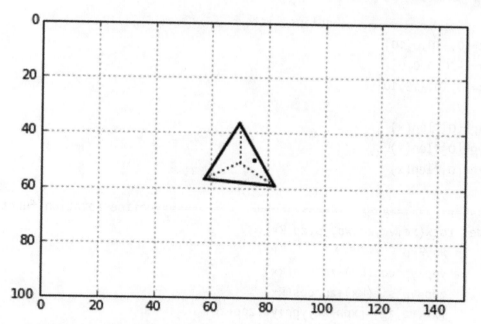

Figure 6-7. *Pyramid with hidden lines removed: Rx=30°, Ry=45°, Rz=-90° (produced by Listing 6-2)*

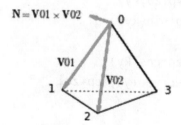

Figure 6-8. *Model for Listing 6-2. N not to scale.*

Listing 6-2. Program HLPYRAMID

```
1    """
2    HLPYRAMID
3    """
4
5    import numpy as np
6    import matplotlib.pyplot as plt
7    from math import sin, cos, radians
```

```
8    #—————————————————define lists
9    x=[0,-10,0,10]
10   y=[-20,0,0,0]
11   z=[0,10,-15,10]
12
13   xg=[0]*len(x)
14   yg=[0]*len(x)
15   zg=[0]*len(x)
16
17   #===============================================define rotation function
18   def rotx(xc,yc,zc,xp,yp,zp,Rx):
19       xpp=xp
20       ypp=yp*cos(Rx)-zp*sin(Rx)
21       zpp=yp*sin(Rx)+zp*cos(Rx)
22       [xg,yg,zg]=[xpp+xc,ypp+yc,zpp+zc]
23       return[xg,yg,zg]
24
25   def roty(xc,yc,zc,xp,yp,zp,Ry):
26       xpp=xp*cos(Ry)+zp*sin(Ry)
27       ypp=yp
28       zpp=-xp*sin(Ry)+zp*cos(Ry)
29       [xg,yg,zg]=[xpp+xc,ypp+yc,zpp+zc]
30       return[xg,yg,zg]
31
32   def rotz(xc,yc,zc,xp,yp,zp,Rz):
33       xpp=xp*cos(Rz)-yp*sin(Rz)
34       ypp=xp*sin(Rz)+yp*cos(Rz)
35       zpp=zp
36       [xg,yg,zg]=[xpp+xc,ypp+yc,zpp+zc]
37       return[xg,yg,zg]
38
39   #====================================define pyramid plotting function
40
41   def plotpyramid(xg,yg,zg):
42       v01x=x[1]-x[0] #——0,1,2 face
43       v01y=y[1]-y[0]
```

```
44      v01z=z[1]-z[0]
45      v02x=x[2]-x[0]
46      v02y=y[2]-y[0]
47      v02z=z[2]-z[0]
48      nz=v01x*v02y-v01y*v02x
49      if nz<=0 :
50          plt.plot([xg[0],xg[1]],[yg[0],yg[1]],color='k',linewidth=2)
51          plt.plot([xg[1],xg[2]],[yg[1],yg[2]],color='k',linewidth=2)
52          plt.plot([xg[2],xg[0]],[yg[2],yg[0]],color='k',linewidth=2)
53      else:
54          plt.plot([xg[0],xg[1]],[yg[0],yg[1]],color='k',linestyle=':')
55          plt.plot([xg[1],xg[2]],[yg[1],yg[2]],color='k',linestyle=':')
56          plt.plot([xg[2],xg[0]],[yg[2],yg[0]],color='k',linestyle=':')
57
58      v03x=x[3]-x[0]  #-0,2,3 face
59      v03y=y[3]-y[0]
60      v03z=z[3]-z[0]
61      nz=v02x*v03y-v02y*v03x
62      if nz<=0 :
63          plt.plot([xg[0],xg[2]],[yg[0],yg[2]],color='k',linewidth=2)
64          plt.plot([xg[0],xg[3]],[yg[0],yg[3]],color='k',linewidth=2)
65          plt.plot([xg[2],xg[3]],[yg[2],yg[3]],color='k',linewidth=2)
66      else:
67          plt.plot([xg[0],xg[2]],[yg[0],yg[2]],color='k',linestyle=':')
68          plt.plot([xg[0],xg[3]],[yg[0],yg[3]],color='k',linestyle=':')
69          plt.plot([xg[2],xg[3]],[yg[2],yg[3]],color='k',linestyle=':')
70
71      nz=v03x*v01y-v03y*v01x  #-0,2,3 face
72      if nz<=0 :
73          plt.plot([xg[0],xg[1]],[yg[0],yg[1]],color='k',linewidth=2)
74          plt.plot([xg[0],xg[3]],[yg[0],yg[3]],color='k',linewidth=2)
75          plt.plot([xg[1],xg[3]],[yg[1],yg[3]],color='k',linewidth=2)
76      else:
77          plt.plot([xg[0],xg[1]],[yg[0],yg[1]],color='k',linestyle=':')
78          plt.plot([xg[0],xg[3]],[yg[0],yg[3]],color='k',linestyle=':')
```

```
79              plt.plot([xg[1],xg[3]],[yg[1],yg[3]],color='k',linestyle=':')
80
81      v21x=x[1]-x[2] #——1,2,3 face
82      v21y=y[1]-y[2]
83      v21z=z[1]-z[2]
84      v23x=x[3]-x[2]
85      v23y=y[3]-y[2]
86      v23z=z[3]-z[2]
87      nz=v21x*v23y-v21y*v23x
88      if nz¡0:
89          plt.plot([x[2],x[1]],[y[2],y[1]])
90          plt.plot([x[1],x[3]],[y[1],y[3]])
91          plt.plot([x[3],x[2]],[y[3],y[2]])
92
93      plt.scatter(xc,yc,s=5,color='k') #——plot a dot at the center
94      plt.axis([0,150,100,0]) #——replot axes and grid
95      plt.axis('on')
96      plt.grid(True)
97      plt.show() #-plot latest rotation
98
99  #========================transform coordinates and plotting fucntions
100 def plotpyramidx(xc,yc,zc,Rx): #———transform & plot Rx pyramid
101     for i in range(len(x)):
102         [xg[i],yg[i],zg[i]]=rotx(xc,yc,zc,x[i],y[i],z[i],Rx)
103         [x[i],y[i],z[i]]=[xg[i]-xc,yg[i]-yc,zg[i]-zc]
104
105     plotpyramid(xg,yg,zg) #———plot
106
107 def plotpyramidy(xc,yc,zc,Ry):
108     for i in range(len(x)): #———transform & plot Ry pyramid
109         [xg[i],yg[i],zg[i]]=roty(xc,yc,zc,x[i],y[i],z[i],Ry)
110         [x[i],y[i],z[i]]=[xg[i]-xc,yg[i]-yc,zg[i]-zc]
111
112     plotpyramid(xg,yg,zg)
```

```
113
114 def plotpyramidz(xc,yc,zc,Rz):
115     for i in range(len(x)): #————transform & plot Rz pyramid
116         [xg[i],yg[i],zg[i]]=rotz(xc,yc,zc,x[i],y[i],z[i],Rz)
117         [x[i],y[i],z[i]]=[xg[i]-xc,yg[i]-yc,zg[i]-zc]
118
119     plotpyramid(xg,yg,zg)
120
121 #————————————————plot pyramids
122 xc=75 #—center coordinates
123 yc=50
124 zc=50
125
126 while True:
127     axis=input('x, y or z?: ') #——input axis of rotation (lower case)
128     if axis == 'x': #——if x axis
129         Rx=radians(float(input('Rx Degrees?: '))) #——input degrees
            of rotation
130         plotpyramidx(xc,yc,zc,Rx) #——call function plotpyramidx
131     if axis == 'y':
132         Ry=radians(float(input('Ry Degrees?: '))) #——input degrees
            of rotation
133         plotpyramidy(xc,yc,zc,Ry)
134     if axis == 'z':
135         Rz=radians(float(input('Rz Degrees?: '))) #——input degrees
            of rotation
136         plotpyramidz(xc,yc,zc,Rz)
137     if axis == ":
138         break
```

6.3 Planes

Next is an example of inter-object hidden line removal. Figure 6-9 shows two planes, (a) and (b); Figure 6-10 shows the same two planes partially overlapping. As you will see shortly, plane (b) is actually beneath the plane (a) and should be partially obscured. Figures 6-11 shows the planes with the hidden lines of plane (b) removed. Figure 6-12 shows another example. Figure 6-13 shows an example with plane (a) rotated.

In this simple model, the two planes are parallel to the x,y plane with plane (b) taken to be located behind plane (a) (i.e. further in the +z direction). You do not need to be concerned with the z component of the planes' coordinates since you won't be rotating them out of plane, (i.e. around the x or y directions), although you will be rotating plane (a) in its plane around the z direction, but for this you do not need z coordinates.

Figure 6-14 shows the model used by Listing 6-3. Plane (a) is drawn in black, plane (b) in blue. Unit vectors $\hat{\mathbf{i}}$ and $\hat{\mathbf{j}}$ are shown at corner 0 of plane (a). You use a ray tracing technique to remove the hidden lines when plane (b) or part of it is behind (a) and not visible. You do so line by line beginning with edge 0-1 of plane (b). Starting at corner 0 of plane (b), you imagine a ray emitting from that point travelling to an observer who is located in the -z direction and looking in onto the x,y plane. If plane (a) does not interfere with that ray (i.e. does not cover up that point), the dot is plotted. If plane (a) does interfere, it is not plotted. The problem thus become one of intersections: determining if a ray from a point on an edge of plane (b) intersects plane (a).

The edges of plane (b) are processed one at a time. Starting with corner 0, you proceed along edge 0-1 to corner 1 in small steps. Vector **H** shows the location of a point h on edge 0-1. Listing 6-3 determines the location of this point and whether or not it lies beneath plane (a) (i.e. if a ray emanating from h strikes plane (a)). If it does not, point p is plotted; if it does, p is not plotted.

In Listing 6-3, lines 14-18 establish the coordinates of the two planes in *global* coordinates, ready for plotting. Lines 21-32 define a function, **dlinea**, that plots the edge lines of plane (a). It does so one edge line at a time. **dlinea** does not do a hidden line check on the edges of plane (a) since you are stipulating that plane (a) lies over plane (b). The calling arguments x1,x2,y1,y2 are the beginning and end coordinates of the edge line. q in line 22 is the length of that line; uxa and uya are the x and y components of a unit vector that points along the edge line from x1,y1 to x2,y2. The loop in lines 27-32 advances the point along the line from x1,y1 to x2,y2 in steps of .2 as set in line 27. hx and hy in lines 28 and 29 are the coordinates of point h along the line. hxstart and hystart permit connecting the points by short line segments, giving a finer appearance than if the points were plotted as dots.

Lines 35-38 plot the edges of plane (a) by calling function **dlinea** with the beginning and end coordinates of each of the four edges. Lines 40-42 establish the distance qa03 from corner 0 of plane (a) to corner 3. uxa and uya in lines 43 and 44 are the x and y components of a unit vector $\hat{\mathbf{u}}$, which points from corner 0 to corner 3. Similarly, lines 46-50 give the components of $\hat{\mathbf{v}}$, a unit vector pointing from corner 0 to 1. They will be required to do the intersection check, as was done in the preceding chapter with line/plane intersections.

Function **dlineb** is similar to **dlinea** except the calling arguments now include agx[0] and agy[0], the coordinates of corner 0 of plane (a). Also, this function includes the interference check, which is between lines 64 and 71. This is labelled the inside/outside check. In line 64, a is the distance between the x coordinate of point h and the x coordinate of corner 0 of plane (a); b in line 65 is the y distance. These are essentially the x and y components of vector **H**. In line 66, the dot (scalar) product of **H** with unit vector $\hat{\mathbf{u}}$ gives up. This is the projection of **H** on the 0-3 side of plane (a). Similarly, the dot product of **H** with unit vector $\hat{\mathbf{v}}$ in line 67 gives vp, the projection of **H** on the 0-1 side of plane (a). The interference check is then straightforward and is summarized in line 68. If all questions in line 68 are true, the point is plotted in line 69 in white, which means it is invisible. If any the questions in line 68 are false, which means the point is not blocked by plane (a), line 71 plots it in black.

You may ask, why use this elaborate vector analysis? Why not just check each point's x and y coordinates as shown in Figure 6-14 against the horizontal and vertical boundaries of plane (a)? You could do that if both planes remain aligned with the x and y axes as shown. But by using the vector approach, you enable either one of the planes to be rotated about the z direction as shown in Figure 6-13.

I have simplified this model a bit by specifying that plane (b) lie under (a). In general, you may not know which plane is closer to the observer and which should be (a) and which (b). This can be accomplished by a simple check on z coordinates. In principle, the hidden line removal process would be similar to what you have done here, although the programming can get complicated trying to keep track of a large assemblage of objects.

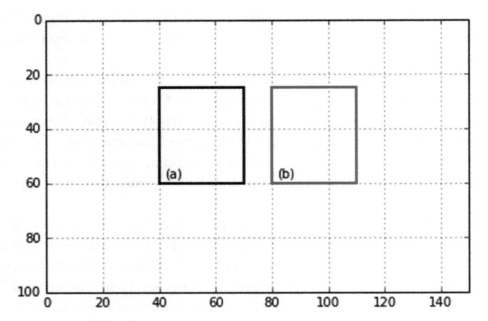

Figure 6-9. *Two planes*

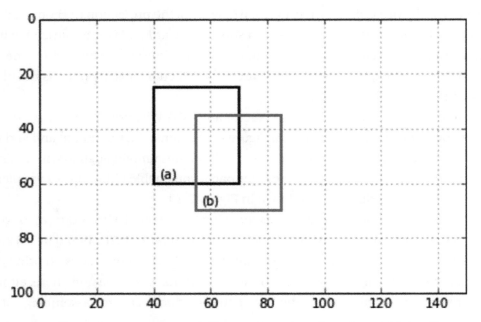

Figure 6-10. *Two planes, one partially overlapping the other, hidden lines not removed. Plane (b) is beneath (a).*

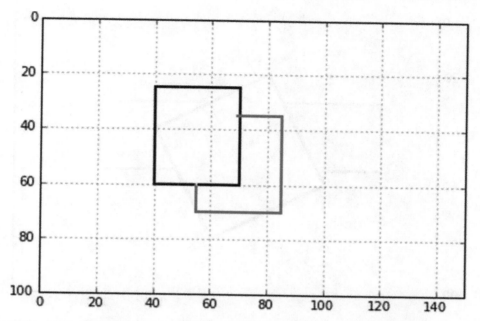

Figure 6-11. *Two planes overlapping, hidden lines removed by Listing 6-3*

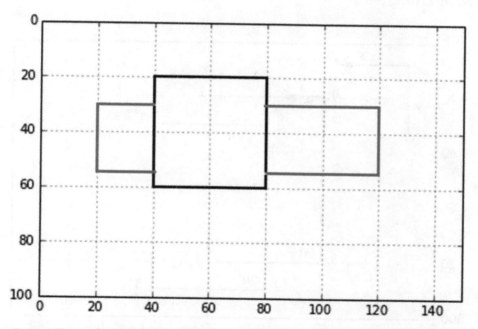

Figure 6-12. *Two planes, one overlapping the other, hidden lines removed by Listing 6-3*

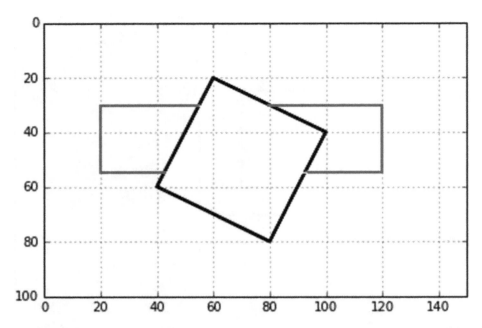

Figure 6-13. *Two planes, one at an angle and overlapping the other, hidden lines removed by Listing 6-3*

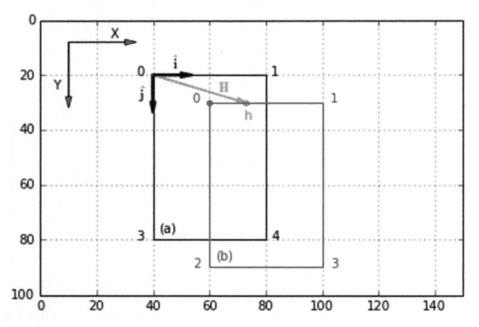

Figure 6-14. *Model for Listing 6-3*

Listing 6-3. Program HLPLANES

```
1    """
2    HLPLANES
3    """
4
5    import numpy as np
6    import matplotlib.pyplot as plt
7    from math import sqrt, sin, cos, radians
8
9    plt.axis([0,150,100,0])
10   plt.axis('off')
11   plt.grid(False)
12
13   #————————————————-define lists
14   axg=[40,80,80,40]
15   ayg=[20,20,60,60]
16
17   bxg=[20,120,120,20]
18   byg=[30,30,55,55]
19
20   #=================================================define function dlinea
21   def dlinea(x1,x2,y1,y2):
22       q=sqrt((x2-x1)**2+(y2-y1)**2)
23       uxa=(x2-x1)/q
24       uya=(y2-y1)/q
25       hxstart=x1
26       hystart=y1
27       for l in np.arange(0,q,.2):
28           hx=x1+l*uxa #————global hit coordinates along the line
29           hy=y1+l*uya
30           plt.plot([hxstart,hx],[hystart,hy],color='k')
31           hxstart=hx
32           hystart=hy
33
```

```
34   #——————————————plane (a)
35   dlinea(axg[0],axg[1],ayg[0],ayg[1]) #——plot plane (a)
36   dlinea(axg[1],axg[2],ayg[1],ayg[2])
37   dlinea(axg[2],axg[3],ayg[2],ayg[3])
38   dlinea(axg[3],axg[0],ayg[3],ayg[0])
39
40   a=axg[3]-axg[0] #——unit vector u plane (a)
41   b=ayg[3]-ayg[0]
42   qa03=sqrt(a*a+b*b)
43   uxa=a/qa03
44   uya=b/qa03
45
46   a=axg[1]-axg[0] #——unit vector v plane (a)
47   b=ayg[1]-ayg[0]
48   qa01=sqrt(a*a+b*b)
49   vxa=a/qa01
50   vya=b/qa01
51
52   #=============================================================lineb( )
53   def dlineb(x1,x2,y1,y2,ax0,ay0):
54       a=x2-x1 #——unit vector line
55       b=y2-y1
56       ql=sqrt(a*a+b*b)
57       uxl=a/ql
58       uyl=b/ql
59       hxglast=x1
60       hyglast=y1
61       for l in np.arange(0,ql,.5):
62           hxg=x1+l*uxl
63           hyg=y1+l*uyl
64           a=hxg-ax0 #——inside/outside check
65           b=hyg-ay0
66           up=a*uxa+b*uya
67           vp=a*vxa+b*vya
```

```
68          if 0<up<qa03 and 0<vp<qa01: #——is it inside (a)?
79              plt.plot([hxglast,hxg],[hyglast,hyg],color='white')
70          else:
71              plt.plot([hxglast,hxg],[hyglast,hyg],color='k')
72      hxglast=hxg
73      hyglast=hyg
74                      '
75  #———————————————plot plane (b)
76  dlineb(bxg[0],bxg[1],byg[0],byg[1],axg[0],ayg[0])
77  dlineb(bxg[1],bxg[2],byg[1],byg[2],axg[0],ayg[0])
78  dlineb(bxg[2],bxg[3],byg[2],byg[3],axg[0],ayg[0])
79  dlineb(bxg[3],bxg[0],byg[3],byg[0],axg[0],ayg[0])
80
81  plt.show()
```

6.4 Sphere

In Chapter 5, you drew a sphere but did not rotate it. The lines on the back side were overlapped by those on the front and thus weren't visible, so removing hidden lines was not an issue. In this chapter, you will draw a sphere and rotate it while removing hidden lines on the back side.

Figures 6-15 and 6-18 show examples of the output from Listing 6-4, which plots a sphere with hidden lines removed. The vertical lines in Figures 6-15 and 6-16, the *longitudes*, are drawn in green; the horizontal *latitudes* are drawn in blue. The program uses a hidden line removal scheme much like the one you used before with boxes and pyramids. If the z component of a vector perpendicular to a point is positive (i.e. pointing away from an observer who is located in the -z direction), the point is not drawn; otherwise it is drawn.

In Listing 6-4, line 14 sets the length of the list g[] to 3. This will be used to return global coordinates xg,yg, and zg from the rotation functions **rotx**, **roty**, and **rotz**, which are defined in lines 24-40 (they are the same as the functions used in previous programs). The longitudes are plotted in lines 55-79. The model is the same as used in Listing 5-5 in Chapter 5. The algorithm between lines 55 and 79 calculates the location of each point on a longitude, one at a time, and rotates it. That is, each point is established and rotated separately; lists are not used other than the g[ ] list. The alpha loop starting in line 55 sweeps the longitudes from $\alpha = 0$ to $\alpha = 360$ in six-degree steps as set in lines 47-49. At each α step a longitude is drawn by the ϕ loop, which starts at -90 degrees and goes to +90 in six-degree steps. The geometry in lines 57-59 is taken from Listing 5-5. The coordinates of a point before rotation (Rx=0, Ry=0, Rz=0) are xp,yp,zp as shown in lines 57-59. This point is located on the sphere's surface at spherical coordinates α, ϕ. Line 60 rotates the point about the x direction by an angle Rx. This produces new coordinates xp,yp,zp in lines 61-63. Line 64 rotates the point at these new coordinates around the y direction. Line 68 rotates it around the z direction. This produces the final location of the point.

Next, you must determine whether or not the point is on the back side of the sphere and hidden from view. If true, it is not plotted. Lines 73-79 perform this function. First, in lines 73-75, you establish the starting coordinates of the line that will connect the first point to the second. You use lines to connect the points rather than dots since lines give a finer appearance. Line 73 asks if phi equals phi1, the starting angle in the phi loop. If it does, the starting coordinates xpglast and ypglast are set equal to the first coordinates calculated by the loop. Next, in line 76, you ask if nz, the z component of a vector from the sphere's center to the point, is less than 0. nz is calculated in line 72. If true, you know the point is visible to an observer situated in the -z direction; the point is then connected to the previous one by line 77.

The **plt.plot()** function in line 77 needs two sets of coordinates: xpglast,ypglast and xpg,ypg. During the first cycle through the loop, the starting coordinates xpglast,ypglast are set equal to xpg,ypg, meaning the first point is connected to itself so the first line plotted will have zero length. After that, the coordinates of the previous point are set in lines 78-79. Line 73 determines if it is the first point. If nz is greater than zero in line 76, the point is on the back side of the rotated sphere and is not visible so it is not plotted. The coordinates xpglast and ypglast must still be updated and this is done in lines 78-79. The latitudes are processed in much the same way, although the geometry is different, as described in Listing 5-5. The colors of the longitudes and latitudes can be changed by changing the **color='color'** values in lines 77 and 104.

When running this program, remember that the rotations are not additive as in some of the previous programs. The angles of rotation specified in lines 51-53 are the angles the sphere will end up at; they are not added to any previous rotations. To rotate the sphere to another orientation, change the values in lines 51-53.

As mentioned in the discussion on concatenation, the sequence of rotations is important. Rx followed by Ry does not give the same results as Ry followed by Rx. This program has the sequence of function calls, Rx,Ry,Rz, as specified in lines 60, 64, and 68 for longitudes and 87, 91, and 95 for latitudes. To change the order of rotation, change the order of these function calls.

The spheres shown in Figures 6-17 and 6-18 have a black background. To achieve this, insert the following lines in Listing 6-4 before any other plotting commands, for example after line 12:

```
#————————————paint the background
for y in np.arange(1,100,1):
    plt.plot([0,150],[y,y],linewidth=4,color='k')
```

This plots black lines across the plotting window from x=0 to x=150 and down from y=1 to y=100. This fills the area with a black background. The color can be changed to anything desired. The **linewidth** has been set to 4 in order to prevent gaps from appearing between the horizontal lines. The background must be painted before constructing the sphere since you are using line segments to do that. New lines overplot old ones, so with this order the sphere line segments will overplot the background lines; otherwise the background lines would overplot the sphere.

In Figures 6-15 and 6-16, the sphere's line widths in program lines 77 and 104 is set to .5. This gives good results on a clear background but the lines are too subdued when the background is changed to black. So, along with inserting the two lines of code above, the line widths in Listing 6-4 should be changed to something greater such as 1.0. The color shown in Figures 6-17 and 6-18 is **'lightgreen'**. Some colors don't plot well against a black background but **color='lightgreen'** seems to work; you just have to experiment.

Listing 6-4. Program HLSPHERE

```
1    """
2    HLSPHERE
3    """
4
5    import numpy as np
6    import matplotlib.pyplot as plt
7    from math import sin, cos, radians, sqrt
8
9    plt.axis([0,150,100,0])
10   plt.axis('off')
```

```
11  plt.grid(False)
12
13  #————————————————lists
14  g=[0]*3
15
16  #————————————————parameters
17  xc=80 #——sphere center
18  yc=50
19  zc=0
20
21  rs=40 #——sphere radius
22
23  #==========================================================
24  def rotx(xc,yc,zc,xp,yp,zp,Rx):
25      g[0]=xp+xc
26      g[1]=yp*cos(Rx)-zp*sin(Rx)+yc
27      g[2]=yp*sin(Rx)+zp*cos(Rx)+zc
28      return[g]
29
30  def roty(xc,yc,zc,xp,yp,zp,Ry):
31      g[0]=xp*cos(Ry)+zp*sin(Ry)+xc
32      g[1]=yp+yc
33      g[2]=-xp*sin(Ry)+zp*cos(Ry)+zc
34      return[g]
35
36  def rotz(xc,yc,zc,xp,yp,zp,Rz):
37      g[0]=xp*cos(Rz)-yp*sin(Rz)+xc
38      g[1]=xp*sin(Rz)+yp*cos(Rz)+yc
39      g[2]=zp+zc
40      return[g]
41
42  #————————————longitudes and latitudes
43  phi1=radians(-90)
44  phi2=radians(90)
45  dphi=radians(6)
```

```
46
47  alpha1=radians(0)
48  alpha2=radians(360)
49  dalpha=radians(6)
50
51  Rx=radians(45)
52  Ry=radians(-20)
53  Rz=radians(40)
54
55  for alpha in np.arange(alpha1,alpha2,dalpha):  #──longitudes
56      for phi in np.arange(phi1,phi2,dphi):
57              xp=rs*cos(phi)*cos(alpha)
58              yp=rs*sin(phi)
59              zp=-rs*cos(phi)*sin(alpha)
60              rotx(xc,yc,zc,xp,yp,zp,Rx)
61              xp=g[0]-xc
62              yp=g[1]-yc
63              zp=g[2]-zc
64              roty(xc,yc,zc,xp,yp,zp,Ry)
65              xp=g[0]-xc
66              yp=g[1]-yc
67              zp=g[2]-zc
68              rotz(xc,yc,zc,xp,yp,zp,Rz)
69              xpg=g[0]
70              ypg=g[1]
71              zpg=g[2]
72              nz=zpg-zc
73              if phi == phi1:
74                  xpglast=xpg
75                  ypglast=ypg
76              if nz < 0:
77                  plt.plot([xpglast,xpg],[ypglast,ypg],linewidth=.5,
                        color='g')
78              xpglast=xpg
79              ypglast=ypg
```

```
80
81  for phi in np.arange(phi1,phi2,dphi):  #————latitudes
82      r=rs*cos(phi)
83      for alpha in np.arange(alpha1,alpha2+dalpha,dalpha):
84          xp=r*cos(alpha)
85          yp=rs*sin(phi)
86          zp=-rs*cos(phi)*sin(alpha)
87          rotx(xc,yc,zc,xp,yp,zp,Rx)
88          xp=g[0]-xc
89          yp=g[1]-yc
90          zp=g[2]-zc
91          roty(xc,yc,zc,xp,yp,zp,Ry)
92          xp=g[0]-xc
93          yp=g[1]-yc
94          zp=g[2]-zc
95          rotz(xc,yc,zc,xp,yp,zp,Rz)
96          xpg=g[0]
97          ypg=g[1]
98          zpg=g[2]
99          nz=zpg-zc
100         if alpha == alpha1:
101             xpglast=xpg
102             ypglast=ypg
103         if nz < 0:
104             plt.plot([xpglast,xpg],[ypglast,ypg],linewidth=.5,
                    color='b')
105         xpglast=xpg
106         ypglast=ypg
107
108 plt.show()
```

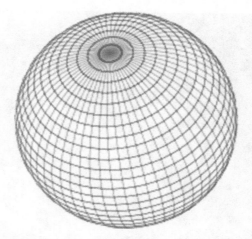

Figure 6-15. *Rotated sphere with hidden lines removed: Rx=55°, Ry=-20°, Rz=-40° (produced by Listing 6-4)*

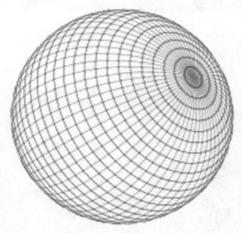

Figure 6-16. *Rotated sphere with hidden lines removed: Rx=40°, Ry=-20°, Rz=40° (produced by Listing 6-4)*

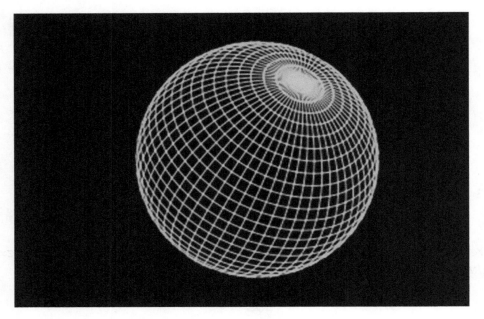

Figure 6-17. *Rotated sphere with hidden lines removed: Rx=40°, Ry=-20°, Rz=40°, black background (produced by Listing 6-4)*

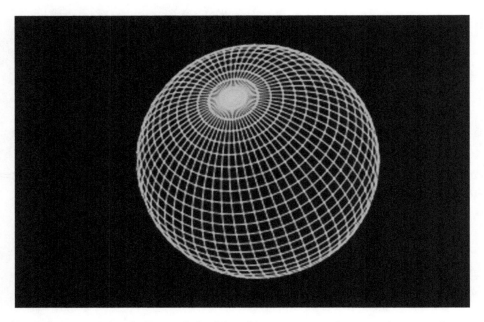

Figure 6-18. *Rotated sphere with hidden lines removed: Rx=60°, Ry=20°, Rz=10°, black background (produced by Listing 6-4)*

6.5 Summary

You learned how to remove hidden lines from single objects and between objects. In the case of single objects, such as the box, the pyramid, and the sphere, you were able to construct algorithms without much trouble. When removing hidden lines from separate objects, such as two planes, you relied on the technique of constructing one of the objects from dots or short line segments that go from one dot to another. In either case, you were still dealing with dots. From a dot on one plane, you drew an imaginary line, a ray, to an observer in the -z direction. Then you checked to see if the ray intersected the other plane. You used the line-plane intersection algorithm developed in Chapter 5. If it did intersect, the dot was hidden and it, or a line segment connected to it, was not drawn. You used two planes to explore this technique. You could have used any of the other shapes you worked with in Chapter 5. For example, you could have easily removed hidden lines from a plane beneath a circular segment by constructing the plane from dots and using the intersection algorithm from Chapter 5. However, you might not know ahead of time which object covers which. You could do a rough check to answer this question. For example, in the case of two planes, if the z coordinates of all four corners of one plane are less than the other, it is closer to the observer, in which case it may cover part of the other plane. In this case, the other plane should be checked for hidden lines.

CHAPTER 7

Shading

In this chapter, you'll learn how to shade three-dimensional objects. Shading produces a much more realistic look and enhances the perception of three-dimensionality. The general idea is to first establish the direction of light rays impacting the object being illuminated and then determine the shading effect the light has on the object's surface. In the case of a box, which I will discuss next, six flat planes comprise the box's surface. The orientation of these planes relative to the direction of the light will determine the degree of shading on each plane. To simulate shading, the planes can be filled with dots or lines. Different intensities of shading can be obtained by changing the intensity of the color of the dots or lines and by color mixing.

Normally an object being plotted will appear on a white background. If a background color is used, such as in Figure 7-13, dots or lines may be used to paint the background. Recall from Chapter 1 that new dots overplot old dots and lines always overplot dots and old lines. This means that whether the object being shaded is constructed of dots or lines, they will overplot the background color if it is painted with dots. The disadvantage of using dots is it takes a lot of time to fill the background with dots. Lines are a better alternative in this regard and are preferred if the object can be constructed of lines. If you must use dots in your object, then you must use dots for your background color.

The heart of a shading program is the intensity function, which relates the shading intensity to the orientation of a plane relative to the incoming light direction. You do not specify the position of a light source; you define the direction of the light rays impacting the object from that source. For example, suppose the program calculates that the angle between a plane and the incoming light rays is 50 degrees. The intensity function converts this angle into a shading intensity, which is used to alter the color intensity of the lines or dots.

A considerable amount of research has been carried out on theories of shading in an effort to produce more lifelike computer-drawn images. These images often have a separate shading function for each primary color and take into account the reflectivity and physical characteristics of the surface material. Smooth surfaces will be highly

© B.J. Korites 2018
B.J. Korites, *Python Graphics*, https://doi.org/10.1007/978-1-4842-3378-8_7

reflective while rough, textured surfaces will scatter the incoming light, producing a higher degree of diffusivity. In your work here, you will keep it simple and use just one shading function and ignore the differences in surface features that can affect the surface's reflectivity and diffusivity, although they could easily be introduced into the program. Also, you assume the shading of a surface is dependent on only the orientation of that surface relative to the light source and not on its orientation relative to the observer who, as usual, you take to be located in the -z direction.

7.1 Shading a Box

Figures 7-1 through 7-7 show samples of output from Listing 7-1. They show a box rotated to different orientations with shading on its surfaces. They are shaded in monochrome black at different intensities ranging from black to white.

Figure 7-1. *Shaded box produced by Listing 7-1, Io=.8*

Figure 7-2. *Shaded box produced by Listing 7-1, Io=1.0*

Figure 7-3. *Shaded box produced by Listing 7-1, Io=1.0*

Figure 7-4. *Shaded box produced by Listing 7-1, Io=1.0*

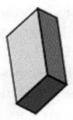

Figure 7-5. *Shaded box produced by Listing 7-1, Io=.8*

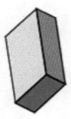

Figure 7-6. *Shaded box produced by Listing 7-1, Io=.6*

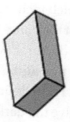

Figure 7-7. *Shaded box produced by Listing 7-1, Io=.4*

Figure 7-9 shows the model used by Listing 7-1. The light source is shown at the upper left. You do not explicitly state its location, only the direction of the light rays emanating from it. You do that by specifying lx,ly, and lz, the components of a unit vector $\hat{\mathbf{l}}$, which is aligned with the light rays. Keep in mind that $\hat{\mathbf{l}}$ is a unit vector so the following relation between its components must be observed:

$$\sqrt{lx^2 + ly^2 + lz^2} = 1$$

(7-1)

237

Looking at the top plane of the box defined by corners 0,1,2,3, you can see a unit normal vector $\hat{\mathbf{n}}$ at corner 0. This points outward from the plane. You shade the box by drawing lines, shown in blue, which extend across the width of the plane from B to E. These lines are drawn from edge 0,1 to 3,2 and then down the plane, thus shading it. The lines on each face will have an intensity that depends on the orientation of $\hat{\mathbf{n}}$ with $\hat{\mathbf{l}}$. You get this orientation by taking the dot product of $\hat{\mathbf{n}}$ with $\hat{\mathbf{l}}$. If $\hat{\mathbf{n}}$ is facing $\hat{\mathbf{l}}$, the dot product will be negative and the intensity of the lines will be less, which means the tone will be lighter; if $\hat{\mathbf{n}}$ is facing away from $\hat{\mathbf{l}}$, the dot product will be positive, the intensity will be greater, and the tone will be darker.

This is illustrated by Figure 7-10, which shows the shading intensity, I, vs. $\hat{\mathbf{n}} \cdot \mathbf{l}$. This is a linear relation. As you will see in the next section, better results can be obtained with a non-linear relation and by mixing (r,g,b) colors. You can get an equation for this linear intensity function by inspection:

$$I = \frac{Io}{2} + \frac{Io}{2}\hat{\mathbf{n}} \cdot \hat{\mathbf{l}} \tag{7-2}$$

$$\boxed{I = \frac{Io}{2}\left(1 = \hat{\mathbf{n}} \cdot \hat{\mathbf{l}}\right)} \tag{7-3}$$

Note the parameter Io. It gives control over the degree of darkness in the shaded areas by increasing or decreasing the intensity of the color. The lines from B to E are plotted with the **plt.plot()** function, which includes the attribute **alpha**. By letting **alpha**=I you can control the intensity of the color. Higher values of **alpha** increase the intensity, making shaded areas appear darker; lower values of **alpha** decrease it, thus creating areas that appear lighter. Note that **alpha** may take on values from 0 to 1, hence I is limited to the same range of values. From Equation 7-3, this means that Io can have a maximum value of 1. Io=1 will give the darkest, most intense hues. To soften the image with more subtle hues, lower Io to something less than 1. To modify the function even more, the left side could be raised, which would darken the lights. If the function were horizontal, all shading would be uniform. To see the effect of Io on the shading, Figures 7-2 through 7-4 have Io=1.0. Figures 7-1, 7-5, 7-6, and 7-7 have Io=.8, .8, .6, and .4, respectively. Colors do not have to be black or primaries; they can be mixed. Figure 7-8 shows the result of using color=(r,g,b) with r=.5, g=0, b=.5,

$$color = (.5,,0,,.5) \tag{7-4}$$

which is a purple mix of equal amount of red and blue. Recall that red, green, and blue in an (r,g,b) mix must each have values between 0 and 1.

You have been applying your shading intensity, I, to monochrome colors. Even if you use r,g,b color mixing, it is still a monochrome shade, although not a primary color. An extension of this method would be to apply separate intensities to each of the three primary colors. For example, when an artist paints a portrait, he/she might render the light side of the face a light pink. To darken the shaded side, he/she would normally add green, the compliment of red, to the mix. If you look closely at the portraits of an accomplished artist, you will see this is usually how it is done. Rarely would one add black to the mix to darken it. In fact, many painters do not even keep a black pigment on their pallet; they achieve darker colors by mixing the hues with their compliment. The compliment of red is green; of yellow it is violet. Color mixing in painting isn't quite that simple, of course, but that is the fundamental idea. To accomplish this in your programming, suppose you are shading a red box using an (r,g,b) color mix. Rather than applying an intensity factor to the red to increase its intensity, thus simulating a darkening, you apply the intensity factor to the green, increasing its contribution in the r,g,b mix, thus darkening the red. For the present, in Listing 7-1 you will keep thing simple and simulate shading by increasing the intensity of the color in the dark areas rather than using color mixing. This works well with a monochrome black image, although it has limitations with colored objects.

The definition of the box in Listing 7-1 is contained in the lists in lines 10, 11, and 12. Lines 14, 15, and 16 open lists for the global coordinates, which are returned by the rotation functions **rotx**, **roty**, and **rotz**. They have the same lengths as the x,y,z lists as specified by **len(x)**.

A new function called **shade()** is defined in Listing 7-1, lines 54-84. The arguments received by **shade()** in line 54 are shown in Figure 7-11. When **shade()** is invoked for a specific plane, the box's corners must follow the order shown in Figure 7-11. As an example, the ordering for plane 1,5,6,2 is shown in Figure 7-12. Some visual gymnastics can be required to orient the six planes of the box such that they conform to the ordering in Figure 7-11. Each of the six planes are drawn and shaded separately by six calls to function **shade()**. They are listed in lines 88-93. The arguments of the calls are the x,y,z coordinates of points a,b,c,d, respectively. Function **shade()** calculates the components of unit vector $\hat{\mathbf{u}}$ in lines 55-61 and $\hat{\mathbf{v}}$ in lines 62-68. Components of unit vector $\hat{\mathbf{n}}$ are calculated in lines 69-71. The dot product on $\hat{\mathbf{n}}$ with the incoming light ray unit vector $\hat{\mathbf{l}}$, the components of which were specified in lines 23-25, is calculated in line 72 as ndotl; the shading intensity in line 73. If nz<=0 (i.e. $\hat{n}$ is pointing toward the observer who is in the -z direction), the edges of the face are plotted in lines 75-78 and the face is shaded in loop 79-84. Line 79 ranges h, shown in Figure 7-11, from 0 to qad, the distance from corner a to d, which was calculated in line 58, in steps of 1. Lines 80-81 calculate the x and y coordinates of the beginning of the line; lines 82 and 83 get the coordinates of the end of the line. Line 84 plots the line. In line 84, **alpha** is equal to the intensity of the shading that was determined in line 73. The box's color is equal to **clr**, which was specified in line 27; for example, **color='k'** will give a black box. An alternative would be to mix primary colors as shown in line 28. This produces the purple box shown in Figure 7-8. To get this color, just remove the # in line 28; otherwise, the shading will be done in black. I will discuss color mixing in more detail in the next section. The maximum intensity Io is specified in line 29. This can be anything between 0 and 1. If nz>0 (i.e. $\hat{n}$ is pointing away from the observer), the face is not plotted. The remainder of Listing 7-1 should be familiar.

Figure 7-8. *Shaded box produced by Listing 7-1, (r,g,b)=(.5,0.,5) color mixing, Io=1.0*

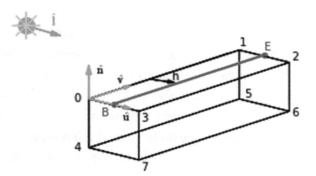

Figure 7-9. *Shading model used by Listing 7-1*

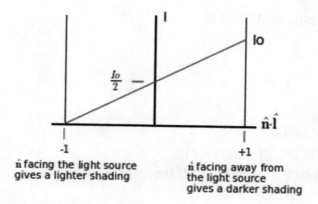

Figure 7-10. *Shading function*

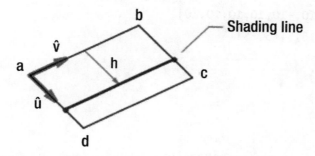

Figure 7-11. *Model of a generic plane used in Listing 7-1*

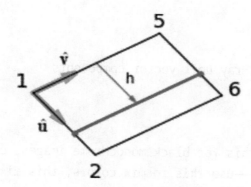

Figure 7-12. *Plane 1,5,6,2*

Listing 7-1. Program SHADEBOX

```
1    """
2    SHADEBOX
3    """
4
5    import numpy as np
6    import matplotlib.pyplot as plt
7    from math import sin, cos, radians, sqrt
8
9    #————————————————lists
10   x=[-20,20,20,-20,-20,20,20,-20]
11   y=[-10,-10,-10,-10,10,10,10,10]
12   z=[5,5,-5,-5,5,5,-5,-5]
13
14   xg=[0]*len(x)
15   yg=[0]*len(x)
16   zg=[0]*len(x)
17
18   #————————————————parameters
19   xc=75 #————center coordinates
20   yc=50
21   zc=50
22
23   lx=.707 #————light ray unit vector components
24   ly=.707
25   lz=0
26
27   clr='k' #————use this for black monochrome images, or use another color
28   #clr=(.5,0,.5) #————use this to mix colors, this mix produces purple
29   Io=.8 #————max intensity, must be 0 < 1
30
31   #=====================================================define rotation
     functions
32   def rotx(xc,yc,zc,xp,yp,zp,Rx):
33       xpp=xp
```

```
34        ypp=yp*cos(Rx)-zp*sin(Rx)
35        zpp=yp*sin(Rx)+zp*cos(Rx)
36        [xg,yg,zg]=[xpp+xc,ypp+yc,zpp+zc]
37        return[xg,yg,zg]
38
39   def roty(xc,yc,zc,xp,yp,zp,Ry):
40        xpp=xp*cos(Ry)+zp*sin(Ry)
41        ypp=yp
42        zpp=-xp*sin(Ry)+zp*cos(Ry)
43        [xg,yg,zg]=[xpp+xc,ypp+yc,zpp+zc]
44        return[xg,yg,zg]
45
46   def rotz(xc,yc,zc,xp,yp,zp,Rz):
47        xpp=xp*cos(Rz)-yp*sin(Rz)
48        ypp=xp*sin(Rz)+yp*cos(Rz)
49        zpp=zp
50        [xg,yg,zg]=[xpp+xc,ypp+yc,zpp+zc]
51        return[xg,yg,zg]
52
53   #================================================================shading
54   def shade(ax,ay,az,bx,by,bz,cx,cy,cz,dx,dy,dz):
55        a=dx-ax
56        b=dy-ay
57        c=dz-az
58        qad=sqrt(a*a+b*b+c*c)
59        ux=a/qad
60        uy=b/qad
61        uz=c/qad
62        a=bx-ax
63        b=by-ay
64        c=bz-az
65        qab=sqrt(a*a+b*b+c*c)
66        vx=a/qab
67        vy=b/qab
68        vz=c/qab
69        nx=uy*vz-uz*vy
```

```
70          ny=uz*vx-ux*vz
71          nz=ux*vy-uy*vx
72          ndotl=nx*lx+ny*ly+nz*lz
73          I=.5*Io*(1+ndotl)
74          if nz<=0:
75              plt.plot([ax,bx],[ay,by],color='k',linewidth=1)
76              plt.plot([bx,cx],[by,cy],color='k',linewidth=1)
77              plt.plot([cx,dx],[cy,dy],color='k',linewidth=1)
78              plt.plot([dx,ax],[dy,ay],color='k',linewidth=1)
79              for h in np.arange(0,qad,1):
80                  xls=ax+h*ux
81                  yls=ay+h*uy
82                  xle=bx+h*ux
83                  yle=by+h*uy
84                  plt.plot([xls,xle],[yls,yle],linewidth=2,alpha=I,
                        color=clr)
85
86  #================================================================
87  def plotbox(xg,yg,zg):
88      shade(xg[0],yg[0],zg[0],xg[1],yg[1],zg[1],xg[2],yg[2],zg[2],xg[3],
            yg[3],zg[3])
89      shade(xg[7],yg[7],zg[7],xg[6],yg[6],zg[6],xg[5],yg[5],zg[5],xg[4],
            yg[4],zg[4])
90      shade(xg[0],yg[0],zg[0],xg[3],yg[3],zg[3],xg[7],yg[7],zg[7],xg[4],
            yg[4],zg[4])
91      shade(xg[1],yg[1],zg[1],xg[5],yg[5],zg[5],xg[6],yg[6],zg[6],xg[2],
            yg[2],zg[2])
92      shade(xg[3],yg[3],zg[3],xg[2],yg[2],zg[2],xg[6],yg[6],zg[6],xg[7],
            yg[7],zg[7])
93      shade(xg[4],yg[4],zg[4],xg[5],yg[5],zg[5],xg[1],yg[1],zg[1],xg[0],
            yg[0],zg[0])
94
95      plt.axis([0,150,100,0]) #——plot axes and grid
96      plt.axis('off')
97      plt.grid(False)
98      plt.show() #——plot latest rotation
```

```
99
100 #===============================================================
101 def plotboxx(xc,yc,zc,Rx): #————transform and plot Rx
102     for i in range(len(x)):
103         [xg[i],yg[i],zg[i]]=rotx(xc,yc,zc,x[i],y[i],z[i],Rx)
104         [x[i],y[i],z[i]]=[xg[i]-xc,yg[i]-yc,zg[i]-zc]
105
106         plotbox(xg,yg,zg) #————plot
107
108 def plotboxy(xc,yc,zc,Ry):
109     for i in range(len(x)): #————transform and plot Ry
110         [xg[i],yg[i],zg[i]]=roty(xc,yc,zc,x[i],y[i],z[i],Ry)
111         [x[i],y[i],z[i]]=[xg[i]-xc,yg[i]-yc,zg[i]-zc]
112
113         plotbox(xg,yg,zg)
114
115 def plotboxz(xc,yc,zc,Rz):
116     for i in range(len(x)): #————transform and plot Rz
117         [xg[i],yg[i],zg[i]]=rotz(xc,yc,zc,x[i],y[i],z[i],Rz)
118         [x[i],y[i],z[i]]=[xg[i]-xc,yg[i]-yc,zg[i]-zc]
119
120         plotbox(xg,yg,zg)
121
122 #——————————————————————-input
123 while True:
124     axis=input('x, y or z?: ') #——input axis of rotation (lower case)
125     if axis == 'x': #-if x axis
126         Rx=radians(float(input('Rx Degrees?: '))) #——input degrees
127         plotboxx(xc,yc,zc,Rx) #——call function plotboxx
128     if axis == 'y':
129         Ry=radians(float(input('Ry Degrees?: '))) #——input degrees
130         plotboxy(xc,yc,zc,Ry)
131     if axis == 'z':
```

```
132          Rz=radians(float(input('Rz Degrees?: '))) #——input degrees
133          plotboxz(xc,yc,zc,Rz)
134     if axis == '':
135          break
```

7.2 Shading a Sphere

In the previous section, you shaded a box using a simple linear relation for the shading function where the intensity of the shading, I, was linearly related to the dot product $\hat{\mathbf{n}} \cdot \hat{\mathbf{l}}$. In this section, you will be mixing the three primary colors and controlling the intensity of each with a non-linear shading function. Results are shown in Figure 7-13, which was produced by Listing 7-2.

Figure 7-13. *Shading a sphere by color mixing with a non-linear intensity function (produced by Listing 7-2)*

Nonlinear shading functions are shown as the red, green, and blue curves in Figure 7-14; the linear one is in black. The non-linear functions give more control over the shading and can produce more realistic effects. They allow you to control the shading by amplifying and extending the lighter shaded areas while more rapidly increasing the transition of intensity into the darker areas. The linear shading function is similar to the one used in Listing 7-1, except that it now starts at I=IA where IA may be greater than zero. The curves begin at I=IA and terminate at I=IB where $\hat{\mathbf{n}} \cdot \hat{\mathbf{l}}$ =+1. IA and IB are parameters that can be adjusted in Listing 7-2. IA>0 will darken the lights. This is sometimes necessary since the tones, when I=0 or close to it, may not transition well to higher regions of I; discontinuities can sometimes be observed. To correct this, start the intensity function at some small value of IA greater than 0. Increasing IA can also be a technique for reducing the brightness of light areas.

Note the difference between $\hat{\mathbf{n}} \cdot \hat{\mathbf{l}}p$ and $\hat{\mathbf{n}} \cdot \hat{\mathbf{l}}$ in Figure 7-14. To get a relation for I vs. $\hat{\mathbf{n}} \cdot \hat{\mathbf{l}}$, you let the function be of the form

$$I = C_1 + C_2 \left(\hat{\mathbf{n}} \cdot \hat{\mathbf{l}}p \right)^n \qquad (7\text{-}5)$$

where C_1 and C_2 are constants and n is a parameter. n can be changed in the program. Noting that I=IA at $\hat{\mathbf{n}} \cdot \hat{\mathbf{l}}p = 0$,

$$IA = C_1 + C_2 (0)^n \qquad (7\text{-}6)$$

$$C_1 = Ia \qquad (7\text{-}7)$$

At $\hat{\mathbf{n}} \cdot \hat{\mathbf{l}}p$ = +2, ($\hat{\mathbf{n}} \cdot \hat{\mathbf{l}}$ = +1), I=IB,

$$IB = IA + C_2 (2)^n \qquad (7\text{-}8)$$

$$C_2 = \frac{IB - IA}{2^n} \qquad (7\text{-}9)$$

With $\hat{\mathbf{n}} \cdot \hat{\mathbf{l}}p = \hat{\mathbf{n}} \cdot \hat{\mathbf{l}} + \mathbf{1}$,

$$I = IA + (IB - IA) \left(\frac{\hat{\mathbf{n}} \cdot \hat{\mathbf{l}} + 1}{2} \right)^n \qquad (7\text{-}10)$$

Equation 7-10 is your intensity function, $I\left(\hat{\mathbf{n}} \cdot \hat{\mathbf{l}} \right)$. You thus have three parameters with which to adjust I: IA, which regulates the intensity of the lightest areas; IB, which adjusts the darkest areas; and n, which adjusts the transition from light to dark. Higher values of n will produce a more rapid transition. Figure 7-14 shows curves for n=1, 2, 3, and 4. When n=1, the curve becomes linear. There are no definite values for n, IA, and IB; they should be adjusted by trial and error to give visually appealing results.

Regarding colors, the background shown in Figure 7-13 is **'midnightblue'**. A good source for color samples is #https://matplotlib.org/examples/color/named_colors.html.

Listing 7-2 creates a sphere by plotting longitudes and latitudes as you did in Listing 6-4. In Listing 6-4, these were spaced six degrees apart. To carry out the shading in Listing 7-2, you will space the longitudes and latitudes closer together, two degrees apart, and adjust their plotting intensity depending on the angle between a local unit vector normal to the surface $\hat{\mathbf{n}}$ and the light source unit vector $\hat{\mathbf{l}}$ at each point on the surface. This will then be used to control the relative r,g,b contributions to the color mix. As before, you establish this relation by taking the dot product $\hat{\mathbf{n}} \cdot \hat{\mathbf{l}}$. $\hat{\mathbf{n}}$ at each point is determined quite simply by obtaining a vector from the sphere's center to the point in question on the sphere's surface and then dividing by the sphere's radius, rs. For example, suppose you are at a point p on the sphere's surface with coordinates xp,yp,zp. A vector **Vp** from the sphere's center at xc,yc,zc to p is

$$\mathbf{Vp} = (xp - xc)\hat{\mathbf{i}} + (yp - yc)\hat{\mathbf{j}} + (zp - zc)\hat{\mathbf{k}} \qquad (7\text{-}11)$$

Vp is normal to the surface at p. A unit normal vector, $\hat{\mathbf{n}}$, is then

$$\hat{\mathbf{n}} = \left(\frac{xp - xc}{rs}\right)\hat{\mathbf{i}} + \left(\frac{yp - yc}{rs}\right)\hat{\mathbf{j}} + \left(\frac{zp - zc}{rs}\right)\hat{\mathbf{k}} \qquad (7\text{-}12)$$

where rs is the sphere's radius. Taking the dot product of $\hat{\mathbf{n}}$ in Equation 7-12 with the incoming light unit vector $\hat{\mathbf{l}}$ gives $\hat{\mathbf{n}} \cdot \hat{\mathbf{l}}$, which you need to determine I from Equation 7-10.

In Listing 7-2, lines 22-24 set the components of the incoming light's unit vector. Lines 26-28 set the intensity function parameters. These values produce Figure 7-13. Lines 37-39 paint the background with dots. Lines 61-101 plot the longitudes. Note in lines 69 and 70 that **dalpha** and **dphi** have been added to **alpha2** and **phi2** since roundoff errors in the **np.arange()** function can sometimes fail to close the sphere; this assures it closes. Lines 86-92 determine the components of the $\hat{\mathbf{n}}$ at the current values of **alpha** and **phi**. Line 93 calculates the dot product $\hat{\mathbf{n}} \cdot \hat{\mathbf{l}}$; line 94 calculates the intensity.

In line 99, the attribute **linewidth** has been increased to 4. When combined with the angular spacing of two degrees in lines 63 and 67, this insures there are no gaps in the surface. Also in line 99 the color statement shows red at 100 percent, green at 80 percent, and blue at 40. The (I-1) factor reflects the impact of the shading function. Recall that when the color mix is (0,0,0), black is produced; conversely, when the mix is

(1,1,1), white is produced. Since you want darks where I is close to or equal to 1 (facing away from the light source), the (I-1) factor accomplishes this since it equals 0 when I=1 producing black. If you did not include the (I-1) factor, the mix (1,.8,.45) would simply produce an unshaded round rusty orange disc.

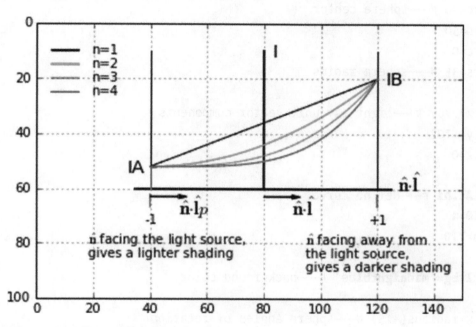

Figure 7-14. *Nonlinear shading function*

Listing 7-2. Program SHADESPHERE

```
1    """
2    SHADESPHERE
3    """
4
5    import numpy as np
6    import matplotlib.pyplot as plt
7    from math import sin, cos, radians, sqrt
8
9    plt.axis([0,150,100,0])
10   plt.axis('off')
11   plt.grid(False)
12
```

```
13   #————————————————lists
14   g=[0]*3
15
16   #————————————————parameters
17   xc=80 #——sphere center
18   yc=50
19   zc=0
20   rs=35 #——sphere radius
21
22   lx=.707 #——light ray unit vector components
23   ly=.707
24   lz=0
25
26   IA=.01 #——define curve
27   IB=1
28   n=2.0
29
30   clrbg='midnightblue' #——background color
31
32   Rx=radians(-15) #——sphere angles of rotation
33   Ry=radians(0)
34   Rz=radians(30)
35
36   #————————————————paint background color
37   for x in np.arange(0,150,1):
38       for y in np.arange(0,100,1):
39           plt.scatter(x,y,s=10,color='clrbg')
40
41   #==============================================================rotation
     functions
42   def rotx(xc,yc,zc,xp,yp,zp,Rx):
43       g[0]=xp+xc
44       g[1]=yp*cos(Rx)-zp*sin(Rx)+yc
45       g[2]=yp*sin(Rx)+zp*cos(Rx)+zc
46       return[g]
47
```

```
48   def roty(xc,yc,zc,xp,yp,zp,Ry):
49       g[0]=xp*cos(Ry)+zp*sin(Ry)+xc
50       g[1]=yp+yc
51       g[2]=-xp*sin(Ry)+zp*cos(Ry)+zc
52       return[g]
53
53   def rotz(xc,yc,zc,xp,yp,zp,Rz):
55       g[0]=xp*cos(Rz)-yp*sin(Rz)+xc
56       g[1]=xp*sin(Rz)+yp*cos(Rz)+yc
57       g[2]=zp+zc
58       return[g]
59
60   #———————————longitudes
61   phi1=radians(-90)
62   phi2=radians(90)
63   dphi=radians(2)
64
65   alpha1=radians(0)
66   alpha2=radians(360)
67   dalpha=radians(2)
68
69   for alpha in np.arange(alpha1,alpha2+dalpha,dalpha):
70       for phi in np.arange(phi1,phi2+dphi,dphi):
71           xp=rs*cos(phi)*cos(alpha)
72           yp=rs*sin(phi)
73           zp=-rs*cos(phi)*sin(alpha)
74           rotx(xc,yc,zc,xp,yp,zp,Rx)
75           xp=g[0]-xc
76           yp=g[1]-yc
77           zp=g[2]-zc
78           roty(xc,yc,zc,xp,yp,zp,Ry)
79           xp=g[0]-xc
80           yp=g[1]-yc
81           zp=g[2]-zc
82           rotz(xc,yc,zc,xp,yp,zp,Rz)
83           xpg=g[0]
```

```
84              ypg=g[1]
85              zpg=g[2]
86              a=xpg-xc
87              b=ypg-yc
88              c=zpg-zc
89              qp=sqrt(a*a+b*b+c*c)
90              nx=a/qp
91              ny=b/qp
92              nz=c/qp
93              ndotl=nx*lx+ny*ly+nz*lz
94              I=IA+(IB-IA)*((1+ndotl)/2)**n
95              if phi == phi1:
96                  xpglast=xpg
97                  ypglast=ypg
98              if nz < 0:
99                  plt.plot([xpglast,xpg],[ypglast,ypg],linewidth=4,
                        color=((1-I),.8*(1-I),.45*(1-I)))
100                 xpglast=xpg
101                 ypglast=ypg
102
103 #———————————————latitudes
104 for phi in np.arange(phi1,phi2+dphi,dphi):
105     r=rs*cos(phi)
106     for alpha in np.arange(alpha1,alpha2+dalpha,dalpha):
107             xp=r*cos(alpha)
108             yp=rs*sin(phi)
109             zp=-rs*cos(phi)*sin(alpha)
110             rotx(xc,yc,zc,xp,yp,zp,Rx)
111             xp=g[0]-xc
112             yp=g[1]-yc
113             zp=g[2]-zc
114             roty(xc,yc,zc,xp,yp,zp,Ry)
115             xp=g[0]-xc
116             yp=g[1]-yc
117             zp=g[2]-zc
118             rotz(xc,yc,zc,xp,yp,zp,Rz)
```

252

```
119        xpg=g[0]
120        ypg=g[1]
121        zpg=g[2]
122        a=xpg-xc
123        b=ypg-yc
124        c=zpg-zc
125        qp=sqrt(a*a+b*b+c*c)
126        nx=a/qp
127        ny=b/qp
128        nz=c/qp
129        ndotl=nx*lx+ny*ly+nz*lz
130        textbfI=IA+(IB-IA)*((1+ndotl)/2)**n
131        if alpha == alpha1:
132            xpglast=xpg
133            ypglast=ypg
134        if nz < 0:
135            plt.plot([xpglast,xpg],[ypglast,ypg],linewidth=4,
                   color=((1-I),.8*(1-I),.45*(1-I)))
136            xpglast=xpg
137            ypglast=ypg
138
139 plt.show()
```

7.3 Summary

While adding a background color can greatly enhance the visual appearance of an object, shading can also be quite effective. In this chapter, you learned techniques for shading an object. Shading implies the presence of an illuminating light source. In your model, you used the direction of the light rays coming from a source but you did not specify the position of the source. In Listing 7-1, you explored the concept of a shading function as shown in Figure 7-10 and how it determines the intensity of shading on a plane. This depends on the orientation of the plane relative to the direction of the incoming light rays, which is determined by taking the dot product of a unit vector normal to the surface, $\hat{\mathbf{n}}$, with a unit vector pointing in the direction of the light rays, $\hat{\mathbf{l}}$. In Listing 7-2, you performed the same shading operations on a sphere. However, you improved on the shading function. Whereas in Listing 7-1 you used a simple linear relation between the shading intensity and the dot product $\hat{\mathbf{n}} \cdot \hat{\mathbf{l}}$, in Listing 7-2 you used a nonlinear relation, as shown in Figure 7-14. This greatly improves the appearance of the shading.

CHAPTER 8

2D Data Plotting

In this chapter, you will look at styles and techniques for plotting two-dimensional data. You will start with some simple plots and then progress to those that include multiple sets of data on the same plot. While Python contains specialized built-in functions that can be quite efficient at this, usually requiring only a few lines of code, you will find that you can embellish your plots by taking a more hands-on approach and being creative by supplementing the specialized Python functions with simple Python commands. For example, the plot in Figure 8-1 requires only three lines of specialized code after the setup and data has been entered. Figure 8-5, on the other hand, can be a challenge to create using just specialized Python commands. The use of simple commands, plus a little creativity, can make the job much easier. Following simple data plots, you will move on to linear regression where you fit a straight line to a data set. You will then see how to fit non-linear mathematical functions to the data. You conclude with splines. A spline is a smooth curve that passes through each data point.

Figure 8-1 shows a plot of a mathematical function. This plot was created by Listing 8-1. In it, line 13 sets the numerical range of the x axis, which in this case goes from 0 to 150 in steps of 1. This means the function will be plotted over that range. The axis definition in line 8 has the same limits, but they could be different. For example, if line 8 was **plt.axis([0,200,0,100])**, the width of the plotting area would be 200 but the function would still be plotted from 0 to 150. This combination would position the function plot toward the left side of the plotting area.

The function being plotted is defined in line 14. This is a simple exponential function of y1 vs. x. Line 17 plots it in blue and attaches the label **'y1'**, which will be used by the **legend()** function in line 20. In line 20, **loc** equals the location of the legend, which can be any combination of upper, middle, lower combined with left, center, right. Here you are using **'upper left'**. If you specify **'best'**, Python will determine the best location for it. As you can see, lines 13, 14, and 17 comprise essentially the entire plotting operation.

B.J. Korites, *Python Graphics*, https://doi.org/10.1007/978-1-4842-3378-8_8

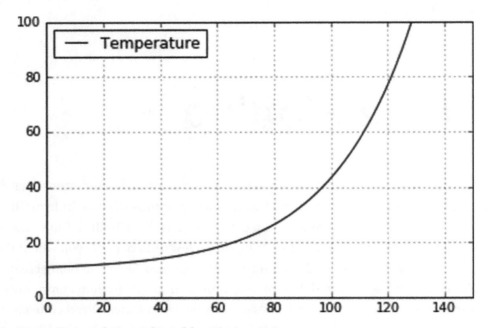

Figure 8-1. *Data plot produced by Listing 8-1*

Listing 8-1. Program DATAPLOT1

```
1   """
2   DATAPLOT1
3   """
4
5   import matplotlib.pyplot as plt
6   import numpy as np
7
8   plt.axis([0,150,0,100])
9   plt.axis('on')
10  plt.grid(True)
11
12  #————————define function y1 vs x
13  x=np.arange(0,150,1)
14  y1=10+np.exp(.035*x)
15
16  #————————plot y1 vs x
17  plt.plot(x, y1,'b',label='y1')
```

```
18
19 #—————————plot the legend
20 plt.legend(loc='upper left')
21
22 plt.show()
```

In Listing 8-2, you plot two functions, y1 and y2, on the same plot. Lines 18 and 19 do the plotting. You add the labels Temperature and Pressure, which will be used by the **legend()** function. In line 25, you add **marker='s'**, which plots a square at each data point of the temperature curve; **marker='*'** in line 26 plots a star at each point of the pressure curve. There are other marker styles available at https://matplotlib.org/api/markers_api.html.

In Figure 8-2, note that the horizontal range of the data plots (20-140) is smaller than the plotting width (0-150). Having the data not bump into the edges of the plot can sometimes make it more readable. To have the data plots span the entire width of the plot, simply change line 8 to **plt.axis([20,140,0,100])**. Similarly, the range of the y values can be changed.

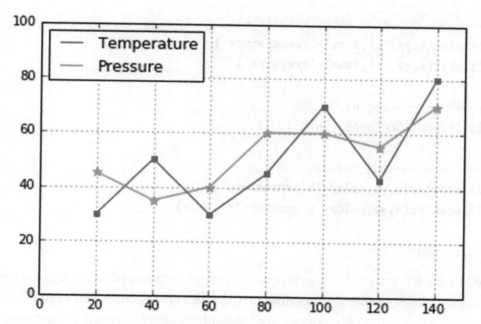

Figure 8-2. *Data plot produced by Listing 8-2*

Listing 8-2. Program DATAPLOT2

```
1   """
2   DATAPLOT2
3   """
4
5   import matplotlib.pyplot as plt
6   import numpy as np
7
8   plt.axis([0,150,0,100])
9   plt.axis('on')
10  plt.grid(True)
11
12  #———————————define data points
13  x=[20,40,60,80,100,120,140]
14  y1=[30,50,30,45,70,43,80]
15  y2=[45,35,40,60,60,55,70]
16
17  #———————————plot lines with labels
18  plt.plot(x,y1,'b',label='Temperature')
19  plt.plot(x,y2,'r',label='Pressure')
20
21  #———————————legend
22  plt.legend(loc='upper left')
23
24  #———————————add markers
25  plt.scatter(x,y1,color='b',marker='s')
26  plt.scatter(x,y2,color='r',marker='*',s=50)
27
28  plt.show()
```

In Listing 8-2, you display two functions, temperature and pressure, against one y axis. This assumes, of course, the values on the y axis are appropriate for both T and p. But what if the values of pressure were either much larger or much smaller than temperature? The plot of pressure might go off the chart or be too small to be discernible. What you need are two vertical scales, one for temperature and another for pressure.

In Listing 8-3, you lower the pressure values as shown in line 14. If plotted against the same vertical scale used for temperature, they would appear too low on the plot. You can remedy this by introducing a second vertical axis. Lines 17-20 plot the temperature data. Line 20 allows you to change the color of the vertical tick marks to any color, red in this case. Line 21 plots a legend in the upper left corner. Lines 24-27 plot a second scale on the right side of the plot. Line 24 establishes a "twin" plotting axis. This twin includes the already established horizontal x axis plus a new vertical y axis on the right side. The rest of the commands in this group refer to this second y axis. Line 26 labels this axis as Pressure. Line 27 changes the tick marks and numbers to blue. Line 28 plots a second legend at the upper right. If you try to plot a single legend for both temperature and pressure, you find the results depend on where in the code you place the **legend()** function. If you use two separate **legends()**, as you are doing here, and locate them at the same position, say upper left, one will overwrite the other. If you try using just one **legend()** at the end of the code, it displays a legend with only the pressure shown. See Figure 8-3. In the next program you will see a way around this problem.

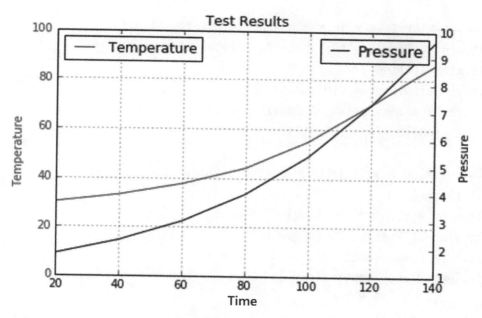

Figure 8-3. *Data plot produced by Listing 8-3*

Listing 8-3. Program DATAPLOT3

```
1   """
2   DATAPLOT3
3   """
4
5   import matplotlib.pyplot as plt
6   import numpy as np
7
8   plt.axis([0,140,0,100])
9   plt.axis('on')
10  plt.grid(True)
11
12  t=[20,40,60,80,100,120,140] #——Time
13  T=[30,33,37.5,44,55,70,86] #——Temperature
14  p=[1.8,2.3,3,4,5.4,7.3,9.6] #——Pressure
15
16  #————Plot T vs t in red on the left vertical axis.
17  plt.plot(t,T,color='r',label='Temperature')
18  plt.xlabel('Time')
19  plt.ylabel('Temperature',color='r')
20  plt.tick}_params(axis='y',labelcolor='r')
21  plt.legend(loc='upper left')
22
23  #————Plot P vs t in blue on the right vertical axis.
24  plt.twinx()
25  plt.plot(t,p,color='b',label='Pressure')
26  plt.ylabel('Pressure', color='b')
27  plt.tick_params(axis='y', labelcolor='b')
28  plt.legend(loc='upper right')
29
30  #————title the plot
31  plt.title('Test Results')
32
33  plt.show()
```

In Listing 8-4, you try to resolve the **legend()** issue you encountered in the previous program. Line 12 sets up a plot called ax1 that will include a subplot. Line 14 plots a grid. Lines 8-10 set up the data lists. Line 16 labels the x axis. Line 18 plots the Temperature curve in red and names it l1. Line 20 sets the scale limits on the left vertical axis, which will range from 0 to 100. Line 21 labels it in red. Line 23 sets up a **twin()** second vertical axis (which includes the x axis) as ax2. Line 25 plots it in blue as the curve l2. Line 27 sets the scale limits to 0-10. Line 28 labels it. Lines 30 and 31 specify the curves that are to appear in the legend. Line 32 plots the legend. The syntax looks a bit cryptic but it works, as you can see in Figure 8-4.

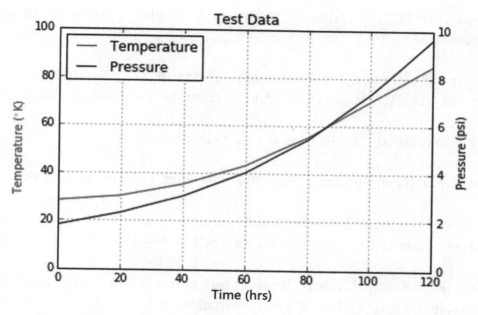

Figure 8-4. *Data plot produced by Listing 8-4*

Listing 8-4. Program DATAPLOT4

```
1    """
2    DATAPLOT4
3    """
4
5    import matplotlib.pyplot as plt
6    import numpy as np
7
```

```
8   t=[0,20,40,60,80,100,120]
9   T=[28,30,35,43,55,70,85]
10  p=[1.8,2.3,3,4,5.4,7.3,9.6]
11
12  fig, ax1 = plt.subplots() #——set up a plot ax1 with subplots
13
14  plt.grid(True) #——draw grid
15
16  ax1.set_xlabel('Time (hrs)') #——label X axis of ax1
17
18  l1=plt.plot(t,T,'r',label='Temperature') #——plot temperature in red as
    curve l1
19
20  ax1.set_ylim([0,100]) #——set Y axis limits of ax1
21  ax1.set_ylabel(r'Temperature (° K)', color='r') #——label Y axis of ax1
22
23  ax2 = ax1.twinx() #——set up ax2 as twin of ax1
24
25  l2=plt.plot(t, p, 'b',label='Pressure') #——plot pressure in blue as curve l2
26
27  ax2.set_ylim([0,10]) #——set Y axis limits of ax2
28  ax2.set_ylabel('Pressure (psi)', color='b') #——label Y axis of ax2
29
30  line1,=plt.plot([1],label='Temperature',color='r') #——line 1 of legend
31  line2,=plt.plot([2],label='Pressure',color='b') #——line 2 of legend
32  plt.legend(handles=[line1,line2],loc='upper left') #——plot legend
33
34  plt.title('Test Data')
```

In Listing 8-5, you plot multiple curves while giving each its own vertical scale. Lines 12-14 define lists for time, temperature, and pressure data. In line 15, you introduce a third dependent variable, **volume v**. Line 17 opens a new list called pp=[ ], which will be used to vertically scale the pressure data. You could simply scale and replace the items in p=[ ] but then you would destroy the original values. That would not be a problem in this program but it's good practice to leave them unchanged. Lines 18-19 scale the original Pressure values contained in p by a factor of 10 and append them to pp. The same is done for v in lines 21-23 where volume data is scaled by a factor of 100. Lines 25-28 plot the curves and plot a legend. Lines 30-33 plot the pressure scale on the right y axis in blue. Lines 35-37 label the three axes. Lines 39-43 plot the volume scale values in green. Lines 45-46 plot the vertical green axis. This is accomplished by plotting the character "|" as text up the right side. Normally you would want to plot a single line from the vertical volume axis from top to bottom but Python does not permit plotting lines or scatter dots outside the main plotting area. It does, however, allow text. So you construct a vertical line from a series of "|" marks. You could add more vertical axes in this manner if you wished. See Figure 8-5.

The approach used in this program is more hands-on than before. Previous programs relied mostly on specialized Python syntax. The advantage to this approach is that it works, it's quite flexible, and it doesn't require many more lines of code. This blend of Python syntax along with a creative use of hands-on techniques is actually quite powerful. Sometimes it pays to think outside the box.

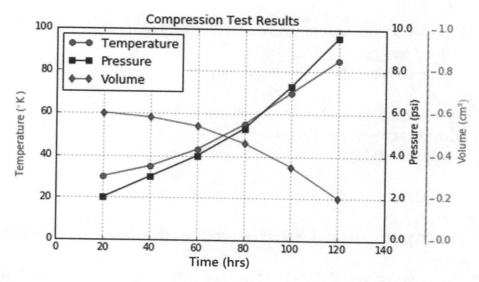

Figure 8-5. *Data plot produced by Listing 8-5*

Listing 8-5. DATAPLOT5

```
1   """
2   DATAPLOT5
3   """
4
5   import matplotlib.pyplot as plt
6   import numpy as np
7
8   plt.axis([0,140,0,100])
9   plt.axis('on')
10  plt.grid(True)
11
12  t=[20,40,60,80,100,120] #——time
13  T=[30,35,43,55,70,85] #——temperature
14  p=[2,3,4,5.3,7.3,9.6] #——pressure
15  v=[.6,.58,.54,.46,.35,.2] #——volume
16
17  pp=[ ] #——list for scaled pressure for plotting
18  for i in np.arange(0,len(p),1):
19          pp.append(p[i]*10) #——scale p by 10
20
21  vv=[ ] #——list for scaled volume for plotting
22  for i in np.arange(0,len(v),1):
23          vv.append(v[i]*100) #——scale volume by 100
24
25  plt.plot(t,T,color='r',label='Temperature',marker='o') #——plot
    temperature
26  plt.plot(t,pp,color='b',label='Pressure',marker='s') #——plot scaled
    pressure
27  plt.plot(t,vv,color='g',label='Volume',marker='d') #——plot scaled volume
28  plt.legend(loc='upper left')
29
30  for y in np.arange(0,100+1,20): #——plot pressure scale values
31          a=y/10
32          a=str(a) #——convert to string for plotting as text
```

```
33       plt.text(142,y,a,color='b')
34
35 plt.xlabel('Time (hrs)') #——label axes
36 plt.ylabel('Temperature °K',color='r')
37 plt.text(151,65,'Pressure (psi)',rotation=90,color='b')
38
39 for y in np.arange(100,-1,-20): #——plot volume scale values
40       a=y/100
41       a=str(a)
42       plt.text(162,y,a,color='g')
43       plt.text(159,y+2,'_',color='g')
44
45 for y in np.arange(1,99,3):
46       plt.text(157,y,'-',color='g')
47
48 plt.text(170,65,r'Volume (cm3)',rotation=90,color='g') #——label volume
   scale
49
50 plt.title('Compression Test Results') #-title
51
52 plt.show()
```

8.1 Linear Regression

Linear regression is the process of fitting a straight line to a set of data points. Referring to
Figures 8-6 and 8-7, the objective is to determine the parameters A and B of a straight line,

$$y = Ax + B \tag{8-1}$$

that result in a best fit to the data points. B is the y axis intercept of the line and A is its
slope. Each data point i has coordinates x_i, y_i. Each has an error e_i with respect to the line.
The best fit of the line to the data points will be the one where A and B result in

$$\sum_{i=1}^{n} e_i^2 = minimum \tag{8-2}$$

where n is the number of data points. This is equivalent to bringing the RMS error to a minimum. e_i is squared in Equation 8-2 to account for negative values of e_i. It can be shown that Equation 8-2 is satisfied when

$$A = \frac{C_3 - nC_1C_2}{C_4 - nC_1C_1} \tag{8-3}$$

$$B = C_2 - AC_1 \tag{8-4}$$

$$C_1 = \frac{1}{n}\sum_{n=1}^{n} t_i \tag{8-5}$$

$$C_2 = \frac{1}{n}\sum_{n=1}^{n} v_i \tag{8-6}$$

$$C_3 = \sum_{n=1}^{n} v_i t_i \tag{8-7}$$

$$C_4 = \sum_{n=1}^{n} t_i t_i \tag{8-8}$$

In Listing 8-6, the regression routine has been added to Listing 8-5 beginning at line 52. It fits a regression line to the green Volume curve. Lines 55-60 calculate the coefficients C1-C4 defined above. **np.sum()** in line 55 sums the elements in list t. **np.multiply()** in line 57 multiplies the elements in lists v and t element by element, producing the list a. Line 58 then adds the elements in a. Lines 62 and 63 calculate A and B in accordance with Equations 8-3 and 8-4. Lines 65-68 plot the regression line using scatter dots; line 66 calculates values of v vs. t as vp, the plotting value of v; line 67 scales vp by 100 for plotting; line 68 does the plotting.

Equation 8-2 state that minimizing $\Sigma e(i)^2$, where e(i) is the deviation of data point i from the regression line, is equivalent to minimizing the RMS value. The RMS value is

$$RMS = \left[\frac{\sum_{1=1}^{n} e(i)^2}{n}\right]^{\frac{1}{2}} \tag{8-9}$$

This is calculated in lines 71-76. e(i) is calculated in line 73. It is squared in line 74 as ee and then summed in line 75 as sumee, producing the numerator in Equation 8-9. RMS is calculated in line 76 in accordance with Equation 8-9. It's obvious that minimizing $\Sigma e(i)^2$ is equivalent to minimizing the RMS value.

The remainder of the program places labels and values on the plot. Line 83 reduces the number of digits of vp1, the beginning value of the regression line; line 84 plots it. Lines 86-88 plot the end value. A and B (Ap and Bp) are similarly plotted in lines 90-96.

There are other ways in Python to reduce the number of digits besides the syntax used in line 83. However, if the number being shortened is negative, the minus sign may not appear on the output. This could be a problem with some versions of Python.

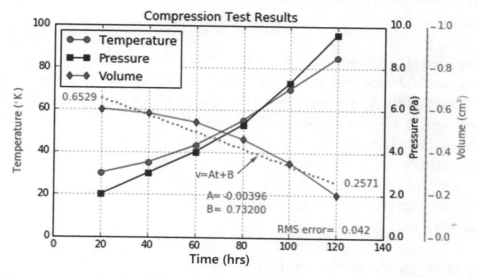

Figure 8-6. *Straight line fit to the volume curve produced by Listing 8-6*

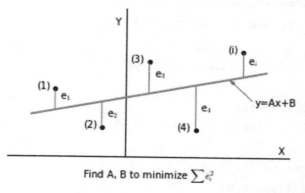

Find A, B to minimize $\sum e_i^2$

Figure 8-7. *Model used by Listing 8-6 showing data points 1,2,3,4...i with straight line fit. e_i=error from straight line for data point i.*

Listing 8-6. REGRESSION1

```
1  """
2  REGRESSION1
3  """
   .
   .
   #————————same as DATAPLOT5—————————
   .
   .
52 #————————————straight line fit to Volume v vs t
53 n=len(v)
54
55 c1=np.sum(t)/n #——sum values of list t and divide by n, =average of t
56 c2=np.sum(v)/n #——sum values of list v and divide by n, =average of v
57 a=np.multiply(v,t) #——multiply list v by t element by element = list a
58 c3=np.sum(a) #——sum elements of a
59 a=np.multiply(t,t) #——multiply list t by t element by element = list a
60 c4=np.sum(a) #——sum elements of a
61
62 A=(c3-n*c1*c2)/(c4-n*c1*c1) #——line parameters A and B
63 B=c2-A*c1
64
65 for tp in np.arange(t[0],t[5],2): #——plot line with scatter dots
66     vp=A*tp+B
67     vp=vp*100 #——scale vp for plotting
68     plt.scatter(tp,vp,color='g',s=1)
69
70 #————————————————calculate RMS error
71 sumee=0
72 for i in range(len(t)):
73     e=(v[i]-(A*t[i]+B))
74     ee=e*e
75     sumee=sumee+ee
76     rms=np.sqrt(sumee/n)
77
```

```
78 #—————————————labels
79 plt.text(60,28,'v=At+B',color='g')
80 plt.arrow(78,30,6,6,head_length=3,head_width=1.5,color='g',linewidth=.5)
81
82 vp1=A*t[0]+B #————beginning v value of line
83 vp1='%7.4f'%(vp1) #————reduce the number of decimal places
84 plt.text(2,64,vp1,color='g') #——plot
85
86 vp2=A*t[5]+B #————end v value of line
87 vp2='%7.4f'%(vp2)
88 plt.text(122,25,vp2,color='g')
89
90 Ap='%7.5f'%(A)
91 plt.text(65,18,'A=',color='g')
92 plt.text(72,18,Ap,color='g') #——print value of A
93
94 Bp='%7.5f'%(B)
95 plt.text(65,12,'B=',color='g')
96 plt.text(73,12,Bp,color='g') #——print value of B
97
98 rms='%7.3f'%(rms)
99 plt.text(95,3,'RMS error=',color='g')
100 plt.text(123,3,rms,color='g') #——print RMS error
101
102 plt.show()
```

8.2 Function Fitting

In Listing 8-6, you plotted a straight line to fit data points that represented measurements of volume vs. time. You were fortunate that there was an analytic solution to this problem represented by Equations 8-2, 8-3, and 8-5. In this section, you will fit an arbitrary function to the same data set. The function is user-defined; that is, you can specify any function you want, whatever you think will give a good fit. In Listing 8-7 you will try the relation

$$v = Ax^2 + B \qquad (8\text{-}10)$$

269

As in the previous section, your task is to find the values of A and B that produce the best fit of this function to the data points. Since you want to be able to use any arbitrary function, it would obviously not be time-effective to derive a closed form solution to the problem for every function you wish to try. Here you will use a brute force approach that involves calculating the values of the parameters A and B in Equation 8-10 for many values of A and B within the expected range of both that results in minimum RMS error. This is a hands-on approach; some insight into the problem is required. For example, inspection of the v(t) curve in Figure 8-8 and Equation 8-10 indicates that parameter B in Equation 8-10, which is the V axis (green) intercept at t=t[0], should lie somewhere between .5 and .7. Similarly, you can assume that A will be very small since Equation 8-10 involves squares of t, which have values as large as t[5]=120. You can also see by inspection that A should be negative. So you can try a range for A of -.001 to 0. Calculate the error for many combinations of values of B between .5 and .7 and A between -.001 and 0. This will give you the A and B corresponding to the almost lowest error between those ranges. I say the "almost" lowest error because, when cycling between the expected ranges of A and B, you do so in small steps. The finer those steps are, the more accurate will be your final solution. While there are automatic iteration techniques that you could use, the process described here is simpler to code but involves user iteration. It works as follows: after guessing initial ranges for A and B, when you get the results, you can make another run with refined values by either closing, opening, or shifting the ranges. You can also change the search increments dB (line 61) and dA (line 64). With just a few of these manual iterations you should be able to get a solution to whatever accuracy you need.

Referring to Listing 8-7, most of it is the same as Listing 8-6. Lines 59-64 define the limits of the search routine B1 and B2, which are the start and end of the B range; A1 and A2 of the A range. dB and dA are the increments. Smaller increments will give more accurate results but will require more processing time. The two nested loops beginning in lines 70 and 71 search first through the B range and then, for each value of B, through the A range. At each combination of A and B the loop starting at line 73 cycles through all the data points, len(t) (=len(v)). Line 74 calculates the error between each data point and the assumed function Equation 8-10; line 75 squares it and line 76 sums the square of the errors in accordance with Equation 8-2. The sum was initially set to zero in line 72. Line 77 says, if the sum of the squares produced by the current combination of A and B is less that the previously calculated sum, then you replace that value with the present one and set the current values of A and B to Amin and Bmin, the values that correspond to the current lowest error. When the A and B loops are first cycled, eemin in line 76 is unknown. It is set to a very high value in line 56. This insures that the first eemin will be less. After the first cycle, it will take on the value corresponding to the latest combination of A and B that produces a lowest value of sumee. The end result of all this is the values of A and B that produce the lowest error between the data points and the assumed function. They are Amin and Bmin. Lines 86-89 plot the function using Amin and Bmin in line 87. Lines 92-97 calculate the corresponding RMS error.

Figure 8-6 shows a straight-line approximation to v(t) and the RMS error of .042, as can be seen printed on that plot. With the non-linear function Ax^2+B, the RMS error is .0132, which is considerably lower.

The remainder of the program places labels on the plot. As you can see from Figure 8-8, the limits of A and B that were set in lines 59-64 are printed in black on the plot as A1, A2, B1, and B2. The values found by the program that result in the lowest error are printed in green as Amin and Bmin. With the assumed values of A1, A2, B1, and B2 in this example, Amin and Bmin fall within the assumed range so you can be confident that you have found the near best values. But let's suppose one of the parameters, say B1, was chosen incorrectly. That is, suppose you had chosen B1=.65 with B2=.7. The result for Bmin calculated by the program would be B1=.65; that is, it would bump up against the lower B limit. That would tell you that B1 is too high and you should lower it for the next run. Similarly, if you had chosen B1=.5 with B2=.6, Bmin would bump up against the upper limit for B, indicating that you should raise B2.

There are other curve fitting functions available similar to the one you are developing here; go to `https://docs.scipy.org/doc/scipy/reference/generated/scipy.optimize.curve_fit.html`. Others can be found with an Internet search. The one you are developing here has the advantage of being open, simple, and easy to use, plus you have control over it.

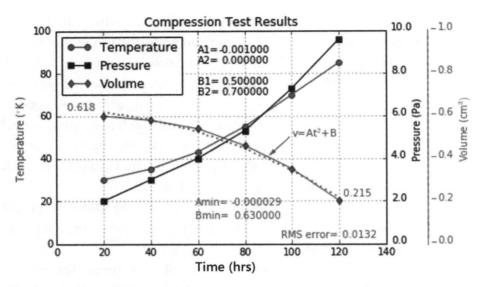

Figure 8-8. *Function fit to volume curve produced by Listing 8-7*

Listing 8-7. Program REGRESSION2

```
"""

REGRESSION2

"""

52 #————————same as REGRESSION1————————
53
54 #————————————parabolic fit to v vs t
55 n=len(v)
56 eemin=10**10 #————starting value of eemin, deliberately set very large
57
58 #——————————loop parameters
59 B1=.5
60 B2=.7
61 dB=.001
62 A1=-.001
63 A2=0.
64 dA=.0000001
65
66 #——————————loop through all combinations of A and B
67 #——————————within ranges defined by loop parameters
```

```
68 #——————————searching for Amin, Bmin that produce
69 #——————————best fit of function to data points
70 for B in np.arange(B1,B2,dB):
71     for A in np.arange(A1,A2,dA):
72         sumee=0
73         for i in range(len(t)):
74             e=(v[i]-(A*t[i]*t[i]+B)) #——error of data point i at A, B
75             ee=e*e #——error squared
76             sumee=sumee+ee #——sum of error squared
77             if sumee < eemin: #——if sum < present minimum eemin then
78                 eemin=sumee #——set new minimum = sumee
79                 Amin=A #——set new Amin = A
80                 Bmin=B #——set new Bmin = B
81
82 #——————————Amin, Bmin above will produce best fit
83
84 #——————————plot best fit function with scatter dots
85 #——————————from t[0] to t[5] in steps=2
86 for tp in np.arange(t[0],t[5],2):
87     vp=Amin*tp*tp+Bmin
88     vp=vp*100 #—scale to plot
89     plt.scatter(tp,vp,color='g',s=1)
90
91 #——————————calculate RMS Error
92 sumee=0
93 for i in range(len(v)):
94     e=(v[i]-(Amin*t[i]*t[i]+Bmin)) #——error at each data point
95     ee=e*e #——error squared
96     sumee=sumee+ee #——sum of squared errors
97     rms=np.sqrt(sumee/n) #——RMS error
98
99 #——————————————labels
100 plt.text(100,50,'v=At+B',color='g')
101 plt.arrow(99,50,-6.5,-6.5,head_length=3,head_width=1.5,color='g',
    linewidth=.5)
```

273

```
102
103 A=Amin
104 B=Bmin
105
106 vp1=A*t[0]*t[0]+B
107 vp1='%7.3f'%(vp1)
108 plt.text(2,63,vp1,color='g')
109
110 vp2=A*t[5]*t[5]+B
111 vp2='%7.3f'%(vp2)
112 plt.text(119,22,vp2,color='g')
113
114 Ap='%8.6f'%(A)
115 plt.text(59,18,'Amin=',color='g')
116 plt.text(74,18,Ap,color='g')
117
118 Bp='%8.6f'%(B)
119 plt.text(59,12,'Bmin=',color='g')
120 plt.text(75.2,12,Bp,color='g')
121
122 rms='%7.4f'%(rms)
123 plt.text(95,3,'RMS error=',color='g')
124 plt.text(120,3,rms,color='g')
125
126 A1='%8.6f'%(A1)
127 plt.text(60,90,'A1=')
128 plt.text(69,90,A1)
129
130 A2='%8.6f'%(A2)
131 plt.text(60,85,'A2=')
132 plt.text(70.2,85,A2)
133
134 B1='%8.6f'%(B1)
135 plt.text(60,75,'B1=')
136 plt.text(70.2,75,B1)
```

```
137
138 B2='%8.6f'%(B2)
139 plt.text(60,70,'B2=')
140 plt.text(70.2,70,B2)
141
142 plt.show()
```

8.3 Splines

The curves shown in Figure 8-9 are called splines. They are characterized by the fact that they pass through their respective data points, which are shown as dots. Each is also a "natural" spline since there is no twisting at the ends. In the parlance of calculus, the second derivative is zero at the end points.

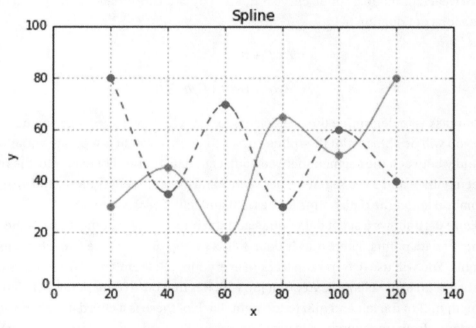

Figure 8-9. *Spline curves produced by Listing 8-8*

Splines constructed of thin slats of wood were at one time commonly used in ship building where it was necessary to produce hull shapes that were smooth. In the lofting room, workers would drive nails into the floor and then bend thin strips of wood around them. The shape of the bent strip was then traced onto paper or plywood beneath. This shape was used to cut full scale molds that were used in the construction process. The word "spline" is thought to derive from the Danish *splind* or North Frisian *splinj*, both ancient boat-building regions. After World War II, the usage of mechanical splines was replaced by mathematically derived curves in both ship building and aircraft design and construction.

The mathematical relation for a spline that you will use here is called a cubic spline. It has the form of

$$x = Axq^3 + Bxq^2 + Cxq + Dx \tag{8-11}$$

Since each point on a spline curve is defined by two coordinates x and y, you need two versions of Equation 8-11:

$$x = Axq^3 + Bxq^2 + Cxq + Dx \tag{8-12}$$

$$y = Ayq^3 + Byq^2 + Cyq + Dy \tag{8-13}$$

Your task is to determine the coefficients Ax → Cx and Ay → Cy. Once you have them, you will be able to plot the spline curve. To do this, you fit a separate equation for x and y between the segment between adjacent data points. For example, the region between point 2 and 3 is a segment; between 3 and 4 is another segment. You also use information about the data points to the right and left of each segment.

Figure 8-10 shows a set of data points and the numbering scheme. nop= is the number of data points. There are six data points so nop=6. There are five inter-point segments. You will use lists to keep track of everything. Remember, Python wants to begin lists with a [o]th element. At point [3], which is the fourth data point, i=3. You see the length q[2] to the left and q[3] to the right. Each of these is a chord length, the straight line distance from one point to the next.

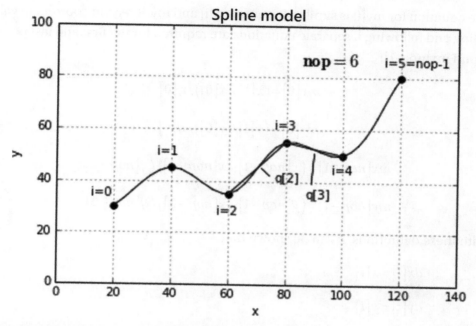

Figure 8-10. *Model used by Listing 8-8*

Referring now to just the x equation in Equation 8-12, you can define a "slope" at point [3], mx[3] as

$$mx[3] = \left(\frac{x[3] - x[2]}{q[2]} + \frac{x[4] - x[3]}{q[3]} \right) * .5 \qquad (8\text{-}14)$$

This is an average at point [3] of the left "slope" and the right. I put "slope" in quotes to emphasize it is not a slope in the traditional sense such as $\Delta y/\Delta x$ but is instead each Δx is divided by a chord length q[ ]. For any point [i],

$$mx[i] = \left(\frac{x[i] - x[i-1]}{q[i-1]} + \frac{x[i+1] - x[i]}{q[i]} \right) * .5 \qquad (8\text{-}15)$$

The equation for my[i] is similar. Because mx[i] and my[i] rely on coordinate values preceding and following i, separate equations are required for the first and last points, mx[0] and mx[nop-1]:

$$mx[0] = (x[1] - x[0]) / q[0] \tag{8-16}$$

$$my[0] = (y[1] - y[0]) / q[0] \tag{8-17}$$

$$mx[nop-1] = (x[nop-1] - x[nop-2]) / q[nop-2] \tag{8-18}$$

$$my[nop-1] = (y[nop-1] - y[nop-2]) / q[nop-2] \tag{8-19}$$

With these definitions, it can be shown that

$$dx[i] = x[i] \tag{8-20}$$

$$dy[i] = y[i] \tag{8-21}$$

$$cx[i] = mx[i] \tag{8-22}$$

$$cy[i] = my[i] \tag{8-23}$$

$$bx[i] = (3x[i+1] - 2cx[i]q[i] - 3dx[i] - mx[i+1]q[i]) / q[i]q[i] \tag{8-24}$$

$$by[i] = (3y[i+1] - 2cy[i]q[i] - 3dy[i] - my[i+1]q[i]) / q[i]q[i] \tag{8-25}$$

$$ax[i] = (mx[i+1] - 2bx[i]q[i] - cx[i] / 3q[i]q[i] \tag{8-26}$$

$$ay[i] = (my[i+1] - 2by[i]q[i] - cy[i] / 3q[i]q[i] \tag{8-27}$$

These coefficients are based on the requirement that, at the intersection of spline segments at a data point, the locations of the splines and their slopes must match from one section to the next. Also, the rate of change of the slopes (second derivative) must match; otherwise there would be angular discontinuities in the shape of the spline. At the beginning point of the spline where i=0, there is no adjacent segment so you require that the rate of change of slope (second derivative of deflection) at that point be zero. This means that if the spline were to continue off to the left side of the first point, it would be a straight line having the same slope as the spline segment at that point. In mechanics of beams, a bending moment called M produces a rate of change of slope y; that is, $d^2y/dx^2 \approx M$. Since there is nothing at either end of the spline to produce a bending moment, $d^2y/dx^2 = 0$ and the slope will not be changed. This is intuitive; if a boat builder is fitting a wooden spline to a set of nails hammered into the floor, and he uses a strip of wooden spline that is too long, the extra length would trail off the end straight at the same angle as the end of the spline at the last nail. This same argument holds for the end of the spline at i=nop-1; there is no constraint on its slope so the second derivative is 0. This provides a "natural" spline. You could specify other end conditions, such as clamped or twisted, but the coefficients above would be different.

The following equations locate a point xp,yp along the spline between points [i] and [i+1]:

$$xp = ax[i]qq^3 + bx[i]qq^2 + cx[i]qq + dx[i] \qquad (8\text{-}28)$$

$$yp = ay[i]qq^3 + by[i]qq^2 + cy[i]qq + dy[i] \qquad (8\text{-}29)$$

where qq is the length of chord i.

When Listing 8-8 plots the spline, it does so segment by segment starting with point [0] and proceeding to point [nop-1]. Referring again to Figure 8-10, if i=3, the above equations would plot the spline segment from point [3] to point [4]. To plot the entire spline from point [0] to [5], the program plots segments starting at [0] and going to [nop-1]. That is, the program automatically plots segments from [0] → [1], [1] → [2],.....[5] → [6].

Referring to Listing 8-8, the calculations and plotting are carried out by function **spline** beginning in line 17. In the function's arguments, x and y, are in a list that is defined in line 73 and 74. Each x,y pair are the coordinates of a data point. **clr** is the color of the spline and **ls** is the line style. The data points are plotted in line 19. **nop** in line 21 is the number of data points. Lines 23-33 are zero lists of length nop. You fill these lists by calculating values item by item. You could have defined empty lists to begin with and appended elements later. By defining the list lengths now, you avoid appending. Either way will work; it's just a matter of preference.

Lines 35-38 calculate the chord lengths q[i]. Line 40 and 41 calculate the slopes at the beginning of the spline. Lines 43-45 calculate the average slopes at 0<i<nop-1. Line 47-48 calculate the slope at the end of the spline. Lines 51-59 evaluate the coefficients in Equations 8-28. Lines 62-70 plot the spline as line segments.

Control of the program takes place in lines 73-83. Here you are plotting two splines. The set of data points for the first spline are contained in the lists in lines 73 and 74. The color and line style desired are set in lines 75 and 76. Line 77 invokes function **spline**. The second spline is created in a similar manner in lines 79-83. More splines could be added by adding more of these routines.

It's an easy matter to print out the x,y values within the range of a spline segment. For example, suppose you want the coordinates of points within the segment between points [2] and [3]. Insert the following lines at line 71:

```
if i==2:
    print(xp,yp)
```

This will print the coordinate's values up to point [3] where i will then become equal to 3.

Listing 8-8. Program SPLINE2D

```
1   """
2   SPLINE2D
3   """
4
5   import matplotlib.pyplot as plt
6   import numpy as np
7   from math import sqrt
8
9   plt.axis([0,140,0,100])
10  plt.axis('on')
11  plt.grid(True)
12
13  plt.xlabel('x')
14  plt.ylabel('y')
15  plt.title('2D Splines')
16
17  def spline(x,y,clr,ls):
18
19      plt.scatter(x,y,s=30,color=clr)
20
```

```
21        nop=len(x)
22
23        q=[0]*nop
24        mx=[0]*nop
25        my=[0]*nop
26        cx=[0]*nop
27        cy=[0]*nop
28        dx=[0]*nop
29        dy=[0]*nop
30        bx=[0]*nop
31        by=[0]*nop
32        ax=[0]*nop
33        ay=[0]*nop
34
35        for i in range(1,nop): #——chords q(i)
36            a=x[i]-x[i-1]
37            b=y[i]-y[i-1]
38            q[i-1]=sqrt(a*a+b*b)
39
40        mx[0]=(x[1]-x[0])/q[0]
41        my[0]=(y[1]-y[0])/q[0]
42
43        for i in range(1,nop-1): #——average m[i]
44            mx[i]=((x[i]-x[i-1])/q[i-1]+(x[i+1]-x[i])/q[i])*.5
45            my[i]=((y[i]-y[i-1])/q[i-1]+(y[i+1]-y[i])/q[i])*.5
46
47        mx[nop-1]=(x[nop-1]-x[nop-2])/q[nop-2]
48        my[nop-1]=(y[nop-1]-y[nop-2])/q[nop-2]
49
50 #————————-calculate coefficients
51        for i in range(0,nop-1):
52            dx[i]=x[i]
53            dy[i]=y[i]
54            cx[i]=mx[i]
55            cy[i]=my[i]
```

```
56          bx[i]=(3*x[i+1]-2*cx[i]*q[i]-3*dx[i]-mx[i+1]*q[i])/(q[i]*q[i])
57          by[i]=(3*y[i+1]-2*cy[i]*q[i]-3*dy[i]-my[i+1]*q[i])/(q[i]*q[i])
58          ax[i]=(mx[i+1]-2*bx[i]*q[i]-cx[i])/(3*q[i]*q[i])
59          ay[i]=(my[i+1]-2*by[i]*q[i]-cy[i])/(3*q[i]*q[i])
60
61   #————————plot the spline
62       xplast=x[0]
63       yplast=y[0]
64       for i in range(0,nop-1):
65           for qq in np.arange(0,q[i],4):
66               xp=ax[i]*qq*qq*qq+bx[i]*qq*qq+cx[i]*qq+dx[i]
67               yp=ay[i]*qq*qq*qq+by[i]*qq*qq+cy[i]*qq+dy[i]
68               plt.plot([xplast,xp],[yplast,yp],linewidth=1,color=clr,
                 linestyle=ls)
69               xplast=xp
70               yplast=yp
71
72   #————————control
73   x=[20,40,60,80,100,120]
74   y=[80,35,70,30,60,40]
75   clr='b'
76   ls='-'
77   spline(x,y,clr,ls)
78
79   x=[20,40,60,80,100,120]
80   y=[30,45,18,65,50,80]
81   clr='g'
82   ls='-'
83   spline(x,y,clr,ls)
84
85   plt.show()
```

8.4 Summary

This chapter covered a range of data plotting techniques: plotting simple points and functions, multiple functions on the same plot, labelling axes with multiple functions, linear regression where you fit a straight line to a data set, function fitting where you fit a user-defined function to a data set, and splines where you fit a smooth curve through each data point. While there are many data plotting routines available within the Python community, which you can find with an Internet search, the approach here has been more hands-on. By understanding how to do it yourself, with a little creativity you can produce plots customized to your own needs. In Chapter 9, you will extend what you have done here to three dimensions.

CHAPTER 9

3D Data Plotting

Extrapolating the techniques developed in Chapter 8, which were used to produce two dimensional splines, to three dimensions is easy: all you need to do is add a few lines to the program. These lines are the bold highlighted lines in Listing 9-1, particularly those in function **plotspline()** from lines 89 to 161. They introduce the z coordinate in a syntax that is essentially the same as used for the x and y coordinates.

Control of Listing 9-1 begins at line 175. The first set of data points are defined by lists x,y, and z in lines 175-177. These have been nullified with the # symbol but are left in place should you want to use them. They produce Figure 9-1. The active lists in lines 179-181 produce Figures 9-2 through 9-4. **nop** in line 183 is the number of data points. This equals **len(x)** which, of course, equals **len(y)** and **len(z)**. The list g in line 85 holds the values returned by the rotation functions **rotx()**, **roty()**, and **rotz()**. The coordinates of the center of rotation xc,yc, and zc are defined in lines 187-189.

The angles of rotation Rxd,Ryd, and Rzd in lines 191-193 could use some explanation. Referring to Figure 9-5, the coordinate system on the right defines the data points and the spline in their rotated (Rxd,Ryd,Rzd) and translated (xc,yc,zc) orientations. The system on the left shows the global coordinate system, which is the one that should be used when specifying rotations. The x and y directions are defined by the **plt.axis()** function in line 9. Since this is a right-handed coordinate system, the +z direction points out of the screen. As an example, a positive rotation around the z direction, Rzd, would rotate the figure on the right in the counter-clockwise direction.

Grid line are shown on the plot primarily as an aid in location for xc,yc,zc. When axes such as the x and z axes in Figure 9-4 lie in the plotting plane, they can be used as a measure of data point and spline coordinate values. However when the plot is rotated, as in Figure 9-3, they do not give true measures but may be used as an aid when locating the center, xc,yc,zc.

© B.J. Korites 2018
B.J. Korites, *Python Graphics*, https://doi.org/10.1007/978-1-4842-3378-8_9

Lines 200-210 plot the axes that define the data points and the spline by invoking function **plotaxis()** that goes from line 33 to 43. Each is 30 units long. The list g in line 43 holds the coordinates of the end of each axis. Line 202 plots the x axis; similarly for the y and z axes.

Without rotation (i.e. Rxd=Ryd=Rzd=0) the axes will appear as on the left side of Figure 9-5. When plotting data, we normally think of z as being a function of x and y (i.e. z=z(x,y)) and we prefer the z axis to point up. To accomplish this, we must rotate the coordinate system such that z points up. As an example, in Figure 9-4, Rx=-90,Ry=0,Rz=0. These values are shown in the upper right corner of the plot. This takes the +z axis, which pointed out of the screen in the unrotated position, and turns it counter-clockwise around the x axis so that it now points upward. +y now points into the screen. This is a good starting orientation. Subsequent rotations around this orientation can give a three dimensional view. Keep in mind, however, that this program has been hard-wired to give rotations in the sequence Rx,Ry,Rz. For example, in function **plotdata()**, which begins at line 46, line 51 does the Rx rotation, next Ry in line 55, and then Rz in line 59.

The data points are plotted in line 213, which invokes function **plotdata()**. This function is straightforward. Each data point is rotated amount Rx, then Ry, followed by Rz in lines 51, 55, and 59. Each point is plotted as a green scatter dot in line 66. Line 64 plots the first point in red. Lines 68-86 plot grey lines from each point down to the x,y plane. The top of each line has the same global plotting coordinates as the data point g[0],g[1]. The z coordinate g[3] is not needed for plotting. The local coordinate of each line's bottom has the same local x,y coordinates as the data point, but now the local z coordinate is zero as specified in line 72. You need these local coordinates to rotate the bottom point of each line. Lines 73, 77, and 81 do the rotations. Line 83 plots the first point in red; line 86 plots the remainder of the points in black with the lines plotted in grey.

Next, the spline is plotted in line 217, which invokes function **plotspline()**. The color is set in line 216. This function is identical to the spline plotting algorithm used in the previous chapter with the exception of the addition of the z axis lines set in bold in the program listing.

The bottoms of the vertical lines are next connected by a spline by invoking function **plotbottomspline()** in line 221. The color is set in line 220. **plotbottomspline()** opens lists for the x,y, and z coordinates of each point: xbottom[ ], ybottom[ ], and zbottom[ ]. The items in each are initially set to zero. They are equated to the x and y data point coordinates in lines 168-171. Since the z coordinate lies in the x,y plane, it is set equal to zero in line 171. These are all local coordinates. Line 172 invokes function **plotspline()**, which was used to plot the main spline, with the arguments being the local coordinates of the bottom points. As before, **plotspline()** will perform the rotations and will plot the spline. The remainder of the program prints data and labels on the plot.

Listing 9-1. Program SPLINE3D

```
1    """
2    SPLINE3D
3    """
4
5    import matplotlib.pyplot as plt
6    import numpy as np
7    from math import sqrt, radians, sin, cos
8
9    plt.axis([0,150,0,100])
10   plt.axis('on')
11   plt.grid(True)
12
13   #=================================================rotation
     transformations
14   def rotx(xp,yp,zp,Rx):
15       g[0]=xp+xc
16       g[1]=yp*cos(Rx)-zp*sin(Rx)+yc
17       g[2]=yp*sin(Rx)+zp*cos(Rx)+zc
18       return[g]
19
20   def roty(xp,yp,zp,Ry):
21       g[0]=xp*cos(Ry)+zp*sin(Ry)+xc
22       g[1]=yp+yc
23       g[2]=-xp*sin(Ry)+zp*cos(Ry)+zc
24       return[g]
25
26   def rotz(xp,yp,zp,Rz):
27       g[0]=xp*cos(Rz)-yp*sin(Rz)+xc
28       g[1]=xp*sin(Rz)+yp*cos(Rz)+yc
29       g[2]=zp+zc
30       return[g]
31
32   #=========================================================plot axis
```

```
33  def plotaxis(xp,yp,zp,Rx,Ry,Rz):
34      rotx(xp,yp,zp,Rx) #-Rx rotation
35      xp=g[0]-xc
36      yp=g[1]-yc
37      zp=g[2]-zc
38      roty(xp,yp,zp,Ry) #-Ry rotation
39      xp=g[0]-xc
40      yp=g[1]-yc
41      zp=g[2]-zc
42      rotz(xp,yp,zp,Rz) #-Rz rotation
43      return[g]
44
45  #================================================plot data points
46  def plotdata(x,y,z,Rx,Ry,Rz):
47      for i in range(0,nop):
48          xp=x[i]
49          yp=y[i]
50          zp=z[i]
51          rotx(xp,yp,zp,Rx)
52          xp=g[0]-xc
53          yp=g[1]-yc
54          zp=g[2]-zc
55          roty(xp,yp,zp,Ry)
56          xp=g[0]-xc
57          yp=g[1]-yc
58          zp=g[2]-zc
59          rotz(xp,yp,zp,Rz)
60          xp=g[0]-xc
61          yp=g[1]-yc
62          zp=g[2]-zc
63          if i==0: #--plot first point red
64              plt.scatter(g[0],g[1],s=25,color='r')
65          else:
66              plt.scatter(g[0],g[1],s=25,color='g')
67          #-------plot vertical lines from data points to the x,y plane
68          xt=g[0] #-global line top coords=rotated data point coords
```

288

```
69          yt=g[1]
70          xp=x[i] #-coords of line bottom (zp=0) before rotation)
71          yp=y[i]
72          zp=0
73          rotx(xp,yp,zp,Rx) #——rotate bottom coords
74          xp=g[0]-xc
75          yp=g[1]-yc
76          zp=g[2]-zc
77          roty(xp,yp,zp,Ry)
78          xp=g[0]-xc
79          yp=g[1]-yc
80          zp=g[2]-zc
81          rotz(xp,yp,zp,Rz)
82          if i==0: #————plot first bottom point red
83              plt.scatter(g[0],g[1],s=25,color='r')
84          else:
85              plt.scatter(g[0],g[1],s=25,color='k')
86          plt.plot([xt,g[0]],[yt,g[1]],color='grey') #——plot line
87
88  #==================================================plot spline
89  def plotspline(x,y,z,Rx,Ry,Rz,clr):
90      q=[0]*nop
91      mx=[0]*nop
92      my=[0]*nop
93      mz=[0]*nop
94      cx=[0]*nop
95      cy=[0]*nop
96      cz=[0]*nop
97      dx=[0]*nop
98      dy=[0]*nop
99      dz=[0]*nop
100     bx=[0]*nop
101     by=[0]*nop
102     bz=[0]*nop
103     ax=[0]*nop
104     ay=[0]*nop
```

```
105    az=[0]*nop
106
107    for i in range(1,nop): #——chords q(i)
108        a=x[i]-x[i-1]
109        b=y[i]-y[i-1]
110        c=z[i]-z[i-1]
111        q[i-1]=sqrt(a*a+b*b+c*c) #——nop=6 gives q[5]
112
113    mx[0]=(x[1]-x[0])/q[0] #——mx[0]
114    my[0]=(y[1]-y[0])/q[0] #——my[0]
115    mz[0]=(z[1]-z[0])/q[0] #——mx[0]
116
117    for i in range(1,nop-1): #——average m[i]
118        mx[i]=((x[i]-x[i-1])/q[i-1]+(x[i+1]-x[i])/q[i])*.5
119        my[i]=((y[i]-y[i-1])/q[i-1]+(y[i+1]-y[i])/q[i])*.5
120        mz[i]=((z[i]-z[i-1])/q[i-1]+(z[i+1]-z[i])/q[i])*.5
121
122    mx[nop-1]=(x[nop-1]-x[nop-2])/q[nop-2] #–mx[nop-1]
123    my[nop-1]=(y[nop-1]-y[nop-2])/q[nop-2] #–my[nop-1]
124    mz[nop-1]=(z[nop-1]-z[nop-2])/q[nop-2] #–mz[nop-1]
125
126    #——————————calculate coefficients
127    for i in range(0,nop-1):
128        dx[i]=x[i]
129        dy[i]=y[i]
130        dz[i]=z[i]
131        cx[i]=mx[i]
132        cy[i]=my[i]
133        cz[i]=mz[i]
134        bx[i]=(3*x[i+1]-2*cx[i]*q[i]-3*dx[i]-mx[i+1]*q[i])/(q[i]*q[i])
135        by[i]=(3*y[i+1]-2*cy[i]*q[i]-3*dy[i]-my[i+1]*q[i])/(q[i]*q[i])
136        bz[i]=(3*z[i+1]-2*cz[i]*q[i]-3*dz[i]-mz[i+1]*q[i])/(q[i]*q[i])
137        ax[i]=(mx[i+1]-2*bx[i]*q[i]-cx[i])/(3*q[i]*q[i])
138        ay[i]=(my[i+1]-2*by[i]*q[i]-cy[i])/(3*q[i]*q[i])
139        az[i]=(mz[i+1]-2*bz[i]*q[i]-cz[i])/(3*q[i]*q[i])
140
```

```
141        #——————————plot spline between data points
142        for i in range(0,nop-1):
143            for qq in np.arange(0,q[i],2):
144                xp=ax[i]*qq*qq*qq+bx[i]*qq*qq+cx[i]*qq+dx[i]
145                yp=ay[i]*qq*qq*qq+by[i]*qq*qq+cy[i]*qq+dy[i]
146                zp=az[i]*qq*qq*qq+bz[i]*qq*qq+cz[i]*qq+dz[i]
147                rotx(xp,yp,zp,Rx) #——Rx rotation
148                xp=g[0]-xc
149                yp=g[1]-yc
150                zp=g[2]-zc
151                roty(xp,yp,zp,Ry) #——Ry rotation
152                xp=g[0]-xc
153                yp=g[1]-yc
154                zp=g[2]-zc
155                rotz(xp,yp,zp,Rz) #——Rz rotation
156                if qq==0: #-plot first point red
157                    xplast=g[0]
158                    yplast=g[1]
159                plt.plot([xplast,g[0]],[yplast,g[1]],linewidth=.7,color=clr)
160                xplast=g[0]
161                yplast=g[1]
162
163 #===============================================plot bottom spline
164 def plotbottomspline(x,y,z,Rx,Ry,Rz,clr):
165     xbottom=[0]*nop
166     ybottom=[0]*nop
167     zbottom=[0]*nop
168     for i in range(0,nop):
169         xbottom[i]=x[i]
170         ybottom[i]=y[i]
171         zbottom[i]=0
172     plotspline(xbottom,ybottom,zbottom,Rx,Ry,Rz, clr)
173
174 #===============================================control
175 #x=[20,40,60,80] #-LOCAL coords-Fig(3D Spline 1)
```

```
176 #y=[30,30,30,30]
177 #z=[15,33,28,17]
178
179 x=[10,30,65,60,80,95,130,140 #-LOCAL coordinates-Figs(3D Splines 2,3
    and 4)
180 y=[20,35,50,32,60,50,65,60]
181 z=[42,30,22,28,45,55,55,55]
182
183 nop=len(x) #-number of data points
184
185 g=[0]*3 #-global plotting coords returned by rotx, roty and rotz
186
187 xc=80 #-origin of X,Y,Z coordinate system
188 yc=20
189 zc=10
190
191 Rxd=-100 #-rotations of X,Y,Z system degrees
192 Ryd=-135
193 Rzd=8
194
195 Rx=radians(Rxd) #----rotations of X,Y,Z system radians
196 Ry=radians(Ryd)
197 Rz=radians(Rzd)
198
199 #------------------------plot X,Y,Z axes
200 plotaxis(30,0,0,Rx,Ry,Rz) #-plot X axis
201 plt.plot([xc,g[0]],[yc,g[1]],linewidth=2,color='k')
202 plt.text(g[0]-5,g[1]-1,'X')
203
204 plotaxis(0,30,0,Rx,Ry,Rz) #-plot Y axis
205 plt.plot([xc,g[0]],[yc,g[1]],linewidth=2,color='k')
206 plt.text(g[0],g[1]-5,'Y')
207
208 plotaxis(0,0,30,Rx,Ry,Rz) #-plot Z axis
209 plt.plot([xc,g[0]],[yc,g[1]],linewidth=2,color='k')
210 plt.text(g[0]-2,g[1]+3,'Z')
```

292

```
211
212 #————————————plot data
213 plotdata(x,y,z,Rx,Ry,Rz)
214
215 #————————————plot spline
216 clr='g' #—————————-spline color
217 plotspline(x,y,z,Rx,Ry,Rz,clr)
218
219 #————————————plot bottom spline
220 clr='b' #—————————bottom spline color
221 plotbottomspline(x,y,z,Rx,Ry,Rz,clr)
222
223 #————————————labels
224 plt.text(120,90,'Rx=')
225 Rxd='%7.1f'%(Rxd)
226 plt.text(132,90,Rxd)
227
228 plt.text(120,85,'Ry=')
229 Ryd='%7.1f'%(Ryd)
230 plt.text(132,85,Ryd)
231
232 plt.text(120,80,'Rz=')
233 Rzd='%7.1f'%(Rzd)
234 plt.text(132,80,Rzd)
235
236 plt.text(90,90,'xc=')
237 xc='%7.1f'%(xc)
238 plt.text(100,90,xc)
239
240 plt.text(90,85,'yc=')
241 yc='%7.1f'%(yc)
242 plt.text(100,85,yc)
243
244 plt.text(90,80,'zc=')
245 zc='%7.1f'%(zc)
246 plt.text(100,80,zc)
```

```
247
248 plt.text(4,90,'x')
249 plt.text(7,90,x)
250 plt.text(4,85,'y')
251 plt.text(7,85,y)
252 plt.text(4,80,'z')
253 plt.text(7,80,z)
254
255 plt.title('3D Spline 4')
256
257 plt.show()
```

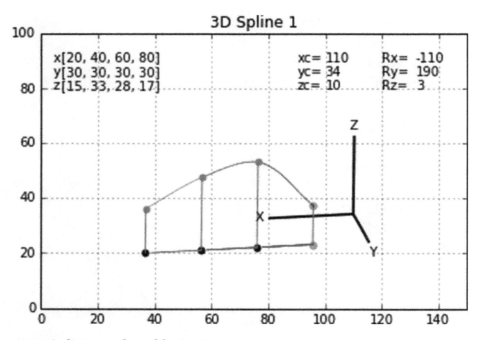

Figure 9-1. *Spline produced by Listing 9-1*

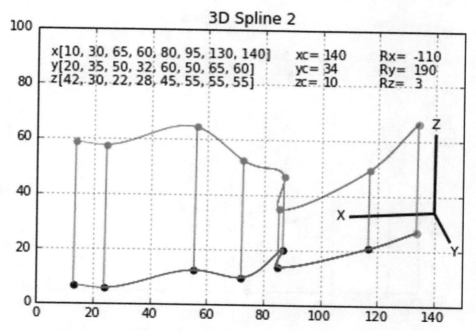

Figure 9-2. *Spline produced by Listing 9-1*

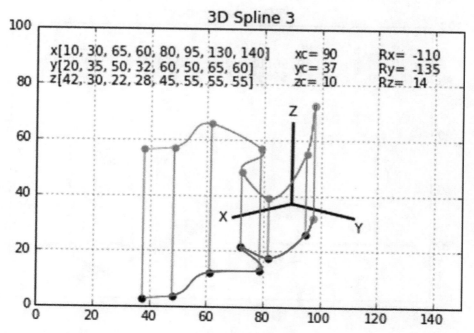

Figure 9-3. *Spline produced by Listing 9-1*

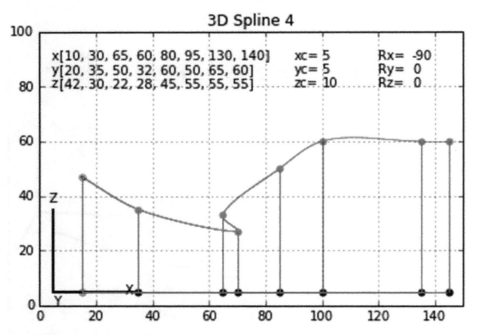

Figure 9-4. *Spline produced by Listing 9-1*

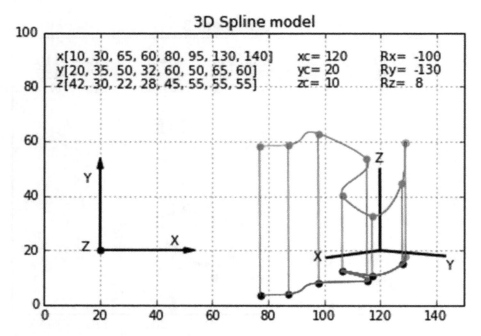

Figure 9-5. *Rotation model used by Listing 9-1*

9.1 3D Surfaces

In the previous section, you saw how to connect data points with splines in three dimensions. In this section, you will use those techniques to create a three-dimensional surface. Figure 9-6 shows a surface z=z(x,y). It is defined by 16 data points in the x,y,z space. To give the appearance of a surface, these points are connected to one another by splines. The green splines connect the points in the y direction, the blue ones in the x direction. Since you already know how to create splines in three dimensions, the problem becomes one of arranging the data points in the proper order.

Listing 9-2 is similar to Listing 9-1 although some of the features of that program have been deleted for simplicity; you do not draw vertical lines from the data points to the x,y plane and you do not plot the projection of the splines on the x,y plane.

The essence of Listing 9-2 is contained in the "control" section beginning in line 140. The 16 data points shown in Figure 9-6 are defined by the lists in lines 168-182. The first group of points in the lists in lines 168-170 define the data points shown in the first y-direction spline (green). This spline lies in the y,z plane where x=0. The points x1[ ], y1[ ],z1[ ] refer to the four points within this spline; x2[ ],y2[ ],z2[ ] refer to the points within the second spline and so on. The first point in the first spline lies at 0,0,0. These coordinates are specified as x1[0],y1[0],z1[0] in lines 168-170. The second point in this first spline lies at 0,10,43. These coordinates are specified as x1[1],y1[1],z1[1]. Similarly, x1[2],y1[2],z1[2] and x1[3],y1[3],z1[3] refer to the third and fourth points in the first y-direction spline. Lines 187-190 plot the data points with these lists as arguments by invoking function **plotdata()**. Lines 194-197 invoke the function **plotspline()**, again with these lists as arguments, which plots the first y-direction spline. Lines 172-174 along with lines 188 and 195 plot the data points and the second green spline at x=20 and so on for the remaining two splines at x=40 and x=60. To plot the x-direction splines, you do the same thing, only you must first redefine the coordinate lists. This takes place in lines 200-214. The blue splines are plotted in lines 218-221.

Of course the coordinate lists could each contain more than four items. The data points defined in the lists in lines 170-184 all lie in a grid. They don't have to.

While it works, the methodology used here to arrange the data for plotting is very cumbersome. It also requires a lot of coding. It is being done this way here to illustrate the procedure used. It could be shortened quite a bit by the use of arrays, which you will use in the next section.

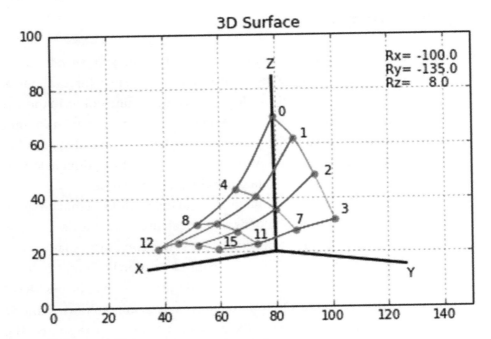

Figure 9-6. *Surface produced by Listing 9-2*

Listing 9-2. Program SURFACE3D

```
1    """
2    SURFACE3D
3    """
4
5    import matplotlib.pyplot as plt
6    import numpy as np
7    from math import sqrt, radians, sin, cos
8
9    plt.axis([0,150,0,100])
10   plt.axis('on')
11   plt.grid(True)
12
13   #=====================================================rotation
     transformations
14   def rotx(xp,yp,zp,Rx):
15       g[0]=xp+xc
```

```
16        g[1]=yp*cos(Rx)-zp*sin(Rx)+yc
17        g[2]=yp*sin(Rx)+zp*cos(Rx)+zc
18        return[g]
19
20    def roty(xp,yp,zp,Ry):
21        g[0]=xp*cos(Ry)+zp*sin(Ry)+xc
22        g[1]=yp+yc
23        g[2]=-xp*sin(Ry)+zp*cos(Ry)+zc
24        return[g]
25
26    def rotz(xp,yp,zp,Rz):
27        g[0]=xp*cos(Rz)-yp*sin(Rz)+xc
28        g[1]=xp*sin(Rz)+yp*cos(Rz)+yc
29        g[2]=zp+zc
30        return[g]
31
32    #===============================================================plot axis
33    def plotaxis(xp,yp,zp,Rx,Ry,Rz):
34        rotx(xp,yp,zp,Rx) #——Rx rotation
35        xp=g[0]-xc
36        yp=g[1]-yc
37        zp=g[2]-zc
38        roty(xp,yp,zp,Ry) #——Ry rotation
39        xp=g[0]-xc
40        yp=g[1]-yc
41        zp=g[2]-zc
42        rotz(xp,yp,zp,Rz) #——Rz rotation
43        return[g]
44
45    #===========================================================plot data
46    def plotdata(x,y,z,Rx,Ry,Rz):
47        for i in range(0,nop):
48            xp=x[i]
49            yp=y[i]
50            zp=z[i]
```

```
51            rotx(xp,yp,zp,Rx)
52            xp=g[0]-xc
53            yp=g[1]-yc
54            zp=g[2]-zc
55            roty(xp,yp,zp,Ry)
56            xp=g[0]-xc
57            yp=g[1]-yc
58            zp=g[2]-zc
59            rotz(xp,yp,zp,Rz)
60            xp=g[0]-xc
61            yp=g[1]-yc
62            zp=g[2]-zc
63            plt.scatter(g[0],g[1],s=25,color='g')
64
65    #========================================================plotspline( )
66    def plotspline(x,y,z,Rx,Ry,Rz,clr):
67        q=[0]*nop
68        mx=[0]*nop
69        my=[0]*nop
70        mz=[0]*nop
71        cx=[0]*nop
72        cy=[0]*nop
73        cz=[0]*nop
74        dx=[0]*nop
75        dy=[0]*nop
76        dz=[0]*nop
77        bx=[0]*nop
78        by=[0]*nop
79        bz=[0]*nop
80        ax=[0]*nop
81        ay=[0]*nop
82        az=[0]*nop
83
84        for i in range(1,nop): #-chords q(i)
85            a=x[i]-x[i-1]
```

```
 86          b=y[i]-y[i-1]
 87          c=z[i]-z[i-1]
 88          q[i-1]=sqrt(a*a+b*b+c*c) #—nop=6 gives q[5]
 89
 90      mx[0]=(x[1]-x[0])/q[0] #—mx[0]
 91      my[0]=(y[1]-y[0])/q[0] #—my[0]
 92      mz[0]=(z[1]-z[0])/q[0] #—mx[0]
 93
 94      for i in range(1,nop-1): #—average m[i]
 95          mx[i]=((x[i]-x[i-1])/q[i-1]+(x[i+1]-x[i])/q[i])*.5
 96          my[i]=((y[i]-y[i-1])/q[i-1]+(y[i+1]-y[i])/q[i])*.5
 97          mz[i]=((z[i]-z[i-1])/q[i-1]+(z[i+1]-z[i])/q[i])*.5
 98
 99      mx[nop-1]=(x[nop-1]-x[nop-2])/q[nop-2] #—mx[nop-1]
100      my[nop-1]=(y[nop-1]-y[nop-2])/q[nop-2] #—my[nop-1]
101      mz[nop-1]=(z[nop-1]-z[nop-2])/q[nop-2] #—mz[nop-1]
102
103      #—————————calculate coefficients
104      for i in range(0,nop-1):
105       dx[i]=x[i]
106       dy[i]=y[i]
107       dz[i]=z[i]
108       cx[i]=mx[i]
109       cy[i]=my[i]
110       cz[i]=mz[i]
111       bx[i]=(3*x[i+1]-2*cx[i]*q[i]-3*dx[i]-mx[i+1]*q[i])/(q[i]*q[i])
112       by[i]=(3*y[i+1]-2*cy[i]*q[i]-3*dy[i]-my[i+1]*q[i])/(q[i]*q[i])
113       bz[i]=(3*z[i+1]-2*cz[i]*q[i]-3*dz[i]-mz[i+1]*q[i])/(q[i]*q[i])
114       ax[i]=(mx[i+1]-2*bx[i]*q[i]-cx[i])/(3*q[i]*q[i])
115       ay[i]=(my[i+1]-2*by[i]*q[i]-cy[i])/(3*q[i]*q[i])
116       az[i]=(mz[i+1]-2*bz[i]*q[i]-cz[i])/(3*q[i]*q[i])
117
118      #—————————plot splines between data points
119      for i in range(0,nop-1):
120          for qq in np.arange(0,q[i],2):
```

```
121                xp=ax[i]*qq*qq*qq+bx[i]*qq*qq+cx[i]*qq+dx[i]
122                yp=ay[i]*qq*qq*qq+by[i]*qq*qq+cy[i]*qq+dy[i]
123                zp=az[i]*qq*qq*qq+bz[i]*qq*qq+cz[i]*qq+dz[i]
124                xp=g[0]-xc
125                yp=g[1]-yc
126                zp=g[2]-zc
127                roty(xp,yp,zp,Ry) #–Ry rotation
128                xp=g[0]-xc
129                yp=g[1]-yc
130                zp=g[2]-zc
131                rotz(xp,yp,zp,Rz) #–Rz rotation
132                if qq==0:
133                    xplast=g[0]
134                    yplast=g[1]
135                plt.plot([xplast,g[0]],[yplast,g[1]],linewidth=.7,color=clr)
136                xplast=g[0]
137                yplast=g[1]
138
139 #=====================================================control
140 g=[0]*3 #–global plotting coords returned by rotx, roty and rotz
141
142 xc=80 #–origin of X,Y,Z coordinate system
143 yc=20
144 zc=10
145
146 Rxd=-100 #-rotations of X,Y,Z system degrees
147 Ryd=-135
148 Rzd=8
149
150 Rx=radians(Rxd) #–rotations of X,Y,Z system radians
151 Ry=radians(Ryd)
152 Rz=radians(Rzd)
153
```

```
154 #————————————plot X,Y,Z axes
155 plotaxis(60,0,0,Rx,Ry,Rz) #—plot X axis
156 plt.plot([xc,g[0]],[yc,g[1]],linewidth=2,color='k')
157 plt.text(g[0]-5,g[1]-1,'X')
158
159 plotaxis(0,60,0,Rx,Ry,Rz) #—plot Y axis
160 plt.plot([xc,g[0]],[yc,g[1]],linewidth=2,color='k')
161 plt.text(g[0],g[1]-5,'Y')
162
163 plotaxis(0,0,60,Rx,Ry,Rz) #—plot Z axis
164 plt.plot([xc,g[0]],[yc,g[1]],linewidth=2,color='k')
165 plt.text(g[0]-2,g[1]+3,'Z')
166
167 #————————define 4 sets of data points at different values of X
168 x1=[0,0,0,0] #——LOCAL coords
169 y1=[0,10,20,30]
170 z1=[50,43,30,14]
171
172 x2=[20,20,20,20]
173 y2=y1
174 z2=[25,23,19,12]
175
176 x3=[40,40,40,40]
177 y3=y1
178 z3=[14,15,13,9]
179
180 x4=[60,60,60,60]
181 y4=y1
182 z4=[7,10,10,9]
183
184 nop=len(x1) #——number of data points
185
186 #————————————plot data points
187 plotdata(x1,y1,z1,Rx,Ry,Rz)
188 plotdata(x2,y2,z2,Rx,Ry,Rz)
```

```
189  plotdata(x3,y3,z3,Rx,Ry,Rz)
190  plotdata(x4,y4,z4,Rx,Ry,Rz)
191
192  #————————————plot Y direction splines
193  clr='g' #————————spline color
194  plotspline(x1,y1,z1,Rx,Ry,Rz,clr)
195  plotspline(x2,y2,z2,Rx,Ry,Rz,clr)
196  plotspline(x3,y3,z3,Rx,Ry,Rz,clr)
197  plotspline(x4,y4,z4,Rx,Ry,Rz,clr)
198
199  #————————redefine the data points at different values of y
200  xx1=[0,20,40,60]
201  yy1=[y1[3],y2[3],y3[3],y4[3]]
202  zz1=[z1[3],z2[3],z3[3],z4[3]]
203
204  xx2=xx1
205  yy2=[y1[2],y2[2],y3[2],y4[2]]
206  zz2=[z1[2],z2[2],z3[2],z4[2]]
207
208  xx3=xx1
209  yy3=[y1[1],y2[1],y3[1],y4[1]]
210  zz3=[z1[1],z2[1],z3[1],z4[1]]
211
212  xx4=xx1
213  yy4=[y1[0],y2[0],y3[0],y4[0]]
214  zz4=[z1[0],z2[0],z3[0],z4[0]]
215
216  #————————————plot X direction splines
217  clr='b' #————————spline color
218  plotspline(xx1,yy1,zz1,Rx,Ry,Rz,clr)
219  plotspline(xx2,yy2,zz2,Rx,Ry,Rz,clr)
220  plotspline(xx3,yy3,zz3,Rx,Ry,Rz,clr)
221  plotspline(xx4,yy4,zz4,Rx,Ry,Rz,clr)
222
223  #————————————————labels
```

```
224 plt.text(120,90,'Rx=')
225 Rxd='%7.1f'%(Rxd)
226 plt.text(130,90,Rxd)
227
228 plt.text(120,85,'Ry=')
229 Ryd='%7.1f'%(Ryd)
230 plt.text(130,85,Ryd)
231
232 plt.text(120,80,'Rz=')
233 Rzd='%7.1f'%(Rzd)
234 plt.text(130,80,Rzd)
235
236 plt.title('3D Surface')
237
238 plt.show()
```

9.2 3D Surface Shading

In the previous section, you constructed a surface by connecting data points with splines. You did not use arrays but relied on a cumbersome system of numbering. While this kept the procedure open and easy to understand, it led to too many lines of code. In this section, you will use the same data set but with two differences: first, you will connect the data points by straight lines; second, you will use arrays to organize your plotting. When you see how simple and elegant the use of arrays can be, you may question which method is the easiest to code and to follow.

Using the same three-dimensional data set as you used in the previous section, the array which defines the data is

$$A = np.array([\quad \overbrace{[0, 0, 50]}^{A[0]=point\ 0}, \ \overbrace{[0, 10, 43]}^{A[1]=point\ 1}, \ [0, 20, 30], \ \overbrace{[0, 30, 14]}^{A[i]=point\ i},$$
$$[20, 0, 25], [20, 10, 23], [20, 20, 19], [20, 30, 12],$$
$$[40, 0, 14], [40, 10, 15], [40, 20, 13], [40, 30, 9],$$
$$[60, 0, 7], \ [60, 10, 10], \ [60, 20, 10], \ [60, 30, 9] \ ]) \tag{9-1}$$

This array is used by Listing 9-3 to produce Figure 9-7. The numbering scheme used to relate A to the surface points is shown in Figure 9-8.

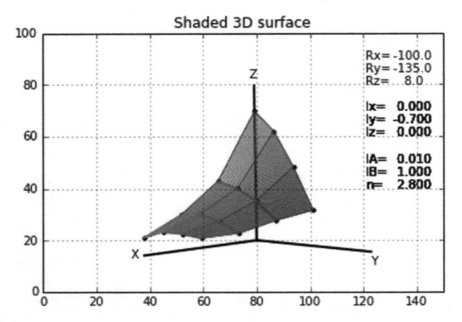

Figure 9-7. *Shaded 3D surface produced by Listing 9-3*

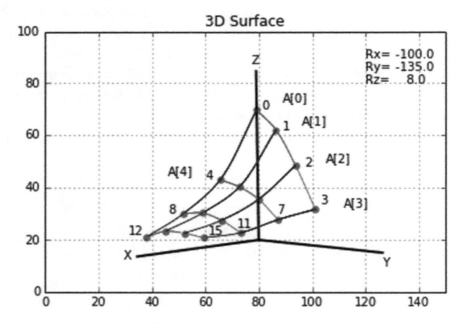

Figure 9-8. *Data point numbering scheme used in Listing 9-3*

Each element in A is a list. There are 16 lists: A[0] through A[15]. List i is referenced as A[i] where i=0→15. For example, A[3]=[0,30,14]. Each list i defines the x,y,z coordinates of data point i. That is

$$A[i,1] = x(i) \tag{9-2}$$

$$A[i,2] = y(i) \tag{9-3}$$

$$A[i,3] = z(i) \tag{9-4}$$

For example, the first point, point 0, has coordinates

$$A[0,1] = x(0) = 0 \tag{9-5}$$

$$A[0,2] = y(0) = 0 \tag{9-6}$$

$$A[0,3] = z(0) = 50 \tag{9-7}$$

This method replaces the list numbering system used in the previous section.

Referring to Figure 9-8, to get the z coordinate of the fourth data point, which is numbered 3, you access the third element of the *fourth* list of array A by letting i=3, j=2. As with lists, the numbering of elements within arrays begins at 0 so the coordinates of the fourth data point are contained in list i=3. The z component is the third element in that list, j=2. Thus the z coordinate of the fourth data point is A[3,2], so

```
print(A[3,2])
```

14

The numbering scheme in Figure 9-8 starts at point 0, which is at the upper corner of the surface at x=0, y=0, z=50, and proceeds in the y direction for a total of 4 data points. It then advances to a new value of x for another grouping of 4 y-direction points. This gives a total of 16 data points. Other numbering schemes could be used. You could, for example, have started at the same point but proceeded in the x direction first rather than the y direction. Or you could have started at a different corner of the surface. As you will see, whatever numbering scheme is chosen, it will have an impact on subsequent operations on that data.

The surface is composed of quadrangles, which are called *patches*. You will be shading these patches. Each patch is defined by four data points. Since these are located in three-dimensional space, the patches will, in general, not be flat. Also, since the sides can have arbitrary lengths, the patches will not necessarily be rectangular. The basic shading techniques used in previous chapters (i.e. coloring the patches by drawing lines across them) will be used but the technique must be modified.

Figure 9-9 shows the model. This is a generic oblique patch defined by four corners numbered $0 \to 3$. q03 and q12 are the lengths of the sides from $0 \to 3$ and $1 \to 2$. As mentioned, these sides are three-dimensional and are not necessarily parallel. As was done in previous chapters on shading, you fill in the patch with color by drawing lines across the quadrangle. The blue lines shown are examples. As shown in Figures 9-10 and 9-11, the algorithm you will be developing here will work with any quadrilateral.

To plot the lines, all you have to do is determine the starting position S of each line along side 0,3 and the end position E alongside 1,2. Since these sides have different lengths, the distance q of S from point 0 alongside 0,3 is not the same as the distance of E from point 1 down along side 1,2. The starting point of the lines S begin at the top of the patch (corner 0) at q=0 and proceed to the bottom at q=q03. To get the corresponding position of E down side 1,2, you ratio the distance q by q12/q03. A line is then drawn between S and E. The blue lines shown in Figure 9-9 are 70%, 80%, and 90% of the way down both sides of the patch.

The unit vector $\hat{n}$ shown in Figure 9-9 is not required for the line drawing but will be needed when you determine the intensity of coloring. This is done as before by taking the dot product of $\hat{n}$ with a light source unit vector $\hat{l}$.

In Listing 9-3, the numbers of the generic patch corners, $0 \to 3$ in Figure 9-9, are replaced by the appropriate numbers for each patch on the surface from array A. The array is defined in the control section in lines 164-167. Line 169 gives the number of data points in A, which is equal to the number of lists, each list defining the location of a point. In this case, nop=16. The data points are plotted in lines 172-194. This simple routine, which illustrates a benefit of using arrays, replaces the data plotting function used in prior programs. Lines 178-185 connect the four y direction points by lines of color **clr** specified in line 177. Function **plotline()** does the line plotting. Lines 188-194 do the same in the x direction.

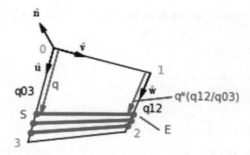

Figure 9-9. *Patch model used in Listing 9-3*

The patches are shaded in lines 197-205 by invoking function **shade()**, which begins in line 65. The arguments are arranged to conform to the generic patch corners shown in Figure 9-9. Lines 197-199 shade the first row of patches in the y direction. The first patch has its upper left corner at A[0,0], the second patch at A[1,0], and so on. In the first cycle through the loop, with i=0, lines 198 and 199 give the following patch corner coordinates, which are used as parameters in the call to function shade:

$A[0, 0] = x[0] = x0 = 0$ *corner 0*

$A[0, 1] = y[0] = y0 = 0$

$A[0, 2] = z[0] = z0 = 50$

$A[1, 0] = x[1] = x1 = 0$ *corner 1*

$A[1, 2] = y[1] = y1 = 10$

$A[1, 3] = z[1] = z1 = 43$

$A[5, 0] = x[5] = x2 = 0$ *corner 2*

$A[5, 1] = y[5] = y2 = 20$

$A[5, 2] = z[5] = z2 = 30$

$A[4, 0] = x[4] = x3 = 0$ *corner 3*

$A[4, 1] = y[4] = y3 = 30$

$A[4, 2] = z[4] = z3 = 14$

In function **shade()**, the arguments in line 65 coincide with the above patch corners 0,1,2 and 3,

$$\left(\underbrace{\overset{A[0]}{x0,\ y0,\ z0,}}_{corner\ 0} \underbrace{\overset{A[1]}{x1,\ y1,\ z1,}}_{corner\ 1} \underbrace{\overset{A[5]}{x2,\ y2,\ z2,}}_{corner\ 2} \underbrace{\overset{A[4]}{x3,\ y3,\ z3,}}_{corner\ 3} \right)$$

When i=1, these same program lines give the corner coordinates for the next patch in the y direction, which has corners 1, 2, 6 and 5. These correspond to the generic patch corners 0, 1, 2, and 3. The remaining cycles of the loop shade the remaining two patches in the y direction. Lines 200-202 and 203-205 advance in the x direction and perform the same operation, thus shading all nine patches.

You may be wondering why the **for** loop in line 197, **for i in range(0,3):**, uses the index *3* instead of *2*. After all, there are only three y direction patches to shade; $0 \rightarrow 3$ would seem to give four. It has to do with the workings of the **range()** function. In general, the syntax is **range(start, stop, step)**. If no **step** is specified, it is assumed to be 1. Range will start at **start**, go to **stop** in steps of **step**, but it will *not* return the value at **stop**. In line 197, 0 is the **start** value, 3 is the **stop** value. This will return i=0, 1 and 2, but *not* 3. This was explained in Chapter 1. You can try this for yourself:

```
for i in range(0,3):
    print(i)
```

```
0
1
2
```

It is tempting to think of **stop** as the number of values to be returned, but it isn't. For example,

```
for i in range(1,3):
    print(i)
```

```
1
2
```

If the **start** value is not specified, it is automatically set to 0:

```
for i in range(3):
    print(i)
```

0

1

2

In this text, I usually included the **start** value for clarity but I do not usually specify the **step** value unless it is different from 1.

In function **shade()**, lines 66-92 evaluate the unit vectors $\hat{u}$, $\hat{v}$, $\hat{w}$, and $\hat{n}$.

Lines 94-96 specify the components of $\hat{l}$, the incoming light direction unit vector, as was done in prior shading programs. Line 98 takes the dot product of $\hat{n}$ with $\hat{l}$. Line 100-103 defines the shading function and establishes the light intensity, I, impacting the patch. Line 105 mixes the r, g, b colors. Lines 107-115 plot the lines across the patch. Line 117 plots the lines. Note that the lines have the color established in line 105.

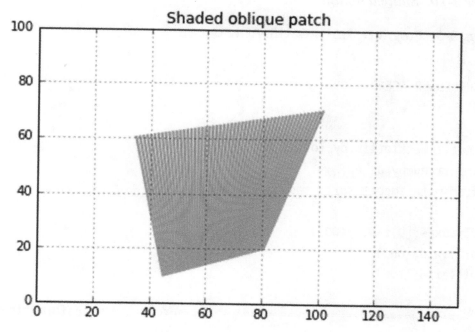

Figure 9-11. *Shaded oblique patch*

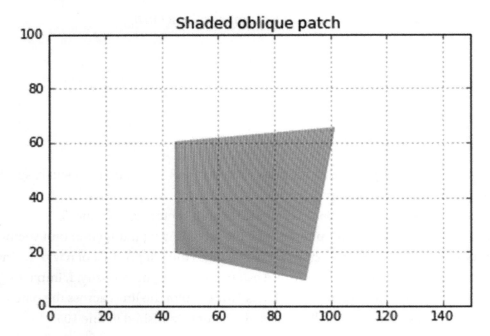

Figure 9-10. *Shaded oblique patch*

Listing 9-3. Program SHADEDSURFACE3D

```
1    """
2    SHADEDSURFACE3D
3    """
4
5    import matplotlib.pyplot as plt
6    import numpy as np
7    from math import sqrt, radians, sin, cos
8
9    plt.axis([0,150,0,100])
10   plt.axis('on')
11   plt.grid(True)
12
13   #=========================================rotation transformations
14
15   #————————same as Listing 9-2, Program SURFACE3D————————
16
```

```
17   #==========================================================plot axes
18
19   #————same as Listing 9-2, Program SURFACE3D————
20
21   #==========================================================plot point
22   def plotpoint(xp,yp,zp,Rx,Ry,Rz,clr):
23       rotx(xp,yp,zp,Rx)
24       xp=g[0]-xc
25       yp=g[1]-yc
26       zp=g[2]-zc
27       roty(xp,yp,zp,Ry)
28       xp=g[0]-xc
29       yp=g[1]-yc
30       zp=g[2]-zc
31       rotz(xp,yp,zp,Rz)
32       plt.scatter(g[0],g[1],s=10,color=clr)
33
34   #==========================================================plotline
35   def plotline(xb,yb,zb,xe,ye,ze,Rx,Ry,Rz,clr):
36       rotx(xb,yb,zb,Rx) #————rotate line beginning coordinates
37       xb=g[0]-xc
38       yb=g[1]-yc
39       zb=g[2]-zc
40       roty(xb,yb,zb,Ry)
41       xb=g[0]-xc
42       yb=g[1]-yc
43       zb=g[2]-zc
44       rotz(xb,yb,zb,Rz)
45       xb=g[0]
46       yb=g[1]
47       zb=g[2]
48
49       rotx(xe,ye,ze,Rx) #————rotate line end coordinates
50       xe=g[0]-xc
51       ye=g[1]-yc
```

313

```
52        ze=g[2]-zc
53        roty(xe,ye,ze,Ry)
54        xe=g[0]-xc
55        ye=g[1]-yc
56        ze=g[2]-zc
57        rotz(xe,ye,ze,Rz)
58        xe=g[0]
59        ye=g[1]
60        ze=g[2]
61
62    plt.plot([xb,xe],[yb,ye],linewidth=.7,color=clr)
63
64    #=================================================shade
65    def shade(x0,y0,z0,x1,y1,z1,x2,y2,z2,x3,y3,z3,Rx,Ry,Rz,clr):
66        a=x3-x0
67        b=y3-y0
68        c=z3-z0
69        q03=np.sqrt(a*a+b*b+c*c)
70        ux=a/q03
71        uy=b/q03
72        uz=c/q03
73
74        a=x1-x0
75        b=y1-y0
76        c=z1-z0
77        q02=sqrt(a*a+b*b+c*c)
78        vx=a/q02
79        vy=b/q02
80        vz=c/q02
81
82        a=x2-x1
83        b=y2-y1
84        c=z2-z1
85        q12=np.sqrt(a*a+b*b+c*c)
86        wx=a/q12
```

```
87      wy=b/q12
88      wz=c/q12
89
90      nx=uy*vz-uz*vy
91      ny=uz*vx-ux*vz
92      nz=ux*vy-uy*vx
93
94      lx=0
95      ly=-.7
96      lz=0
97
98      ndotl=nx*lx+ny*ly+nz*lz
99
100     IA=.01
101     IB=1
102     n=2.8
103     I=IA+(IB-IA)*((1-ndotl)/2)**n
104
105     clr=(1-I,.4*(1-I),.6*(1-I))
106
107     r=q12/q03
108     dq=q03/50
109     for q in np.arange(0,q03+1,dq):
110         xb=x0+ux*q
111         yb=y0+uy*q
112         zb=z0+uz*q
113         xe=x1+wx*q*r
114         ye=y1+wy*q*r
115         ze=z1+wz*q*r
116
117         plotline(xb,yb,zb,xe,ye,ze,Rx,Ry,Rz,clr)
118
119     plt.text(121,70,'lx=')
120     lx='%7.3f'%(lx)
121     plt.text(130,70,lx)
```

```
122
123        plt.text(121,65,'ly=')
124        ly='%7.3f'%(ly)
125        plt.text(130,65,ly)
126
127        plt.text(121,60,'lz=')
128        lz='%7.3f'%(lz)
129        plt.text(130,60,lz)
130
131        plt.text(121,50,'IA=')
132        IA='%7.3f'%(IA)
133        plt.text(130,50,IA)
134
135        plt.text(121,45,'IB=')
136        IB='%7.3f'%(IB)
137        plt.text(130,45,IB)
138
139        plt.text(121,40,'n=')
140        n='%7.3f'%(n)
141        plt.text(130,40,n)
142
143 #=========================================================control
144 g=[0]*3 #——global plotting coords returned by rotx, roty and rotz
145
146 xc=80 #——origin of X,Y,Z coordinate system
147 yc=20
148 zc=10
149
150 Rxd=-100 #——-rotations of X,Y,Z system degrees
151 Ryd=-135
152 Rzd=8
153
154 Rx=radians(Rxd) #——rotations of X,Y,Z system radians
155 Ry=radians(Ryd)
156 Rz=radians(Rzd)
```

```
157
158 #————————————plot X,Y,Z axes
159
160 #————same as Listing 9-2, Program SURFACE3D————
161
162 #————————define data point array A
163
164 A=np.array([ [0,0,50], [0,10,43], [0,20,30], [0,30,14],
165             [20,0,25], [20,10,23], [20,20,19], [20,30,12],
166             [40,0,14], [40,10,15], [40,20,13], [40,30,9],
167             [60,0,7], [60,10,10], [60,20,10], [60,30,9] ])
168
169 nop=len(A) #————number of data points
170
171 #————————————plot data points
172 clr='k'
173 for i in range(0,16):
174     plotpoint(A[i,0],A[i,1],A[i,2],Rx,Ry,Rz,clr)
175
176 #—————————connect data points in Y direction
177 clr='k' #————line color
178 for i in range(0,3):
179     plotline(A[i,0],A[i,1],A[i,2],A[i+1,0],A[i+1,1],A[i+1,2],Rx,Ry,Rz,
        clr)
180 for i in range(4,7):
181     plotline(A[i,0],A[i,1],A[i,2],A[i+1,0],A[i+1,1],A[i+1,2],Rx,Ry,Rz,
        clr)
182 for i in range(8,11):
183     plotline(A[i,0],A[i,1],A[i,2],A[i+1,0],A[i+1,1],A[i+1,2],Rx,Ry,Rz,
        clr)
184 for i in range(12,15):
185     plotline(A[i,0],A[i,1],A[i,2],A[i+1,0],A[i+1,1],A[i+1,2],Rx,Ry,Rz,
        clr)
186
187 #————————————connect data points in X direction
```

```
188 clr='k' #———————line color
189 for i in range(0,4):
190     plotline(A[i,0],A[i,1],A[i,2],A[i+4,0],A[i+4,1],A[i+4,2],Rx,Ry,Rz,clr)
191 for i in range(4,8):
192     plotline(A[i,0],A[i,1],A[i,2],A[i+4,0],A[i+4,1],A[i+4,2],Rx,Ry,Rz,clr)
193 for i in range(8,12):
194     plotline(A[i,0],A[i,1],A[i,2],A[i+4,0],A[i+4,1],A[i+4,2],Rx,Ry,Rz,clr)
195
196 #———————————————shade patches
197 for i in range(0,3):
198     shade(A[i,0],A[i,1],A[i,2],A[i+1,0],A[i+1,1],A[i+1,2],A[i+5,0],
199         A[i+5,1],A[i+5,2],A[i+4,0],A[i+4,1],A[i+4,2],Rx,Ry,Rz,clr)
200 for i in range(4,7):
201     shade(A[i,0],A[i,1],A[i,2],A[i+1,0],A[i+1,1],A[i+1,2],A[i+5,0],
202         A[i+5,1],A[i+5,2],A[i+4,0],A[i+4,1],A[i+4,2],Rx,Ry,Rz,clr)
203 for i in range(8,11):
204     shade(A[i,0],A[i,1],A[i,2],A[i+1,0],A[i+1,1],A[i+1,2],A[i+5,0],
205         A[i+5,1],A[i+5,2],A[i+4,0],A[i+4,1],A[i+4,2],Rx,Ry,Rz,clr)
206
207 #———————————————labels
208 plt.text(121,90,'Rx=')
209 Rxd='%7.1f'%(Rxd)
210 plt.text(130,90,Rxd)
211
212 plt.text(121,85,'Ry=')
213 Ryd='%7.1f'%(Ryd)
214 plt.text(130,85,Ryd)
215
216 plt.text(121,80,'Rz=')
217 Rzd='%7.1f'%(Rzd)
218 plt.text(130,80,Rzd)
219
220 plt.title('Shaded 3D Surface')
221
222 plt.show()
```

9.3 Summary

In this chapter, you saw how to plot data in three dimensions. To do so, you changed the usual orientation of your axes with z pointing into the screen to z pointing up; x and y are in the horizontal plane. This is the common way of displaying data where Pz=f(Px,Py); Px,Py, and Pz being the coordinates of a data point. In Listing 9-1, you connected the data points by splines. As an aid to visualization, you projected the spline down onto the x,y plane. It could be projected onto the other coordinate planes without much difficulty. The 3D spline algorithm you used is an extrapolation of the 2D spline presented in Chapter 8. In Listing 9-2, you constructed a surface by connecting points by splines in the x and y directions. Then you shaded the three-dimensional surface. This required connecting the data points by straight lines rather than splines. The result was an assemblage of oblique patches, which are not necessarily planar; each of them may be twisted out of plane. You learned how to shade the surface by shading each patch. This required development of an algorithm capable of shading a non-planar oblique quadrilateral. The shading was carried out by plotting lines across the surface of each patch; the intensity of the color was determined by the orientation of the patch with respect to the direction of the illuminating light rays.

CHAPTER 10

Demonstrations

In this chapter, you will apply some of the techniques developed in previous chapters to produce some interesting images. These images should give you some idea of the things that can be accomplished with Python graphics.

10.1 Saturn

Saturn is famous for its rings. While Jupiter, Saturn, Uranus, and Neptune also have rings, Saturn's are the largest, brightest, and most well known in our solar system. They consist of particles as small as dust up to boulder-sized objects. These objects are composed mostly of ice and are thought to have originated when a comet or large asteroid collided with one of Saturn's moons, shattering both into small pieces. Saturn has been known from ancient times but in 1610 Galileo was the first to observe it with a telescope. The planet is named after Saturn, the Roman god of agriculture, as is our sixth day, Saturday.

Listing 10-1 builds on an earlier program, Listing 7-2 from Chapter 7. That program is left mostly intact here except for the introduction of algorithms that construct Saturn's rings and the shadow of the planet on the rings.

Figures 10-1 through 10-5 show images produced by Listing 10-1. They are at different angles of orientation, which are listed in the captions. Also listed are the unit vector components of the incoming light rays. For example, lx=+.707, ly=+.707, lz=0 indicates a source in the upper left quadrant; lx=-1, ly=0, lz=0 indicates a light source coming from the right. In the images, please notice the shadow cast by the planet on the rings, especially in Figure 10-5, which shows the curvature of the planet.

For comparison, a photographic image of Saturn can be found at www.jpl.nasa.gov/spaceimages/?search=saturn&category=#submit.

© B.J. Korites 2018
B.J. Korites, *Python Graphics*, https://doi.org/10.1007/978-1-4842-3378-8_10

Figure 10-1. *Saturn with rings and shadow 1: Rx=-20, Ry=0, Rz=-10, lx=1, ly=0, lz=0 (produced by Listing 10-1)*

Figure 10-2. *Saturn with rings and shadow 2: Rx=-8, Ry=0, Rz=30, lx=.707, ly=.707, lz=0 (produced by Listing 10-1)*

Figure 10-3. *Saturn with rings and shadow 3, Rx=-20, Ry=0, Rz=25, lx=.707, ly=.707, lz=0 (produced by Listing 10-1)*

Figure 10-4. *Saturn with rings and shadow 4: Rx=-10, ry=0, Rz=25, lx=-.707, ly=-.707, lz=0 (produced by Listing 10-1)*

Figure 10-5. *Saturn with rings and shadow 5: Rx=20, Ry=0, Rz=30, lx=-1, ly=0, lz=0 (produced by Listing 10-1)*

Figure 10-6 shows the model used to construct the rings. In Chapter 7, you developed the shaded sphere algorithm by first creating an upright sphere. That is, the longitudes were vertical and the latitudes were horizontal (i.e. parallel to the x,z plane). From this starting orientation you rotated the sphere around the x,y, and z axes. You do a similar thing here for the rings. You create horizontal rings, which are parallel to the x,z plane, and then rotate them through the same angles along with the spherical planet body. The rings lie in a plane that passes through the sphere's center so both the sphere and the rings have the same center of rotation.

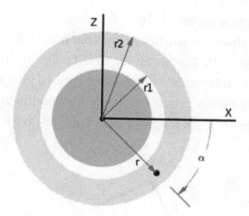

Figure 10-6. *Rings model: top view of planet and rings looking down on the x,z plane with Rx=0, Ry=0, Rz=0*

The band is drawn as a series of adjacent concentric circles, each of which is composed of short line segments. Referring to Figure 10-6 and Listing 10-1, program lines 42 and 43 set the inner and outer radii of the rings. Line 44 sets the distance between circles. The rings are divided into seven annular bands (not shown in Figure 10-6) to accommodate different colors; their width is **deltar** in line 45.

Each line segment is rotated and plotted separately. Line 48 starts a radial direction loop from r1 to r2 plotting the circle segments. Line 49 starts a loop plotting in the circumferential direction. Lines 50-61 do the rotating producing global plotting coordinates xpg and ypg in lines 62 and 63. The rotation functions are the same as in previous programs.

Next, you set the colors of the segments. The rings are arranged in bands of different colors, which are a result of their physical composition as seen in the NASA image. This is done in lines 66-75. The first band, which goes from r=r1 to r1+**deltar**, has color **clr**=(.63,.54,.18) and so on for the remaining bands. You omit the fifth band, which is empty; the background color shows through. The sixth band is twice as wide as the others. This provides the colors for the seven bands.

For a given light direction, in most orientations the planet's body will cast a shadow on the rings. Referring to Figure 10-7, your objective is to determine if point p lies inside or outside the planet's shadow zone. The spherical planet casts a circular shadow. The shadow's diameter will equal the size of the planet, or more precisely, the sphere's "great circle." This is the largest circle that can be obtained by cutting a sphere with a plane through its center. It's like cutting an orange in half; what you see is the orange's great circle. In Figure 10-7, the shadow could as well be caused by a circular disk of this size as by the spherical planet; the shadow will have the same size in either case. The side view of Saturn's great circle is shown as the heavy line that passes through the plane's center. From the geometry in Figure 10-7, you can see that if p lies in a position such that $|\mathbf{B}| > \text{rs}$, where rs is Saturn's radius, it is outside the shadow zone; if $|\mathbf{B}| < \text{rs}$, p is inside the shadow zone. Once you determine where p is, if it is inside the shadow zone, when you plot the rings you will color that point grey. If it is outside, you will give it one of the band colors set in lines 66-75.

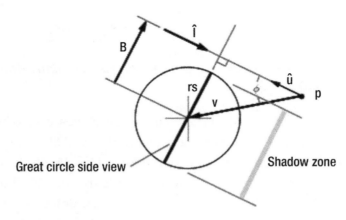

Figure 10-7. *Shadow model*

Your job now is to get $|\mathbf{B}|$ for a given position of p. You see from Figure 10-7 that

$$|\mathbf{B}| = |\mathbf{V}|sin(\phi) \tag{10-1}$$

You know that

$$\mathbf{V} \times \hat{\mathbf{u}} = |\mathbf{V}||\hat{\mathbf{u}}|sin(\phi) \tag{10-2}$$

where $\hat{\mathbf{u}}=-\hat{\mathbf{I}}$. Combining the above equations with $|\hat{\mathbf{u}}|=1$,

$$\mathbf{B} = \mathbf{V} \times \hat{\mathbf{u}} \tag{10-3}$$

$$|\mathbf{B}| = |\mathbf{V} \times \hat{\mathbf{u}}| \tag{10-4}$$

In Listing 10-1, line 78 establishes the length of the incident light vector, $\hat{\mathbf{I}}$. This should equal 1, but it may not if the components entered in lines 23-25 do not compute to 1 (i.e. $\sqrt{lx^2 + ly^2 + ly^2} \neq 1$). Lines 79-81 then reestablish the components if necessary.

Lines 82-84 establish the components of vector **V**. Lines 85-87 compute components of **B**. Line 88 gives its magnitude magB=|**B**|. Line 89 determines if p lies within the shadow zone. If it does, line 90 is executed. This is the dot product of **V** with **î**. It determines whether p lies on the side of the planet that is toward the light source, in which case it is opposite the dark side of the planet and not in the shadow zone. This is necessary since the shadow algorithm in lines 78-89 does not make this distinction. If p does lie on the dark side within the shadow zone, the color is set to a medium grey in line 91.

You will notice in the images above that there is a dark band within the rings. This is because Saturn's rings have a void in that band: there are no particles there to reflect light; what you see is the background color, **'midnightblue'**, showing through. This creates a problem since the shadow color will overplot the background color in that void. Lines 93 and 94 reestablish it as **'midnightblue'**.

Now that the band colors have been established, you can plot the rings. This is done by plotting short line segments. Lines 97-100 compute the starting location of the first segment. Referring to Figure 10-6, lines 100-101 determine if the segment is in front of the planet, in which case it is plotted. Lines 103-108 determine if it is behind the planet, in which case it is not plotted. This is done by calculating the distance c of the point's global coordinates from the planet's center. Line 107 says, if c is greater than the sphere's radius times 1.075, then plot the segment. The factor of 1.075 is included to prevent the line segments from nibbling into the sphere's edges. It is necessary to go through this logic; otherwise the front visible segments, which are within the radius of the sphere, won't be plotted.

Two things can be noted regarding the above images produced by Listing 10-1. First is the color. The NASA photographic image shows a greyish hue, almost devoid of color. But many observers of Saturn have described it as having a golden hue, hence my choice of colors. As any photographer knows, capturing an object's true colors in a photographic image is difficult; so much depends on the color of the incident light and the image-capturing medium. Perhaps it is best to rely on the observations of stargazers. If you do not agree with the colors in the images produced by Listing 10-1, you can tinker with them by altering the **clr** definitions in the program. The second thing to notice is the curvature of the shadow that follows the planet's curvature in Figure 10-5. It shows that the shading algorithm works as expected.

Regarding use of the program, you can change the direction of the incident light in lines 24-26 and the angles of rotation in lines 32-34. Listing 10-1 takes a while to run so be patient.

Listing 10-1. Program SATURN

```
1    """
2    SATURN
3    """
4
5    import numpy as np
6    import matplotlib.pyplot as plt
7    from math import sin, cos, radians, sqrt
8
9    plt.axis([0,150,100,0])
10   plt.axis('off')
11   plt.grid(False)
12
13   print('running')
14   #————————————parameters
15   g=[0]*3
16
17   xc=80 #——sphere center
18   yc=50
19   zc=0
20
21   rs=25 #——sphere radius
22
23   lx=-1 #——light ray unit vector components
24   ly=0
25   lz=0
26
27   IA=0
28   IB=.8
29   +n=2
30
31   Rx=radians(-20)
32   Ry=radians(0)
33   Rz=radians(30)
34
```

```
35   #————————same as SHADESPHERE————-
36
37   #————————————rings
38   alpha1=radians(-10)
39   alpha2=radians(370)
40   dalpha=radians(.5)
41
42   r1=rs*1.5
43   r2=rs*2.2
44   dr=rs*.02
45   deltar=(r2-r1)/7 #————ring band width
46
47   #————————rotate ring point p which is at r, alpha
48   for r in np.arange(r1,r2,dr):
49       for alpha in np.arange(alpha1,alpha2,dalpha):
50           xp=r*cos(alpha)
51           yp=0
52           zp=-r*sin(alpha)
53           rotx(xc,yc,zc,xp,yp,zp,Rx)
54           xp=g[0]-xc
55           yp=g[1]-yc
56           zp=g[2]-zc
57           roty(xc,yc,zc,xp,yp,zp,Ry)
58           xp=g[0]-xc
59           yp=g[1]-yc
60           zp=g[2]-zc
61           rotz(xc,yc,zc,xp,yp,zp,Rz)
62           xpg=g[0]
63           ypg=g[1]
64
65   #————————————select ring band color
66       if r1 <= r < r1+1*deltar:
67           clr=(.63,.54,.18)
68       if r1+1*deltar <= r <= r1+2*deltar:
69           clr=(.78,.7,.1)
```

```
70      if r1+2*deltar <= r <= r1+3*deltar:
71          clr=(.95,.85,.1)
72      if r1+3*deltar <= r <= r1+4*deltar:
73          clr=(.87,.8,.1)
74      if r1+5*deltar <= r <= r1+7*deltar:
75          clr=(.7,.6,.2)
76
77  #————————————————shadow
78      magu=sqrt(lx*lx+ly*ly+lz*lz)
79      ux=-lx/magu
80      uy=-ly/magu
81      uz=-lz/magu
82      vx=xc-xpg
83      vy=yc-ypg
84      vz=zc-zpg
85      Bx=uy*vz-uz*vy
86      By=uz*vx-ux*vz
87      Bz=ux*vy-uy*vx
88      magB=sqrt(Bx*Bx+By*By+Bz*Bz)
89      if magB < rs: #————————if in the shadow region
90          if vx*lx+vy*ly+vz*lz <= 0: #————if v points toward light source
91              clr=(.5,.5,.2) #————shadow color
92
93      if r1+4*deltar <= r <= r1+5*deltar: #————overplot empty band
94          clr='midnightblue' #————with background color
95
96  #————————————————plot line segment
97      if alpha == alpha1:
98          xstart=xpg
99          ystart=ypg
100     if zpg <= zc: #-front (z axis points into the screen)
101         plt.plot([xstart,xpg],[ystart,ypg],linewidth=2,color=clr)
102
```

```
103    if zpg >= zc: #-back
104        a=xpg-xc
105        b=ypg-yc
106        c=sqrt(a*a+b*b)
107        if c > rs*1.075: #—plot only the visible portion of rings
108            plt.plot([xstart,xpg],[ystart,ypg],linewidth=2,color=clr)
109        xstart=xpg
110        ystart=ypg
111
112 plt.show()
```

10.2 Solar Radiation

This section illustrates a typical scenario: using Python to plot and label curves that represent mathematical functions. Here you plot Max Planck's spectrum of radiation. You use it to represents the energy spectrum emitted by the Sun, calculate the Sun's total power output, and the amount that reaches Earth, which is called the *solar constant*. The scientific aspects of this section are quite interesting, as is the history of their development. The major benefit from a Python programming aspect is seeing how the programs perform numerical integration, set up the plots, and display numerical data.

10.2.1 Photons and the Sun

The Sun, like all radiating bodies, emits electromagnetic energy in the form of photons. We know that photons are emitted at different frequencies or wavelengths, a wavelength being inversely proportional to frequency, as in

$$\lambda = \frac{s_m}{\nu} \tag{10-5}$$

where λ is the wavelength, s_m is the speed of light within the medium, and ν is the frequency of a wave travelling in that medium. Since we are concerned primarily with light travelling through empty space, (i.e. from the Sun to Earth), $s_m = c$ where c is the speed of light in empty space, Equation 10-5 thus becomes

$$\lambda = \frac{c}{\nu} \tag{10-6}$$

A function such as solar power, when represented over a range of frequencies or wavelengths, is called a *spectrum*. In the case of electromagnetic radiation, we are mostly concerned with the power of light at different frequencies or equivalently, wavelengths. This is called a *power spectrum*. An example is the curve shown in Figure 10-8 where the power spectral density, often called simply the power spectrum, S(λ), is plotted vs. wavelength λ. This curve originated from Equation 10-7.

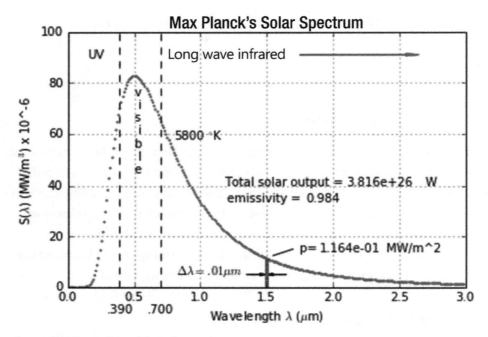

Figure 10-8. *Max Planck's Solar Spectrum*

Most of the frequencies emitted by the Sun, which range from high frequency, short wavelength ultraviolet to low frequency, long wavelength infrared, are invisible to our human eyes. We are able to see only a small range of the spectrum which, fortunately for us, lies near the peak of the Sun's emitted power spectrum. This must have pleased our hunter-gatherer ancestors since it enabled them to hunt and gather earlier and later in the day. While we can thank the shape of the Sun's power spectrum for this, it is also a characteristic of our eyes' biology which, if we believe Charles Darwin, probably evolved to be optimized at the frequencies near the Sun's maximum power output.

10.2.2 Max Planck's Black Body Radiation

As mentioned, light is photons. But what is a photon? We know photons are quantized forms of electromagnetic energy. But in the late 19th century, that was still a mystery. There were many attempts to explain the light spectrum that was emitted from heated materials. For example, when we heat up an iron poker, at first we don't see any change in color but then, after a certain temperature is reached, we visually observe it glowing through a progression of colors: dull red, brighter red, orange, yellow, white, blue, and then violet. These colors correspond to different frequencies of the electromagnetic radiation emitted by the object. Early attempts to explain this phenomenon were based on the classical theory at that time called Maxwell's Equations. These equations describe an electromagnetic field where the electromagnetic energy is assumed to be a smooth continuum. Despite many attempts, this approach failed to explain what was being observed.

Many scientists at the time struggled with this problem. Then in 1900, Max Planck, a German physicist, sent a postcard to a colleague. On the back he had written an equation that accurately described the spectrum. Plank's breakthrough was to assume, contrary to the prevailing theories at the time, that the electromagnetic field was not a continuum of energy. Rather, he guessed that electromagnetic energy exists in discrete packets and not as a continuous field, as was assumed by Maxwell's equations. This led to his breakthrough formulation, shown in Equation 10-7. He presented his idea to the German Physical Society on December 14, 1900, a date that has become known as the birth of quantum mechanics. His equation is known as the *blackbody radiation formula*. You will see more of it later.

In 1901, Planck published his results in an article in *Annalen der Physik* in which he hypothesized that electromagnetic energy could only be released by a source, such as the Sun, in the form of discrete packets of energy rather than as continuous waves. Since it was known that light exhibits wave characteristics, in 1905 Albert Einstein extended this idea by suggesting Planck's discrete "packets" could only exist as discrete "*wave*-packets." He called such a packet a *Lichtquant* or "light quantum." Later, in 1928, Arthur Compton used the term "photon" which derives from *Phos*, the Greek word for light.

Planck also assumed that the source of the wave packets are thermally excited charges, each emitting a packet of electromagnetic energy, a photon, at a particular frequency. The more charges emitting photons at the same frequency, the greater the power of the emitted light at that frequency. He further theorized that the energy of a wave packet could only occur at specific fixed energy levels or states.

Returning to 1900, the equation Planck wrote on the back of a postcard, which predicts the power spectrum of light S(λ) emitted by a black body is

$$S(\lambda) = \frac{2\pi c^2 h}{\lambda^5} \frac{\varepsilon}{e^{\frac{hc}{\lambda kT}} - 1} \quad J/s/m^3 = W/m^3 \qquad (10\text{-}7)$$

where c is the speed of light (m/s), h is Planck's Constant (J·s), λ is the wavelength (m), k is Boltzman's Constant (J/K), T is temperature (K), and ε is the emissivity of the radiating body's surface. ε is essentially a measure of the effectiveness of a surface's radiating ability. It can range from 0 to 1. As you might imagine, there was a lot of thought behind the development of this equation, which I won't go into here.

Over the past 100+ years this relation has withstood the test of time and gives very accurate results. Displayed in Figure 10-8, it is often referred to as *Planck's black body radiation formula.* It applies equally well to all radiating bodies as well as the Sun. Even though the Sun certainly doesn't *look* like a black body, as far as its radiation characteristics are concerned it behaves like one—a very hot one. As an analogy, you might think of the Sun as being a very hot (about 5800°K) black stove glowing very brightly.

Figure 10-8 shows the solar output spectrum (red curve) of the Sun as predicted by Equation 10-7. This is called a power spectral density, or simply a power spectrum. Each point on the curve gives the power density S(λ) at a corresponding wavelength λ. The green band shown in the figure will be explained later.

10.2.3 The Sun's Total Power Output

The quantity S(λ) displayed in Figure 10-8 is a *power density*. What is a *power density* and how does it differ from a simple power? Notice in Equation 10-7 that the units of S(λ) are power per cubic volume. These are the units of a density. You might think of this "density" as analogous to mass density that has units of mass per cubic volume. In the case of S(λ) you are dealing with a power density.

The feature of Equation 10-7 that makes the power spectrum resemble the Sun's output, and not that of any other black body, is the temperature T. For the Sun, T is approximately 5800°K. To get the power emitted by the Sun, P(λ), over a bandwidth λ_1 to λ_2, it is necessary to sum S(λ) across that band. In calculus, this amounts to taking the integral of S vs. λ, which is equivalent to finding the area under the $S(\lambda)$ curve between these limits.

$$P_{\lambda_1 \to \lambda_2} = \int_{\lambda_1}^{\lambda_2} S(\lambda)d\lambda \quad J/s/m^2 = W/m^2 \tag{10-8}$$

With Equation 10-7 this becomes

$$P_{\lambda_1 \to \lambda_2} = 2\pi c^2 h \int_{\lambda_1}^{\lambda_2} \frac{\lambda^{-5}\varepsilon}{e^{\frac{hc}{\lambda kT}} - 1} d\lambda \quad J/s/m^2 = W/m^2 \tag{10-9}$$

Equation 10-9 gives the power emitted by the Sun over the bandwidth λ_1 to λ_2. It equals the integral of $S(\lambda)$ times the infinitesimally small bandwidth $d\lambda$. In other words, if you pick a point along the $S(\lambda)$ curve, as shown in Figure 10-9, and multiply it by $d\lambda$ and then sum all those values from λ_1 to λ_2, you would get the total electromagnetic power emitted by the wavelengths in the waveband λ_1 to λ_2. This is the area under the $S(\lambda)$ curve from λ_1 to λ_2.

To get the power generated by the entire solar spectrum, you integrate Equation 10-9 from wavelengths beginning at $\lambda=0$ and extending to $\lambda=\infty$. For those who prefer to integrate Equation 10-9 mathematically, I show how to do so in Appendix B. Integration is simply finding the area under the $S(\lambda)$ curve. You can avoid the math by doing it numerically. To do so, replace the infinitesimally small wave band $d\lambda$ with a small band of finite width $\Delta\lambda$ and replace the integral with a summation, as in

$$P(\lambda) = 2\pi c^2 h \sum_{i=1}^{i=N} \frac{1}{\lambda_i^5} \frac{\varepsilon}{e^{\frac{hc}{\lambda_i kT}} - 1} \Delta\lambda \quad J/s/m^2 = W/m^2 \tag{10-10}$$

where i refers to the ith band centered at λ_i and N is the number of bands of width $\Delta\lambda$ between λ_i and λ_N. A typical band of width $\Delta\lambda$ is illustrated in Figure 10-9. The width of the band shown is exaggerated for illustrative purposes. In reality, it should appear much narrower.

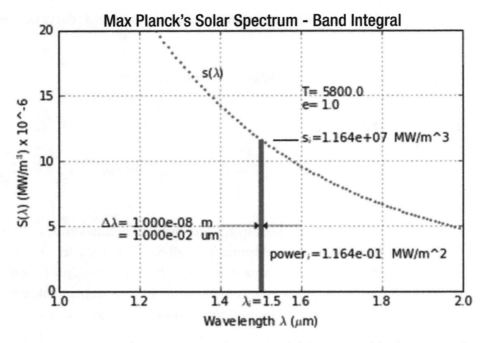

Figure 10-9. *Numerical integration of power S(λ)dλ emitted by spectrum band$_i$ across a .01 μm bandwidth at λ$_i$=1.5 (produced by Listing 10-2)*

Equation 10-10 is an approximation to Equation 10-9 because it assumes the value of S(λ) is constant across the width of each band Δλ. However, if Δλ is chosen small enough, the curve S($λ_i$ − Δλ/2) → S($λ_i$ + Δλ/2) can be approximated by the constant value S($λ_i$) across the bandwidth Δλ, in which case the results can be quite accurate. With this simple integration scheme, the power in the band equals the band's rectangular area. While there are more sophisticated integration schemes you could use, this one is simple, easy to program, and adequate for your purposes.

Let's calculate the power P(λ) emitted by the wavelengths across the small band Δλ. Figure 10-9 shows an enlargement of the band shown in Figure 10-8 centered at λ=1.5 um. This might be considered a typical band$_i$ in Equation 10-10. Listing 10-2 evaluates the power generated by the wavelengths across this bandwidth. The curve S(λ) has been generated according to Equation 10-7. According to this simplified integration scheme, the power generated by this band, which is just its rectangular area, is given by

$$P(\lambda) = S(\lambda)\Delta\lambda \qquad J/s/m^2 = W/m^2 \qquad (10\text{-}11)$$

In Listing 10-2, which plots Figure 10-9, the area of the band is calculated according to Equation 10-11. The magnitude of $\Delta\lambda$ is arbitrary. In the program, it is the parameter **dla**, which is set to .01x10^{-6} meters or .01 μm. Whether $\Delta\lambda$ is large or small, the power it emits will be the power radiated by the wavelengths across that bandwidth. Wider bandwidths will generate proportionally more power, narrower ones less. Later, when you do a numerical integration of the area under the entire S(λ) curve to get the total power radiated by the Sun across its entire spectrum, choosing a small value of $\Delta\lambda$ will lead to more accurate results.

In Figure 10-9, the band is shown at λ=1.5 um. The corresponding value of S, as calculated by the program, is 1.164x10^7 MW/m^3. With a bandwidth of .01 μm, which equals 1.0x10^{-8} meters, the power generated by this band is (1.164x10^7)x(1x10^{-8})=.1164 MW/m^2, about what a small power plant produces.

Note that the units of S(λ) will be consistent with those of the input parameters: speed of light, Planck's Constant, Boltzman's Constant, and wavelength λ. The units of these parameters should be consistent with one another. To avoid confusion, in this work you will keep all of these quantities in the spatial dimension of meters when evaluating Equation 10-7. S(λ) will then have the units (J/s)/m^3, which is the same as W/m^3. If output is needed in another power dimension, such as kW or MW, the conversion can be done after S(λ) has been evaluated by multiplying S(λ) in watts by 10^{-3} to get kilowatts or 10^{-6} to get megawatts. When calculating power emitted across a waveband, the width of that band $\Delta\lambda$ should also be in meters. For example, 1.5μm should be specified as 1.5x10^{-6}m. Conversion from meters back to micrometers μm for display or other purposes later can be done by multiplying λ meters by 10^{+6}. This is shown in Listing 10-2 in the section **plot s curve** in line **lag=la*10**6**.

In the figure, S$_i$ is shown with a value of 1.164x10^7 MW/m^3. The S(λ) axis indicates a value of 11.64 MW/m^{3}x10^{-6}, which indicates that the value of 11.64 has been multiplied by 10^{-6} for display purposes. This would make its actual value 11.64x10^{+6}, which equals the value calculated by the program. This is displayed on the plot as 1.164x10^{+7} MW/m^3.

In Listing 10-2, which created Figure 10-9, the section **plot S curve** solves Equation 10-7 for values of wavelength la, which go from la=lamin to lamax in increments **dla**. The comments within the code trace the evolution of the units of S. As given by Equation 10-7, when the parameters are as indicated in section **establish parameters**, the units of s start off as Joules/second per cubic meter (remember s(λ) is a density). Since one Joule per second defines the watt, the units are watts per cubic meter. These are converted to megawatts per cubic meter and then scaled to be plotted against the vertical axis in the units $(MW/m^3)x10^{-6}$ as the variable sg. The 10^{-6} factor indicates the actual values have been multiplied by that amount. Next, the green band is plotted and the values of temperature and emissivity are displayed.

The value of $S(\lambda)$ at $\lambda=1.5$ is calculated using Equation 10-7, converted to MW/m^3, and then multiplied by the bandwidth $dl=.01x10^{-6}$ to get pl MW/m^2, the power within that bandwidth. The remainder of the program displays the data and cleans up the plot.

Listing 10-2. Program BANDINTEGRAL

```
"""

BANDINTEGRAL
"""

import numpy as np
import matplotlib.pyplot as plt

#---------------------------------------------------------- set up axes
ymax=20
plt.axis([1.,2.,0,ymax])
plt.xlabel('Wavelength $\lambda$ ($\mu$m)')
plt.ylabel('S($\lambda$) (MW/m$^{3}$) x 10$^{-6}$')
plt.grid(True)
plt.title('Max Planck's Solar Spectrum - Band Integral')

#------------------------------------------------ establish parameters
c=2.9979*(10.**8)          # speed of light in a vacuum m/s
h=6.63*(10.**-34)          # Planck's Constant J.s
kb=1.38*(10**-23)          # Boltzmann's Constant J/K

t=5800.                    # temperature K
e=1.0                      # emissivity

lamin=.01*10**-6           # starting wavelength m
lamax=2.*10**-6            # ending wavelength m
dla=.01*10**-6             # incremental wavelength m

#------------------------------------------------------ plot s curve
for la in np.arange(lamin,lamax,dla):
    a1=2.*np.pi*c*c*h/(la**5.)
```

```
        a2=h*c/(la*kb*t)
        sl=e*a1/(np.exp(a2)-1.)              # J/s/m^3 = W/m^3
        sl=sl*10**-6                         # MW/m^3
        slg=sl*10**-6                        # scale plot at 10^-6 scale
        lag=la*10**6                         # scale to plot at 10^6 scale
        plt.scatter(lag,slg,s=1,color='r')
#─────────────────────────────────────────── plot band
plt.plot([1.495,1.495],[0.,11.64],color='g')
plt.plot([1.4975,1.4975],[0.,11.64],color='g')
plt.plot([1.5,1.5],[0,11.64],color='g')
plt.plot([1.5025,1.5025],[0.,11.64],color='g')
plt.plot([1.5005,1.505],[0.,11.64],color='g')

#───────────────────────────── plot temperature and emissivity
d=str(t)
plt.text(1.6,15,'T=')
plt.text(1.65,15,d)
plt.text(1.6,14,'e=')
d=str(e)
plt.text(1.65,14,d)

#──────────────────── calculate s and band power pl at lambda=1.5
la=1.5*10**-6
a1=2.*np.pi*c*c*h/(la**5.)
a2=h*c/(la*kb*t)
sl=e*a1/(np.exp(a2)-1.)   # J/s/m^3 = W/m^3
sl=sl*10**-6             # MW/m^3
dl=.01*10**-6            # bandwidth m
pl=sl*dl

#──────────────────────── plot results and labels
plt.plot([1.53,1.59],[11.6,11.6],'k')
plt.text(1.6,11.5,'si=')
d='%7.3e'%(sl)
plt.text(1.65,11.5,d)
plt.text(1.83,11.5,'MW/m^3')
```

```
plt.arrow(1.4,5,.085,0,head_width=.5,head_length=.01,linewidth=.2)
plt.arrow(1.6,5,-.085,0,head_width=.5,head_length=.01,linewidth=.2)

plt.text(1.15,5,'$\Delta \lambda$=')
dle='%7.3e'% (dl)
dls=str(dle)
plt.text(1.18,5,dls)
plt.text(1.35,5,'m')')

plt.text(1.145,4,'=')
dl=dl*10**6
dle='%7.3e'%(dl)
dls=str(dle)
plt.text(1.18,4,dls)
plt.text(1.35,4,'um')

plt.text(1.35,16.5,'s($\lambda$)')
plt.text(1.52,2.5,'power$_{i}$=')
pl='%7.3e'%(pl)
pl=str(pl)
plt.text(1.65,2.5,pl)
plt.text(1.823,2.5,'MW/m^2')
plt.text(1.45,-1.1,'$\lambda_{i}$=1.5')

plt.show()
```

Next, let's look at Max Planck's entire black body spectrum as shown in Figure 10-8. It's titled as "Max Planck's *Solar* Spectrum" since the temperature used is that of the Sun, approximately 5800° K.

The program that produced this plot, Listing 10-3, follows the logic in the preceding program, Listing 10-2, but here you sum the individual band powers from $\lambda=.01\text{x}10^{-6}$ to $10.\text{x}10^{-6}$ meters $(.01\mu\text{m}$ to $10.\mu\text{m})$ to get the area under the entire (almost) $S(\lambda)$ curve. The band you looked at in Listing 10-2 is shown at $\lambda=1.5$ um.

The process used here is to simply advance along wavelengths, calculate the value of $S(\lambda)$ at each wavelength, multiply it by $\Delta\lambda$ to get the power within that band, and then sum the power generated by each band in accordance with Equation 10-10. This will give you the total power emitted by all wavelengths.

You extend the range of integration to 10x10⁻⁶ meters in order to get a more accurate measure of the total power under the S(λ) curve. This will be the total spectral power emitted by each square meter of the Sun's surface. Then you multiply that by the Sun's spherical surface area to get the total power emitted by the Sun, which is known as the *solar luminosity*. In Figure 10-8, it is called the "total solar output." As shown on the plot, its value as calculated by the program is 3.816×10^{26} watts. This is in close agreement with published values.

Many researchers use e=1.0 for emissivity, which is an idealization that assumes the Sun is a perfect radiator (you can assume it isn't). Here you use an emissivity of e=.984. When you use Planck's spectrum to calculate the solar constant, which has been measured by satellite (next section), you must either reduce the temperature of the Sun in your calculations or lower its emissivity to less than 1.0 in order to get the results to agree with measured values. If you choose to stay with a Sun temperature of 5800°K, then you must lower the emissivity to .984 in order to obtain agreement. Another option, as you will see, is to keep e=1.0 and lower the Sun's temperature to 5777° K.

Listing 10-3. Program PLANCKSSOLARSPECTRUM

```python
"""

PLANCKSSOLARSPECTRUM
"""


import numpy as np
import matplotlib.pyplot as plt
#----------------------------------------------------- set up axes
ymax=100
plt.axis([0,3,0,ymax])
plt.xlabel('Wavelength _ (_m)')
plt.ylabel('S(λ) (MW/m^{3}) x 10^-6')
plt.grid(True)
plt.title('Max Planck\'s Solar Spectrum')
#------------------------------------------- establish parameters
c=2.9979*(10.**8)          # speed of light in a vacuum m/s
h=6.63*(10.**-34)          # Planck's Constant J.s
kb=1.38*(10**-23)          # Boltzmann's Constant J/K
e=.984                     # emissivity
```

```
t=5800.                       # K
lamin=.01*10**-6              # m
lamax=10.*10**-6              # m
dla=.01*10**-6                # m
st=0.                         # set area under s curve to zero
#————————————————————————— plot s curve and calculate area
for la in np.arange(lamin,lamax,dla):
    a1=2.*np.pi*c*c*h/(la**5.)
    a2=h*c/(la*kb*t)
    sl=e*a1/(np.exp(a2)-1.)                # W/m^3
    sl=sl*10**-6                           # MW/m^3
    bandarea=sl*dls                        # band area MW/m^2
    st=st+bandarea                         # sum band areas MW/m^2
    slg=sl*10**-6                          # scale to plot
    lag=la*10**6                           # scale to plot
    plt.scatter(lag,slg,s=1,color='r')
#————————————————————————— multiply the Sun's surface area
ds=1.39*10**9            # Sun's diameter m
spas=np.pi*ds**2.       # Sun's spherical area m^2
to=spas*st              # Sun's total output MW
to=to*10**6             # Sun's total output W
#————————————————————————————— plot results
plt.text(.8,58.,'5800')
plt.text(1.05,58, '°K')
plt.plot([.39,.39],[-0.,100.],'b-')
plt.plot([.7,.7],[-0.,100.],'b-')
plt.text(.3,-10,'.390')
plt.text(.6,-10,'.700')
plt.text(.15,90.,'UV')
plt.text(.8,90.,'long wave infrared')
plt.arrow(1.75,91.,.8,0.,head_width=1.,head_length=.1,color='r')
plt.text(1.2,40.,'total solar output =')
so='dd=str(so)
plt.text(2.1,40,dd)
plt.text(2.7,40,'W')
```

```
plt.text(1.2,34,'emissivity =')
e=str(e)
plt.text(1.8,34,e)
plt.text(.5,75.,'v')
plt.text(.53,70.,'i')
plt.text(.5,65.,'s')
plt.text(.53,60.,'i')
plt.text(.5,55.,'b')
plt.text(.53,50.,'l')
plt.text(.5,45.,'e')
plt.plot([1.49,1.49],[0.,11.61],color='g')
plt.plot([1.5,1.5],[0.,11.61],color='g')
plt.plot([1.51,1.51],[0.,11.61],color='g')
#——————————— calculate s at la=1.5x10^-6 m and band power pband
laband=1.5*10**-6
a1=2.*np.pi*c*c*h/(laband**5.)
a2=h*c/(laband*kb*t)
sband=a1/(np.exp(a2)-1.)
sband=sband*10**-12
pband=sband*dla # MW/sq meter
pband=pband*10**6 # W/sq meter
#—————————————————————————— plot band
plt.plot([1.55,1.7],[12.5,15.],color='k')
plt.text(1.72,14.,' p=')
pband='pband=str(pband)
plt.text(1.9,14,pband)
plt.text(2.4,14,'MW/m^2')
plt.arrow(1.35,5,.1,0,head_width=1, head_length=.05, ec='k', fc='k')
plt.arrow(1.65,5,-.1,0,head_width=1, head_length=.05, ec='k', fc='k')
plt.text(.82,4.9,'Δλ = :01μm' )

plt.show()
```

10.3 Earth's Irradiance

Figure 10-10 shows the spectrum of solar radiation that reaches Earth. Figure 10-11 shows the Earth orbiting the Sun. This is the model used to calculate the amount of the Sun's total power output that is intercepted by Earth, the *solar constant*. The distance between the two orbs is an average of 1 AU, about 93,000,000 miles. It varies during an orbit. The circular disk labelled A_p has an area equal to the Earth's cross-section. The solar power intercepted by A_p is responsible for heating the Earth.

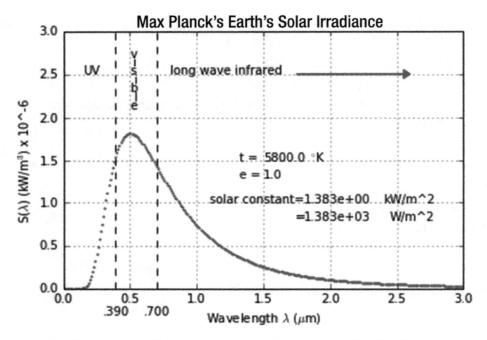

Figure 10-10. *Svpectrum of solar power reaching Earth, the Earth's solar irradiance, produced by Listing 10-3, which has been modified by inclusion of the inverse square law*

Notice how much lower the values are than in Figure 10-8. This is because the power *intensity* of the Sun's output that reaches Earth and is intercepted by A_p diminishes over the distance from Sun to Earth according to the inverse square law of

$$p_p = p_s \left(\frac{r_s}{r_{es}} \right)^2 \tag{10-12}$$

where p_s is the intensity of power at the Sun's surface, p_p is the *intensity* intercepted by A_p, r_s is the radius of the Sun, and r_{es} is the distance from the Sun to the Earth. The total power intercepted by A_p is thus

$$P_p = A_p p_p \tag{10-13}$$

$$P_p = A_p p_s \left(\frac{r_s}{r_{es}} \right)^2 \tag{10-14}$$

When Equation 10-13 is included in Listing 10-3, the spectrum reduces to Figure 10-10. Again, notice how much lower the values are than in Figure 10-8 as a result of the inverse square law.

P_p, which is the solar power reaching the top of the Earth's atmosphere, is called the *solar constant*. Its value as measured by satellite is about 1361 W/m². About 30% of this is reflected off the Earth's surface and atmosphere by albedo effects such as snow, ice, clouds, water, etc. The remainder is absorbed by the Earth. Much of that is reradiated back into space, allowing the planet to reach a thermal equilibrium. The Earth is also a hot (warm) body and it exhibits its own thermal radiation out into space. But some of what should be reradiated is blocked by greenhouse gasses including $CO2$, contributing to global warming. All this is, as we know, being actively investigated by climate researchers.

10.3.1 The Earth Sun Model

Figure 10-11 shows the Earth orbiting the Sun and Listing 10-4 contains the code.

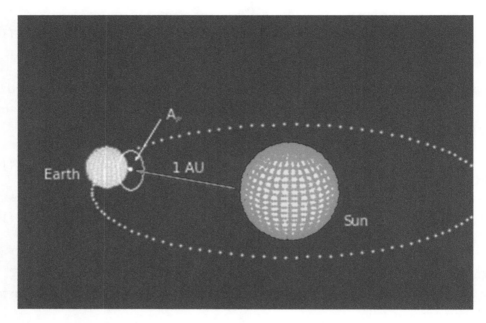

Figure 10-11. *The Earth-Sun Model produced by Listing 10-4*

Listing 10-4. Program EARTHSUN

```
"""

EARTHSUN
"""

import matplotlib.pyplot as plt
import numpy as np
from math import radians, sin, cos, sqrt

plt.axis([-100,150,-100,150])

plt.grid(False)
plt.axis('off')
sfx=2.5/3.8
```

```
#———————————————background
for x in range(-100,150,2):
    for y in range(-100,150,2):
        plt.scatter(x,y,s=40,color='midnightblue')

phimin=0.
phimax=2.*np.pi
dphi=phimax/100.

rs=40.
re=20.

ys=15.
ye=2.

xos=50.
yos=0.
zos=0.

#———————————————Sun's core
plt.scatter(xos,yos,s=4300,color='yellow')

#———————————————Sun horizontals
rx=radians(20)

for ys in np.arange(-rs,rs,5):
    for phi in np.arange(phimin,phimax,dphi):
        rp=np.sqrt(rs*rs-ys*ys)
        xp=rp*np.sin(phi)
        yp=ys
        zp=rp*np.cos(phi)
        px=xos +sfx*xp*1. +yp*0. +zp*0.
        py=yos +xp*0. +yp*np.cos(rx) -zp*np.sin(rx)
        pz=zos +xp*0. +yp*np.sin(rx) +zp*np.cos(rx)
        if pz > 0 :
            plt.scatter(px,py,s=1,color='red')
```

```
#————————————————Sun verticals
alphamin=0.
alphamax=2.*np.pi
dalpha=alphamax/30.

for alpha in np.arange(alphamin,alphamax,dalpha):
    for phi in np.arange(phimin,phimax,dphi):
        xp=rs*np.sin(phi)*np.sin(alpha)
        yp=rs*np.cos(phi)
        zp=rs*np.sin(phi)*np.cos(alpha)
        px=xos +sfx*(xp*1. +yp*0. +zp*0.)
        py=yos +xp*0. +yp*np.cos(rx) -zp*np.sin(rx)
        pz=zos +xp*0. +yp*(np.sin(rx)) +zp*np.cos(rx)
        if pz > 0 :
            plt.scatter(px,py,s=1,color='red')

#————————————————Earth's clouds
xoe=-50.
yoe=20.
zoe=-10.

plt.scatter(xoe,yoe,s=800,color='white')

#———————————————— Earth horizontals
rx=20.*np.pi/180.
dphi=phimax/100.

for ys in np.arange(-re,re,2):
    for phi in np.arange(phimin,phimax,dphi):
        rp=np.sqrt(re*re-ys*ys)
        xp=rp*np.sin(phi)
        yp=ys
        zp=rp*np.cos(phi)
        px=xoe +sfx*(+xp*1. +yp*0. +zp*0.)
        py=yoe +xp*0. +yp*np.cos(rx) -zp*np.sin(rx)
```

```
        pz=zoe +xp*0. +yp*(np.sin(rx)) +zp*np.cos(rx)
        if pz > 0 :
            plt.scatter(px,py,s=.1,color='#add8e6')
#————————————————Earth verticals
alphamin=0.
alphamax=2.*np.pi
dalpha=alphamax/30.

for alpha in np.arange(alphamin,alphamax,dalpha):
    for phi in np.arange(phimin,phimax,dphi):
        xp=re*np.sin(phi)*np.sin(alpha)
        yp=re*np.cos(phi)
        zp=re*np.sin(phi)*np.cos(alpha)
        px=xoe +sfx*(xp*1. +yp*0. +zp*0.)
        py=yoe +xp*0. +yp*np.cos(rx) -zp*np.sin(rx)
        pz=zoe +xp*0. +yp*(np.sin(rx)) +zp*np.cos(rx)
        if pz > 0 :
            plt.scatter(px,py,s=.1,color='#add8e6')
plt.arrow(xos-rs*sfx-3,yos+2,xoe-(xos-rs*sfx)+re+3,yoe-yos-6.2,color='r',
                          head_length=4.,head_width=3.)
plt.text(-14,16,'1 AU',color='white')
plt.text(80,-29,'Sun',color='white')
plt.text(-84,10,'Earth',color='white')

#————————————————front orbit
deltamin=0.*np.pi/180.
deltamax=195.*np.pi/180.
ddelta=deltamax/60.

for delta in np.arange(deltamin,deltamax,ddelta):
    r=108./sfx
    xp=r*np.cos(delta)
    yp=0.
    zp=r*np.sin(delta)
    px=xos +sfx*(xp*1. +yp*0. +zp*0.)
    py=yos +xp*0. +yp*np.cos(rx) -zp*np.sin(rx)
```

```
    pz=zos +xp*0. +yp*(np.sin(rx)) +zp*np.cos(rx)
    plt.scatter(px,py,s=1,color='white')

#——————————————————back orbit
deltamin=220.*np.pi/180.
deltamax=360.*np.pi/180.

for delta in np.arange(deltamin,deltamax,ddelta):
    r=108./sfx
    xp=r*np.cos(delta)
    yp=0.
    zp=r*np.sin(delta)
    px=xos +sfx*xp*1. +yp*0. +zp*0.
    py=yos +xp*0. +yp*np.cos(rx) -zp*np.sin(rx)
    pz=zos +xp*0. +yp*(np.sin(rx)) +zp*np.cos(rx)
    plt.scatter(px,py,s=1,color='white')

#——————————————Ap disc
xoc=xoe+re*sfx
yoc=yoe-2.5
zoc=zoe
rc=.83*re
phi1=0
phi2=2*np.pi
dphi=(phi2-phi1)/200
ry=-25*np.pi/180

for phi in np.arange(phi1,phi2,dphi):
    xc=xoc
    yc=rc*np.sin(phi)
    zc=rc*np.cos(phi)
    px=xoc+zc*np.sin(ry)
    py=yoc+yc
    pz=zoc+zc*np.cos(ry)
    plt.scatter(px,py,s=.03 ,color='white')
```

```
plt.scatter(xoe+re*sfx,yoe-2,s=6,color='white')

plt.arrow(-20,60,(xoe+re*sfx)+24,(yoe+re/2)-60-2,color='white',
                              linewidth=.5,head_width=2.,head_length=3)
plt.text(-18,60,'Ap',color='white')

plt.show()
```

10.4 Summary

In this chapter you have seen some typical applications of Python graphics programming. In the first section you saw how relatively easy it is the create the image of Saturn. The planet's body utilized the sphere and shading algorithms developed in earlier chapters; the bands were developed by constructing concentric rings flat in the x,z plane. The shadow algorithm required a bit of original geometry. The whole thing was then rotated in space about the x,y,z axes. In the section on solar radiation you learned about the physics of solar radiation, especially Max Planck's black body radiation formula, and Python's ability to construct technical illustrations. Of special note are the techniques used to scale variables for plotting. Then you learned how to build images such as Figure 10-8 which displays the model used to understand Earth's solar irradiance.

APPENDIX A

Where to Get Python

There are several places on the Internet where you can download various versions of Python. I use Anaconda with Spyder[2] and Python 3.5. This is available for download from Continuum Analytics at `https://docs.continuum.io/anaconda/install`.

It's free and easy; just follow the instructions. While I use Python 3.5, I recommend using the latest version.

An icon should appear on your desktop. If it doesn't, look in your list of installed programs and drag it to the desktop. Double-click it to get the environment to run. You will be entering Python script in the left pane. After entering code for a program, click the Run button at the top or press the F5 key on your keyboard. You may be told to open a new console. Click the Consoles button at the top then select the "Open an IPython console" option to do so. Try to run it again. Results should appear in the pane at the lower right.

There is a pane at the upper right that shows the state of variables. I never use it; in fact, I close it to allow more room for output. If I want to see what a particular variable is doing, I usually put a **print** statement in the program. The variable's history will appear in the output pane.

If you find your program is doing unexpected things, it can sometimes help to open a new console and rerun the program.

© B.J. Korites 2018
B.J. Korites, *Python Graphics*, https://doi.org/10.1007/978-1-4842-3378-8_11

APPENDIX B

Planck's Radiation Law and the Stefan-Boltzmann Equation

In Chapter 10, you were introduced to Max Planck's famous equation of black body radiation:

$$S(\lambda) = \frac{2\pi c^2 h}{\lambda^5} \frac{\varepsilon}{e^{\frac{hc}{\lambda kT}} - 1} \quad J/s/m^3 = W/m^3 \tag{B-1}$$

The power emitted by a surface over a bandwidth $\lambda_1 \rightarrow \lambda_2$ is

$$P_{\lambda_1 \rightarrow \lambda_2} = \int_{\lambda_1}^{\lambda_2} S(\lambda) d\lambda \quad J/s/m^2 = W/m^2 \tag{B-2}$$

With Equation B-1, this becomes

$$P_{\lambda_1 \rightarrow \lambda_2} = 2\pi c^2 h \int_{\lambda_1}^{\lambda_2} \frac{\lambda^{-5}\varepsilon}{e^{\frac{hc}{\lambda kT}} - 1} d\lambda \quad J/s/m^2 = W/m^2 \tag{B-3}$$

© B.J. Korites 2018
B.J. Korites, *Python Graphics*, https://doi.org/10.1007/978-1-4842-3378-8_12

In Chapter 10, you numerically integrated Equation B-3. Here you will mathematically integrate it and show that it can be used to derive the Stefan-Boltzmann Law of black-body radiation

$$p = \frac{\varepsilon 2\pi^5 k_B^4}{15 h^3 c^2} T^4 \tag{B-4}$$

where T is the surface's absolute temperature, p is power radiated per unit area, k_B is Boltzmann's Constant, h is Planck's Constant, c is the speed of light, and ϵ is the surface's emissivity. The power radiated from a surface of area A is then

$$P = pA = \varepsilon A\sigma T^4 \tag{B-5}$$

where

$$\sigma = \frac{2\pi^5 k_B^4}{15 h^3 c^2} = 5.6696 x 10^{-8} \; W/m^2/K^4 \tag{B-6}$$

σ is known as the Stefan-Boltzmann Constant. Equation B-4 relates power intensity radiated by a surface to the fourth power of its temperature, T. This equation is commonly used in science and engineering.

To carry out the integration that results in Equation B-4, you start with Planck's radiation equation (also shown in 12-1 above):

$$S(\lambda) = \frac{2\pi h c^2}{\lambda^5} \frac{\varepsilon}{e^{\frac{hc}{\lambda \kappa_B T}} - 1} \tag{B-7}$$

You want to integrate this from $\lambda=0$ to $\lambda=\infty$ to get the total power per unit area p radiated by all wavelengths. Letting $C_1 = \epsilon 2\pi h c^2$ and $C_2 = \frac{k_B T}{h}$, you get

$$p = C_1 \int_0^\infty \frac{\lambda^{-5} d\lambda}{e^{\frac{1}{C_2 \lambda}} - 1} \tag{B-8}$$

If you make the following substitutions

$$x = C_2\lambda, \quad dx = C_2 d\lambda \tag{B-9}$$

after a little fussing around you have

$$p = C_1 C_2^4 \int_0^\infty \frac{dx}{x^5 \left(e^{\frac{1}{x}} - 1\right)} \tag{B-10}$$

Using the well-known :) relation

$$\int_0^\infty \frac{dx}{x^5 \left(e^{\frac{1}{x}} - 1\right)} = \frac{\pi^4}{15} \tag{B-11}$$

and substituting C_1 and C_2 into Equation B-10, you get

$$p = \frac{\varepsilon 2\pi^5 k_B^4}{15 h^3 c^2} T^4 \tag{B-12}$$

which is the same as Equation B-4 above.

Index

A

arange() function, 52

B

Black body radiation
    Boltzmann's Constant, 356
    Stefan-Boltzmann Law, 356
Bottom-up programming, 134
Box, 203
    shading objects, 236

C

Circular arcs
    dots, 52
    line segments, 59
Corner numbering
       scheme, 114

D

2D data plotting
    function fitting, 269–271
    legend() function, 255
    linear regression, 265–269,
       272–273, 275
    program, 256–258, 260–262,
       264–265
    splines, 275–282
    twin plotting axis, 259

3D data plotting
    plotdata() function, 286
    plotspline() function, 285–293, 295
    plt.axis() function, 285–286
    rotation model, 296
        x direction, 109–110
        y direction, 106–109
        z direction, 111
    surfaces, 297–305
    surface shading, 305–318
Dot art, 50
Dot discs, 64
2D rotation model
    circles, 93, 97
    column vectors, 81
    components, 80
    corner coordinates, 91
    definitions, 81
    2DROTCIRCLE1 program, 94–96
    2DROTCIRCLE2 program, 98–100
    2DROT1 program, 83
    2DROTRECTANGLE program, 87–90
    equation, 80
    global coordinate system, 78
    local system, 79
    matrices, 81
    model creation, 78, 93
    radians() function, 83
    unit vectors, 79
    vectors, 82
2D translation, 75

E

Ellipses
    ELLIPSEMODEL program, 73–75
    line equation, 69
    major and minor
        dimensions, 68
    model creation, 70
    polar coordinates, 69
    program, 71

F, G

Functional programming, 134

H

Hidden lines
    box, 203
    inter-object, 203
    intra-object, 203
    planes, 218
    pyramid, 212
    sphere, 225

I, J

Inter-object hidden line, 203
Intersections
    line
        circle, 180
        circular sector, 181
        rectangular plane, 153
        sphere, 187
        triangular plane, 166
    overview, 153
    plane sphere, 196
Isometric projections, 105–106
    vs. perspective views, 143

K

Keyboard data entry
    bottom-up programming, 134
    coding, 136
    functional programming, 134
    input() function, 134
    plotcircle() function, 134
    top-down programming, 134

L, M

len(x) function, 205
Line intersection
    circle, 180
    circular sector
        in-bounds/out-of-bounds
            test, 183–184
        LCSTEST program, 184–187
        line intersection, 181
        local coordinates, 182
    rectangular plane, 153
        coordinate, 160
        data input, 159
        definitions, 159
        dot product, 158
        geometry plane, 154
        hit point lies, 157
        LRP program, 161–166
        out-of-bounds geometry, 158
        parameters, 159
        plane's boundaries, 160
        rectangle's boundaries, 160
        relations, 154
        rotation functions, 159
        unit vector, 154, 156
    sphere, 187
        components, 189
        coordinates, 190

latitudes, 190, 192

longitude, 191

LS program, 192–196

model for, 188

unit vector, 189

triangular planes

expression, 167

geometry, 166

Heron's formula, 167

hit produce, 169

LTP program, 175–180

out of bounds test, 168

THT1 program, 169–172

vector result, 173

N, O

np.scatter() function, 59, 61

np.sin() and np.cos() function, 52

P, Q

Perspective view

function, 147

imaginary rays, 144

vs. isometric view, 143

pinhole camera *vs.* computer
projection, 144

primitive camera, 143

program, 148–150

projection geometry, 146

relations, 144

side view of projection
geometry, 147

Vermeer's interior, 151

z position, 146

Pinhole camera *vs.* computer
projection, 144

Planes

hidden lines, 218

intersections, 196

Plotting area

axis labels, 13–14

background color, 23

colors, 15

intensity, 19–20

mixing, 16–19

coordinate axes, 29–30

custom grid lines, 11–12

displaying, 8

grid, 8, 9

importing commands, 6–7

overplotting, 20–22

saving, 8

shape distortions

circle, 26

plt.axis(), 27–28

scale factor, 27

square, 23–25

size of, 4–5

technical graphics, 3

tick marks, 9–10

title, 14–15

two-dimensional coordinate
system, 3

Plotting commands and functions

arange() function, 42

arrays, 41

arrows, 33–34

line styles, 32

lists, 36–40

points and dots,
scatter(), 31–32

range(), 43

text, 34–36

tuples, 38, 41

plt.plot() function, 226
Power density, 334
Programming style, 2–3
Pyramid, 212

R

radians() function, 52, 83, 87
Rectangular plane, 153
Right-hand rule, 101–102
RMS value, 266

S

Saturn, 1, 321
    center of rotation, 324
    components, 327
    midnightblue, 327
    program, 328–331
    rings model, 325
    rotation functions, 325
    shading algorithm, 327
    shadow cast, 321–323, 326
    side view, 326
Shading objects
    box, 236
    dots/lines, 235
    generic plane, 241
    overview, 235
    shade() function, 239
    sphere, 246
    theories, 235
Solar radiation, 331
    Earth's irradiance
        power intensity, 345
        solar constant, 344–345
        Sun model, 346–350

Max Planck's black body radiation
    birth of quantum mechanics, 333
    blackbody radiation
        formula, 333–334
        Maxwell's equations, 333
        wave packets, 333
    photons and the Sun, 331–332
    solar constant, 331
    Sun's total power output
        BANDINTEGRAL program, 338–340
        dla parameter, 337
        integration, 335–336
        mass density, 334
        Planck's spectrum program, 341–343
        power density, 334
        solar luminosity, 341
Sphere
    hidden lines, 225
    line intersection, 187
    plane intersections, 196
    shading objects
        equation, 247
        non-linear intensity function, 246
        nonlinear shading function, 249
        np.arange() function, 248
        plotting longitudes and latitudes, 248
        SHADESPHERE program, 249–253
        unit vector, 248
Stefan-Boltzmann Constant, 356

T, U, V, W, X, Y, Z

Three-dimensions
    4BOXES program
        coding, 117
        corner numbering scheme, 114
        plotbox function, 116–117

rotx function, 115
roty function, 116
4BOXESUPDATE program
    coding, 122–123
    corner coordinates, 121
    sequence rotations, 123
coordinate system, 103
3D rotation model (*see* 3D data
    plotting)
foreshortening, 105
isometric projections, 105–106
keyboard data entry (*see* Keyboard
    data entry)
matplotlib system, 103
matrix concatenation
    order of rotation, 130–132
    SEQUENTIALCIRCLESUPDATE
        program, 132–133
perspective view, 105–106
projection of, 104
right-hand rule, 101–102
SEQUENTIALCIRCLES program, 124

Top-down programming, 134
Triangular planes, 166
Two-dimensional images
    circles, 60
    circular arcs
        dots, 52
        line segments, 59
    dot art, 50
    dot discs, 64
    ellipses, 68
    lines from dots
        attributes, 45
        coordinate values, 47
        DOTLINE program, 48–49
        line creation, 45
        scalar components, 46
        unit vector, 46
    numpy, 50
    plt.plot() line segments, 60
    random library, 50
    rotation (*see* 2D rotation model)
    translation, 75

CPSIA information can be obtained
at www.ICGtesting.com
Printed in the USA
LVHW06s0839080818
586260LV00004B/52/P